Praise for
Beyond Fairy Tales

"Karris offers an engaging, resource-rich book to bring life to stale or shaky relationships. In a practical, at-times humorous, and always-down-to earth style, he creates a roadmap for a rewarding journey towards love. You are certain to enrich yourself as a person and as a partner by reading this book!"

> — **Lorrie Brubacher**, M.Ed., Director of the Carolina Center for Emotionally Focused Therapy, author of *Stepping into Emotionally Focused Therapy: Key Ingredients of Change*, 2nd ed. (2025)

"In this comprehensive, well-written, and inspiring guide to revitalizing connection between partners in an intimate relationship, Mark covers everything from romance to the operating manual for different attachment styles to personal well-being. I highly recommend this book for couples who are suffering and therapists who are helping them."

> — **Polly Young-Eisendrath**, Ph.D., Author of *Love Between Equals* and *Dialogue Therapy for Couples and Real Dialogue for Opposing Sides*

"Wondering what good couples therapy looks like? This book beautifully illuminates the process and possibilities. Filled with sage, practical advice, and understanding, this book is a gift to couples everywhere."

> — **Michelle Becker**, author of *Compassion for Couples: Building the Skills of Loving Connection*

"I want to offer my enthusiastic support for *Beyond Fairytales*. I find the straightforward language, fresh ideas and practical solutions to be ones from which *any* couple can benefit."

— **David Mars**, Ph.D., Director of the Center for Transformative Therapy, Developer of Transformative Couples Therapy®

"*Beyond Fairy Tales* provides readers with a quenching gulp from the deep wisdom well of attachment theory. Mark expertly guides partners through difficult conversations and delivers the practical and innovative tools necessary to take their relationship to the next level."

— **George Faller**, LMFT, EFT trainer, president of the New York Center for Emotionally Focused Therapy (NYCEFT), and coauthor of *Emotionally Focused Family Therapy*

"It is extremely refreshing to have a guidebook for couples that addresses the real stressors and impossible expectations that modern-day couples face.*" And "*The step-by-step strategies and real-life examples in *"Beyond Fairy Tales"* provide a roadmap for couples to get to the root of issues and put a stop to the negative patterns."

— **Jackie Wielick**, LMFT, Owner of Therapy by Jackie, PLLC, and **Jennine Estes Powell**, LMFT, Founder of Estes Therapy, Coauthors of "*Help for High Conflict Couples: Using Emotionally Focused Therapy and the Science of Attachment to Build Lasting Connection*"

"Karris' humility and pragmatism, honed by years of experience as a couples' therapist guides the reader in taking their relationship from distress to recovery.

— **Clare Rosoman**, author of *Repairing Attachment Injuries in Close Relationships: An Emotionally Focused Guide to Moving Beyond Betrayal* (2025)

"Beyond Fairy tales gives you the compassionate guidance and hope necessary to create lasting change."

— **Shane Birkel,** Host of the *Couples Therapist Couch* podcast

"There are many books about relationships with practical pointers and some based on solid science, but very few that truly have both. This book does both and is a huge gift to our culture, which is often quite disoriented about what actually makes relationships work. "*Beyond Fairy Tales*" is a difference-maker, and I am excited to see its impact on readers!"

— **Ryan Rana**, President and Founder of the Arkansas EFT Center, Co-host of the *Leading Edge in Emotionally Focused Therapy* podcast and *successinvulnerability.com*

"Beyond Fairy Tales is a playful and invigorating exploration for couples, offering a powerful resource to strengthen relationships. Karris provides fresh insights, empathetic compassion for the challenges couples face, and practical strategies for growing stronger together."

— **Jim Thomas**, EFT Trainer Emeritus, Clinical Fellow, LMFT

"Mark creates an approachable framework for harnessing and transforming emotional experience into forces for connection and relational satisfaction for any couple willing to do the work."

— **Michael Barnett,** author of *The Emotionally Focused Therapy Workbook for Addiction: How to Heal the Loneliness and Shame That Trigger Addictive Behaviors*

"Beyond Fairy Tales delivers! It is a compassionately tailored guidebook for everyday couples who are in need of refreshment and change in their relationship."

— **Anabelle Bugatti** 'Dr. Belle', PhD, LMFT, Author of *Relentless Empathy in the Therapeutic Relationship*, President of Southern NV EFT

"Filled with wisdom, compassion, and practical direction, *Beyond Fairy Tales* guides you on an honest, informed, and inspiring journey through the trials and triumphs of love."

— *James Furrow*, PhD, Couple and Family Therapy Program, Seattle University, co-author of *Emotionally Focused Family Therapy: Restoring Connection and Promoting Resilience*

"Beyond Fairy Tales is wonderful! In his clear and humorous way, Dr. Kerris presents some of the most valuable insights and tools from the world of couple therapy and research."

— **Scott R Woolley**, PhD, distinguished professor at Alliant International University, EFT trainer, and founding director of the San Diego Center for EFT and TRIEFT Alliant

Beyond Fairy Tales

A Couple's Guide to Finding Clarity, Doing the Work, and Building a Lasting Relationship

Dr. Mark Gregory Karris

SacraSage

Print book: 978-1-958670-59-0

Hardcover book: 978-1-958670-60-6

E-book: 978-1-958670-58-3

Printed in the United States of America

Library of Congress Cataloguing-in-Publication Data

Beyond Fairy-Tales: A Couple's Guide to Finding Clarity, Doing the Work, and Building a Lasting Relationship

Contact: MarkGKarris@gmail.com

MarkGregoryKarris.com

Contents

Introduction   ix

Part One
Setting the Stage

1. The End of Fairy Tales and Embracing the Real Us   3
2. Discovering Each Other's Operating Manual   26
3. Awakening the Gift of Reflective Empathic Compassion   60

Part Two
Mapping Negative Patterns

4. What Is Your Negative Cycle?   87
5. What Is the Anatomy of Your Negative Cycle?   101

Part Three
Deepening Your Bond

6. Strengthening Your Connection   127
7. Employing Effective Communication   149
8. Unleashing Your Inner Cycle Slayer   165
9. Cultivating a Healthier You (For A Healthier We)   187
10. Revitalizing Your Sexual Connection   220

Epilogue   245

Notes   247
Acknowledgments   251
About the Author   253

Introduction

If you've found your way to *Beyond Fairy Tales*, chances are you've discovered that the fairy tale of never-ending romantic bliss is a myth. In the idyllic early days of the honeymoon stage, you may have experienced your version of a life complete with lazy afternoons sipping intoxicating margaritas and engaging in hours of passionate lovemaking. However, if you have reached for this book, you have probably come to realize that the reality of romantic partnerships isn't always as magical as you may wish.

Your relationship journey may have begun with the naive optimism of *Hopeville*, where everything felt perfect and your partner completed you in many wondrous ways, to now visiting the harsh reality of *Doomsville*. Unfortunately, Doomsville may feel eerily similar to Tolkien's Middle-Earth realm of Mordor, and your partner may have morphed into someone more akin to Sauron, the embodiment of evil.

Okay, I might be a tad dramatic. Hopefully, your partner isn't truly "evil" (if they are, then RUN! FAST!). However, you may have reached a point in your relationship where something just doesn't feel right. The mysterious and potent spark that once ignited wonder and connection in your relationship may now feel like a mere flutter in the air. This change may well leave you with a deep longing to return to what once was.

You may find yourself caught in the ache of yearning for more in your relationship, more in your life. This constant awareness of loss may tug at your attention like a persistent splinter, constantly provoking you, reminding you that change is necessary.

For some, the splinter is small. There is still plenty of love left in your relationship, but you know that you both deserve to break free from the pattern of disconnection that can kick your ass on occasion. For others, the splinter in your relationship has become a pulsating and infected wound, requiring urgent attention. Those of you in this situation might find yourselves frightened that, if things don't improve, the relationship may slowly wither and die.

You may have found this book while seeking a relationship tune-up to inject more vitality into your partnership. You may have reached for this book as a last-ditch effort as you find yourself on the brink of giving up and contemplating divorce. Whatever the reason that brought you to these pages, *Beyond Fairy Tales* can help breathe new life into your relationship.

The complexity of today's world adds to the challenge of thriving within a healthy, balanced relationship. Modern life was difficult enough with the constant demands of incessant smartphone pings, overpacked schedules, the demands of raising children, and ongoing financial instability. As we add the challenge of navigating an ever-complicated global landscape, our lives and ability to cling to love become increasingly difficult. As we are challenged by the shifting cultural complexities of our daily lives, we must work to maintain the balance in our romantic relationships. We all find ourselves struggling in the aftermath of a global pandemic, a time in which so many face an epidemic of aloneness. Adding to these challenges, the modern intricacies of gender, race, religion, wars, and politics make sustaining a predominantly happy relationship feel like an Olympic-sized endeavor. However, maintaining a stable relationship amidst this chaos is not just feasible; it's crucial.

This book aims to guide you in finding your way back to one another. Here, you will learn to slice through the clutter and reclaim connection, sanity, and love. We will explore ways to revive feelings of empathy, the necessary elixir for secure relationships. You will also learn to transcend the individual fantasies that we often project upon one another. These Disneyesque fairy tale projections often obstruct mature love by promoting a grasp on idealized versions of our partners rather than accepting their true, imperfect, and at times annoying selves.

Most importantly, *Beyond Fairy Tales* is here to help you nurture a genuine sense of connection and *attachment* security. When you see the word "attachment," think of it as "someone with whom I have a close, intimate, and affectionate bond." This book is packed with transformational principles of connection and practical, everyday practices to boost your confidence in being able to rely on each other, have each other's backs, embrace your differences, and deepen your connection. You'll learn to break free from the damaging negative cycles and unhealthy patterns that chip away at your relationship. As you journey through these pages, you'll transform from adversaries or distant partners into compassionate friends and teammates, navigating this unpredictable, rapidly changing world together.

Even though it would be wonderful if both you and your partner could dive into this book and embark on this journey of change together, let's be real: that's probably not going to happen for most of you. But here's the good news: even if your partner never cracks open these pages, you'll still walk away with insights and strategies that can bring you closer and create a healthier connection. You'll find that as you begin to shift your own thoughts, feelings, and behaviors, your partner might just start to shift right along with you.

Beyond Fairy Tales is *not* intended for individuals living in abusive relationships. Love shouldn't be a perpetual battlefield where one profoundly wounded partner uses gaslighting, intimidation, exploitation, coercion, control, and violence as weapons against another. My years working as a domestic violence victim advocate have helped me understand the devastating impact all forms of partner abuse and their repeated patterns inflict. My heart aches for anyone trapped in a loveless cycle of torment. However, this book will *not* be an ideal resource for people in these situations.

This book assumes that there is a level of safety and healthiness within the relationship of those using it. If you are wondering if this book is for you, consider whether you have an established sense of security and trust in your relationship (even if those qualities feel like they're hanging by a few fraying threads). If your relationship feels unsteady at times, has grown stale, or if you find yourselves stuck in conflict that doesn't cross into the territory of abuse, this book is for you.

To those who are *not* in a predominant pattern of abuse and who seek to build healthy, secure connections, even amidst the beautiful and chaotic mess of real life, let this book be your road map for navigating the exciting, challenging, and ultimately rewarding journey to a mature, imperfect love.

As a therapist specializing in couples therapy, I've spent the last decade knee-deep in the trenches, researching and applying the most empirically validated models. My approach is about cutting through the jargon and creating a straightforward, no-nonsense, and compassionate resource, distilling these concepts into simple, digestible nuggets that couples can actually use in their everyday lives. I hope this book empowers you and your partner to become more whole, both as unique individuals and as a united couple.

For your convenience, all the exercises and worksheets from this book, including the attachment quiz, are compiled into a downloadable workbook. You can easily access it by visiting:

https://markgregorykarris.com/beyond-workbook/

In my work with couples, witnessing life and love emerge from the depths of a couple's pain and trauma is profoundly sacred. It fills my heart with immense gratitude and continually reaffirms my calling as a wounded healer. I've seen the healing journey of countless couples, and watched in awe as they rediscovered love. Let me be your guide on this wild and wondrous journey, as you seek to grow in profound empathy, meaningful depth, and enduring connection.

Part One
Setting the Stage

FAIRY TALE

Chapter 1
The End of Fairy Tales and Embracing the Real Us

"Your problem is not that you have (necessarily) chosen the wrong person but that you have not yet stepped out of idealization into the realities of love."

— Polly Young-Eisendrath, *Love Between Equals*

W e're all familiar with the ending of the story of *Snow White* and the sentiment echoed at the close of many beloved fairy tales: "And they lived happily ever after." Yet, aside from the rare couples who appear to exist in perpetual honeymoon bliss until their final breath, the relational reality for most of us is significantly different. The elusiveness of such an ending is especially true for those of us who never received modeling for healthy relationships. Sure, we will all experience amazing heart-soaring moments of joy (otherwise, why bother tying the knot?). However, most of us will acknowledge that describing our relationships as perpetually "happy" is stretching the reality a bit.

As we go through our relationship challenges, wouldn't it feel validating to read sequel titles like "Snow White: After the Honeymoon" or

"The Frog Prince: Couples Therapy Edition"? After all, imagine the PTSD (posttraumatic stress disorder) Snow White must have grappled with. Can you imagine the anxiety that stemmed from her experiences with her narcissistic stepmother, the Queen? Imagine what nightmares all those attempts on her life—being strangled by her lace clothing, being poisoned by a comb, and being poisoned by a tantalizing apple—must have created. Simply being forced into exile in a frightening forest to survive the elements must have brought with it real and lasting mental health challenges. Despite Snow White's apparent resilience, it's hard to imagine these traumas not creating symptoms that she would have to face and that would affect her relationship.

I can imagine *Snow White's* husband shaking his head in the middle of an argument about sour milk and saying, "Hey, Snow. Why are you so reactive? You sure have some trust issues. For the millionth time, I am not out to poison you. I thought the milk was still fresh. I promise. I will make sure to check it next time."

The same could be said of the prince from the tale "*The Frog Prince.*" Talk about an identity crisis. Can you imagine the trauma of finding yourself a prince one moment and a squishy frog the next? I don't care if you had done something truly heinous, finding yourself transformed into a lower life-form by a scorned witch must be over-whelming. Imagine the heightened alertness needed for survival in the wild—dodging slithering snakes, evading hungry birds, and avoiding fungal infections. Let's not even talk about learning to eat insects. It's a lot to handle. The story may end with a festive wedding, but how did the prince's trauma symptoms manifest in his marriage? This must have been especially trying since there would have been no therapists specializing in cross-species trauma to help the couple cope. The poor prince couldn't even visit the local library to pick up the famous trauma book *The Body Keeps the Score.*

I can imagine the prince and his wife sitting in couples therapy and his wife frustratingly talking to him about an argument they had a few days before. "I don't know what I said that would cause you to go into an angry shame spiral, causing you to get up and just leave the table. I just said about your finding a new job, 'Sometimes you have to take a *leap* of faith and trust that everything is going to work out.' I know, I shouldn't have said 'leap,' but I didn't purposely try to upset you. Why are you so easily reactive?"

Meanwhile the couple's quirky therapist with an odd sense of humor must have thought to herself, "This is so *ribbiting*. I mean, riveting." Despite her inner dialogue, ever the consummate professional, she would likely have turned to the wife, saying, "It sounds like you didn't mean to upset the prince, and you are still struggling as to why he reacted that way. Let's find out." She might have then turned to the prince and gently asked him, "Prince, what did you feel when your beloved used a word that reminded you of your past trauma?"

The reality is, once we leave the honeymoon phase, over time—some more slowly than others—we start to realize that we aren't living in a *Disney* film. The illusion that we live in a romantic bubble with the perfect partner begins to waver in the harsh light of reality. The person we thought we were in a relationship with begins to change as the glow of the honeymoon phase of our relationship takes on a real-life hue.

Our partner's once charming quirks start to grate on our nerves. That initial excitement? The relationship dims into the everyday mundane. You will find that this is especially true once you begin having kids. And don't get me started on how our own baggage—yeah, those childhood traumas we thought we had in check—starts to erupt into everyday life, turning us into someone we barely recognize. And, of course, our baggage isn't all we have to worry about. We are also affected by our partner's ghastly ghosts from the past. As we traverse the trials of life, both our own ghosts and those of our partner will begin to make their appearances. As they emerge, there is a true possibility of their scaring away the captivating butterflies of loving sentiments we once held dear.

Myths About Modern-Day Love

One of the problems that accompany fairy tales and cultural myths is the fact that they can fill our heads with shallow beliefs that create and perpetuate suffering and relationship disconnection. While simple stories may be greatly entertaining for children, they aren't the stuff upon which to build your relationship patterns. What we believe about relationships matters. Holding fewer myths can increase our ability to build a mature, authentic, and secure relationship with the one we love (and are commonly frustrated at). So, let's explore some of those pesky myths and the "myth-busting truths" you'll need to reject them.

Myth #1: Love Should Not Be Hard

Occasionally, I meet someone who, after getting married, genuinely believes they should be happy with their partner *all* the time. Their naïveté toward the challenging realities of a daily partnership is rarely conscious. These people are usually shocked into awareness of their unconscious belief when they experience a relational reality check. This newfound awareness is often only obtained after some very hard conflicts.

Such individuals often experienced a sheltered upbringing. They may have been protected from a lot of suffering and had most of their needs readily met. At times, you find this outlook rooted within a religious context. In such instances these expectations of continual happiness may be immersed in a prosperity gospel type of narrative, characterized by beliefs such as "If I engage in the right religious behaviors and believe in the correct theological truths, then perpetual peace and blessings are mine to claim!" While these sincere people do exist, I more frequently meet folks who hold the belief that relationships shouldn't be hard, at least *most* of the time.

The problem with believing that love shouldn't be hard is the same problem you will find with most relational myths—those myths lead to internal angst, relational disappointment, and relational disconnection.

Why is that?

Well, in this case, the moment things get tough, folks start thinking there's a glitch in the matrix of their relationship. Negative thoughts, such as "I'm supposed to be happy," "This is too hard," and "Something is catastrophically wrong with our relationship," start rolling in like unyielding sentinels. Then the momentum picks up and the thoughts move to "Something is wrong with my partner." The next milestone along this path is the belief that "We aren't supposed to be together." Next, thoughts turn to "I shouldn't have married my partner." Then, "Gosh, I should have married my college sweetheart." This line of thinking may ultimately lead to the thought that "I should connect with that old flame on Facebook," and to a pit that holds every negative belief one can hold about their partner and the future of their relationship.

Our thoughts affect our emotions and physiology. Thus, once we have formulated and bought into these thoughts, we can start to feel down. We can begin to experience a heaviness in our bodies that slackens the skip in our step. In an effort to protect ourselves from getting hurt, we then may find ourselves placing another brick in the wall of our defenses. Here, we create a strong and endurable fortress, one brick at a time, that keeps our partner from reaching our innermost being. As the walls grow, so does the distance between us.

When our partner experiences our distancing, our behavior can trigger a negative cycle of further disconnection. As each of us withdraws for self-protection, the gully lying between us expands ever further. This process leaves us feeling more alone and frustrated with the relationship—which is precisely the experience we want less of.

Let's be clear: we all possess intuitions, a sense of internal fairness, and our own "what feels good" meter. Indeed, some relationships are abusive, toxic, or, at the other extreme, utterly devoid of life. There's a line that, once crossed, necessitates listening to our thoughts and feelings. It is this boundary that steers us back toward what feels safe, loving, and true. Of course, there are those relationships where things aren't perfect—where you get on each other's nerves and have unresolved issues, yet both of you continue trying hard to find better ways to heal and connect, persisting even amidst accumulated hurts and perhaps a sense of hopelessness. That's who I aim to reach with this book.

For those dedicated to the long haul, those seeking to rediscover empathy and deepen their connection, those aiming for less conflict, let me share two myth busters. These truths can create some mental wiggle room and reduce your inclination to cling to the notion that love shouldn't be hard.

Myth-Busting Truth: Life Is Hard

Who among us can say, "Life is easy?" It's honestly a rare person who can. While life is certainly more difficult for some than for others, for most of us, life is hard. The challenge of life may come from the myriad of curveballs life throws at us. When life is challenging, maintaining a consistent loving connection with our partners becomes harder.

Some of us will be confronted with the harrowing effects of cancer. This life-altering diagnosis will impact not only our lives but those of our families, friends, and colleagues. Others of us will endure the profound sorrow of losing someone dear. Some of us bear scars from traumas dating back decades, while others navigate the uncertainties of existential crises. Experiences of racism or being on the receiving end of any other kind of "ism," whether overt or subtle, keep some of us trapped in a perpetual state of alert. Beautiful yet wonderfully wild children test the patience of many.

Meanwhile, long COVID persists for some of us, just as addictions and mental illnesses do for others. The news of loved ones caught in conflict zones abroad deeply affects many, while complicated relation-ships with parents or in-laws trouble others. Then there are those who struggle alongside partners wrestling with pregnancy loss or financial stress. And for those in draining, soul-sucking jobs, the struggle of life is relentless. Life, in all its complexity, is undeniably tough. In a world so full of hurdles, expecting love to flow smoothly is, well, simply a fairy tale.

How does life's inherent toughness challenge our ability to keep a secure bond with our partner? Just as plants flourish with sunlight, water, and nutrients, there are a few essential elements for the mainte-nance and growth of our relationships. A loving bond is nurtured by dedicated time, deep empathy, intentional effort, shared joy, and a decent set of conflict-resolution skills. Each of these elements requires a substantial investment of emotional, mental, physical, and for some, spiritual resources. When we lack these essential elements, our relation-ships become stunted or even begin to wither. The many hurdles we encounter amid the hustle and bustle of life are like constant shrieking shadows. Much like a dark impenetrable bank of clouds that blocks out a plant's much-needed rays of sun, these shadows make it tough to grow a loving connection.

It's hard to love when we have been hurt. On top of this, when we're bogged down by fatigue, stress, or existential concerns about our meaning and purpose, it's difficult to manage our impulsive and reactive behaviors. Being exceptional lovers for our partners necessitates ample food for our brain's executive functions—simply put, the mental skills needed to control our thoughts, emotions, and actions. We need to recognize when we're on edge, with our mental reserves running low. By acknowledging and addressing these challenges, which leave us prone to irritability and reactivity, we create the space and capacity to love more effectively.

When we find ourselves in depleted states, especially as we move further into the evening hours, we can become the worst versions of ourselves. In these moments and mental states our ability to love well becomes limited. Each of us has a limited capacity, and that capacity depends on what's happening in our lives. This isn't a knock against us. Even a luxurious Mercedes running on fumes will eventually lose its ability to move forward.

Recognizing our limits is crucial, not just for ourselves but also for understanding the strains our partners face. Each person's capacity to love is shaped by their unique burdens and the inner and outer battles they confront. When we acknowledge that life is hard, and in turn accept that love is hard, we can soften the harsh and judgmental view we often hold of ourselves, our partner, and our relationship. If we start viewing life's stressors as the enemy instead of going at each other's throats, and stop dumping all of life's annoyances on our partners like they're the cause, we'll live in a happier place.

Appreciating our common humanity in life's struggles stirs empathy for ourselves and our partners. This shift in perspective helps us realize that most of us are doing the best we can with the tools and bandwidth available to us. While we may not all be in the same boat as those around us, we are all navigating the same choppy and chaotic waters of life. Before we can arrive at another destination, such as a more secure and healthy relationship, we must first fully arrive at where we are currently, with greater clarity and empathy for our journey.

Myth-Busting Truth: We Are Different

Throughout our lives, we've made decisions that have greatly influenced the complex web of causes and effects forming our past and shaping who we are today. However, as much as we would like to revel in the notion that we're the sole masters of our universe, relishing the idea that we alone crafted ourselves into the amazing people we think we are, much of who we have become was beyond our control.

From the very beginning, the stage of life was set without our consent. We didn't choose the womb in which we were born, the DNA that spirals within us, where we grew up, or the way our primary care-givers related to us. In our youth, which schools we attended was not our decision to make. Whether we would grow up to be emotionally savvy (right-brained leaning) or more analytic (left-brained leaning) was largely beyond our control. Likewise, the prefrontal cortex—the command center for making choices that align with our higher selves, especially when temptation pulls us astray—was molded by our early relationships, our environment, and our socioeconomic status. As we grew, even our spiritual and secular leanings were more inherited than chosen. Research clearly shows that all of our early experiences work together to shape us into the people we are today. Introduce different variables along the path that is our past, and we become very different individuals.

The tapestry of our personalities—our preferences, aversions, strengths, and areas ripe for growth—is woven from the myriad experiences and influences that precede us. Similarly, our partners emerge as unique individuals, shaped by their own distinct combination of circumstances and choices. Our differences can enrich our lives, yet they may also present challenges.

How could love flow easily when we are so different from one another? While opposites may attract, for many of us, especially those who have known their partners for a while, our differences can drive us mad. We tend to want our partners to see, behave, think, and feel the same way we do, even though we know they aren't carbon copies of ourselves. Sameness can often reduce friction and facilitate smoother interactions; it is true. Research indicates that it's not the differences in values, thoughts, quirks, behaviors, triggers, and joys themselves that are the problem; rather, it's how we handle these differences. However, for many of us, our expectations and handling of our differences make it challenging to maintain a consistent sense of perceived love.

Couples often face common differences, ranging from the trivial, like how the toilet paper hangs, to the more profound, such as beliefs regarding finances, parenting styles, and the ideal amount of time spent with in-laws. Beyond these clear issues, there are less obvious differences that can lead to feelings of disconnection.[1]People may experience differences in their philosophy of life and their preferred pace of life. For instance, one partner might be full of energy, constantly seeking adventure and thrilling experiences, while the other prefers a slower pace and focuses on relaxation and leisure. Differences in the perception of time can also emerge. One partner may focus on living in the present, while the other lives more in the past. Punctuality, too, can become a battleground, with one partner perpetually on time and the other seemingly in a constant state of delay. And then, of course, there's the eternal divide between early birds and night owls.

Our brains and nervous systems are as different as our personalities and backgrounds. This may be an obvious statement, yet, amidst the emotional triggers of daily life, we rarely pause to consider the neurobiological difference between ourselves and others. This is especially true in our close romantic relationships. Our failure to recognize and accept the differences that exist between ourselves and our partners can lead to profound misunderstandings and heartache.

Take Brian and Taylor, for instance. Brian, a thirty-four-year-old engineer, thrives on facts, figures, and solving problems. Taylor, a twenty-nine-year-old hairstylist, values art, creativity, and emotional depth. Their love story, which began in their late twenties, has led to a marriage lasting seven years. Despite their deep affection for one another, they often find themselves clashing over expectations of how to support each other during tough times.

For example, Taylor seeks understanding and empathy during moments of hurt. She often feels dismissed by Brian, who believes he is being helpful. This often results in Brian feeling that his efforts never seem to satisfy Taylor. This disconnect leads to heightened moments where the couple shoots verbal bullets at each other. Feeling frustrated, Taylor calls Brian a "robot" and "emotionally stunted." In response, Brian, matching Taylor's anger, views Taylor's emotional expressions as exaggerated. He goes so far as to label them as "crazy" and "over the top" and suggests that Taylor might benefit from seeing a therapist individually. Brian and Taylor both pathologize one another's behavior, convinced there is something inherently wrong with the other.

This situation highlights significant issues related to *neurodiversity*, the range of variations upon which an individual's behavioral traits and brain functions exist. Our understanding of the wide range of normal behaviors and traits an individual may exhibit allows us to understand that differing brain types are normal and should be respected.

However, when not understood or appreciated within relationships, the differences an individual exhibits may cause massive friction. Brian and Taylor have vastly different life experiences and neurobiological make-ups, including genetics, nervous systems, and brain features, which predispose them to engage in either more logical and rational discussions or emotionally heartfelt ones.

For Brian, emotional expressions might not come naturally. These proclivities may lead him to rely on logic and dismiss what doesn't make sense to him. Taylor, on the other hand, experiences emotions deeply and seeks emotional connection as a form of validation and understanding. Left unattended, the neurodivergence of this couple may create difficulty in their ability to communicate and maintain a strong emotional connection. Difficulties in communication and closeness may lead to the couple misunderstanding each other's needs and intentions.

Is it really fair for Taylor to criticize Brian as somehow lesser for putting logic above emotional intelligence, or for not naturally engaging with feelings the way she does? And should Brian go around thinking

Taylor's "cray cray" and dismiss her needs as a character flaw of being too caught up in emotions? No way! How is that helpful, anyway? It's easy to assume a position of superiority, to believe oneself to be the epitome of a perfect romantic partner ("If only they were more like me."). However, becoming caught up in our own perfection does very little to support a strong relationship. It is more productive to embrace the differences we find lurking in our relationships with grace and under-standing, instead of judgment and criticism. Looking at your partner with an eye of love will allow both of you to maintain an openness and growth potential that will get you closer to where you want to be. Failing to acknowledge your partner's unique way of being and insisting that they think, feel, and behave exactly as you do, is a recipe for ongoing frustra-tion and relationship disaster. Inviting them to love you well while considering your operating system and love tank is one thing; demanding that they do so while you are coming from a position of superiority and harsh judgment is quite another.

Maintaining the spark in our relationships can be complicated. This isn't simply due to life's difficulties. Many of our relationship struggles evolve due to our differences. Let's deconstruct one other myth that can burrow into our minds and hearts, contributing to more intense struggle and suffering in our relationships.

Myth #2: The Perfect Partner Will Complete and Perfect Us

Certain relational myths are so deeply embedded in our unconscious and intricately entwined with our psyche that unraveling them can feel like the aftermath of heart surgery. Among these myths is the belief that our one perfect partner will rescue us from our existential dilemmas, making us feel whole. In other words, they are to be godlike, offering salvation from our loneliness and insecurities. They are expected to heal our inner aches and wounds, thereby making us feel complete and wrapped in an ideal state of happiness. Polly Young-Eisendrath discusses this phenomenon of unconscious idealizing projection, noting:

At the beginning of a romance when you are idealized and look into your lover's eyes, you wholly enjoy seeing an image of yourself as "amazing" and "wonderful" reflected back. When the idealization is going both ways, there is a mutual elation and intoxication about the possibilities for the future. You both feel something like "you are the fairest of them all" and "anything is possible.[2]

Of course, no one on their dating journey, looking for love, asks prospective partners, "Before we move forward, are you perfect?" or "Can you complete me and make me happy?" Such questions would surely backfire and ensure that this would be the last time we saw that potential partner. Yet, we must acknowledge that seeking a partner isn't an altruistic endeavor. Meaning, we're not just looking to give; we're also looking to gain. It's this deeper question of "Why did I want to be with my partner?" that can offer us a glimpse into our savior-seeking inclinations.

When people ask why you chose your partner, the go-to answers usually sound something like "Because they're loving," "Because they're kind," "Because they're sexy as hell," "Because they've got a career," or "Because they have a wonderful sense of humor." These reasons all zoom in on our partner's traits and qualities. Then, there's the side of the coin that's all about us, like when we say, "I just love how they make me feel." This is where we touch base with our own, let's call it "self-interested," reasons for being with someone. And hey, "self-interested" isn't a dirty word here—it's totally normal to gravitate toward people because of how they make us feel. It is okay to have needs, longings, and desires in relationships. It's only when we forget to balance our needs and desires with the consideration for our partner's preferences that being self-interested veers off into "selfish" territory.

It's common to believe that we choose our companions for their ability to enrich our lives or to awaken a sense of aliveness within us. Yet, for many, a deeper, more honest reason prevails. Were our partners to ask us why we're with them, and were we to take a truth serum and speak directly from our unconscious, we might admit:

I wish to be with you—not precisely who you are, but rather a version of you that exists in my unconscious fantasy. This imagined version of you is the one I believe will fulfill the needs that went unmet in my childhood, providing the unconditional love, affection, and acceptance I've always yearned for.

This unconscious projection of our ideal partner is especially prominent in the honeymoon phase of our relationships. It may resurface periodically throughout the relationship but often becomes somewhat dormant during parenthood, when much of our time and energy are focused on raising children. However, after the children have grown and left the nest, it may reemerge with a vengeance, especially if we find ourselves in a midlife crisis filled with existential concerns.

When we've done a fair amount of work to address and integrate our past traumas, cultivated a healthy and balanced view of self, developed self-regulation skills for stressful situations, recognized our strengths and limitations, developed a strong sense of purpose, and embraced a significant level of self-compassion, we become less inclined to seek salvation in someone else. Conversely, the extent to which we haven't done this work matches our inclination to cling to the myth of a perfect partner who will complete us and bring us perpetual happiness.

There is no judgment here. Who can blame us? We desire to love and be loved. We want to feel a sense of being okay in the world. If we were deprived of the necessary nurturing ingredients in our formative years, when we longed to be the apple of our parent's eye, we may have found ourselves desperately seeking that experience in the eyes of another. We may have gazed into that gleaming eye yearning for a glimmering reflection of ourselves in all our glory—perfectly wonderful, capable, sexy, and utterly worthy of respect. However, expecting our partner to give us in the here and now, what we didn't get in the then and there of the past, can only cause perpetual frustration.

Who can live up to our relational fantasies and perpetual mirroring? No one. We can't live up to our partner's either. While these fantasies help us feel like we live on cloud nine in the early stages of our relationship, they won't sustain a mature and lasting relationship with the imperfect partners we find before us. The desire for the eternal perfect relationship will inevitably create too much pressure. This pressure will in turn create power struggles and feelings of rejection, anger, and heartache.

Myth-Busting Truth: Our Imperfect Partner Can't Complete and Perfect Us

I recall a period in my life where my idealistic projections created significant issues with my wife. I harbored unrealistic expectations that she would always be available for me whenever I needed her. I fantasized that after a tough day, she would be there to rub my head, affirm my worth, and assure me that I would overcome any challenges. I expected that whenever I felt desire, she would reciprocate with open arms, whispering praises of my "earth-shattering manliness." If I achieved success, I believed she would bask in my joy with me. If I was sad, I thought she would offer her shoulder for me to cry on, dedicating all her time to me.

Despite my wife's genuine efforts to express love and make me feel valued (which were plenty), expecting her to consistently fulfill these roles was not just unrealistic—my expectation was unfair. My demands placed an immense burden on her, leading me to sulk like a disappointed or rejected child when she couldn't meet my desires exactly as I had expected. This cycle only pushed us further apart. As I pressed harder and harder for an unrealistic amount of connection and affection, particularly given that she had a life of her own and limited emotional bandwidth, she withdrew further and further. The more she withdrew, the more I poked and pouted. As she withdrew, I clung tighter to my unrealistic expectations, feeling hurt and angry that she couldn't be who I wanted her to be.

I am sure your partner has amazing qualities. You would never have chosen them if they didn't. Yet, the truth remains: they are imperfect, they can't complete you, and, while they can contribute to your happiness, they can't make you perpetually happy. As a matter of fact, it is almost a given that our partners will cause us pain. Relationship expert Terry Real puts it plainly when addressing the reality of relationships:

"Disillusionment comes with the cold realization that not only will your partner not directly heal you, but they are exquisitely designed to stick the burning spear right into your eyeball."[3] Even though we know this deep down, we still cling to the fairy tale of the perfect healing partner, even in subtle ways.

For example, why do we have such strong reactions when our partners can't be there for us in the way we want? Why do we become so despairing after a fight? We can get so hurt and reactive that our minds spiral into thoughts about how terrible our partners are and how bleak the future looks. Sure, there are perfectly valid neuroscience-based explanations for these reactions (many of which we'll discuss later), but they're also fueled by the myths we hold about relationships.

We should expect relationships to involve a never-ending cycle of rupture and repair. As imperfectly perfect partners, journeying with our equally imperfectly perfect partners, we are guaranteed to be hurt by them (and them by us). These hurts will, of course, cause a rupture in our connection. However, the hope is that, on this romantic journey, there will be an equal number of, or more, moments of repairing those ruptures and feeling the secure connection once again.

Let me be clear, and I'll emphasize this often: I am not talking about the kind of hurt that constitutes abuse. Absolutely not! Abuse is intolerable, and you should never accept it. What I'm talking about are those everyday moments when we forget to do something our partner asked, reject their desire to connect because we're exhausted and say it too bluntly, forget to pick up the milk, withdraw without warning when we should be communicating, get irritable in tense moments, or criticize instead of supporting our partners. These are the times when we are not our best selves. We will hurt our partners, and they will hurt us—until death or divorce do us part.

Myth-Busting Truth: If Parents Disappoint Us, Surely Our Partners Will

We understand, on some level, that our partners can't always be in a chipper mood, engage in deep philosophical, theological, or political discussions when uninspired, or be ready to connect with us emotionally or sexually exactly when we wish them to. We know that life's challenges, our unique differences, and the inherent imperfections in people mean friction, and unmet expectations are inevitable in any relationship. It's natural to experience ups and downs, feel disappointed, face rejection, and argue from time to time, given the complexities of life. Yet, when confronted with our partner's differences, quirks, lack of emotional intelligence, or inability to be present when we wish, we often find ourselves jolted, surprised, or filled with judgment and contempt.

It's almost as if we're unconsciously searching for a perfect, idealized parent—always attuned, continually in touch with what we seek, loving us with all they have. Yet, in truth, many of us would admit that even our parents couldn't always provide the support we needed. Do we expect more from our partners than we received from our parents?

Psychologists talk about "good enough" parenting, which is the notion that children can thrive when their parents are responsive and attuned to their needs about 30% of the time. That doesn't mean parents can be abusive the other 70% of the time. It's within the context of imperfect yet loving parents, living life, doing the best they can, yet having moments where they were busy, not in the greatest mood, stressed, and neglectful of some of the emotional and physical needs of the child. So, if this is the reality of "good enough" parenting, why do we expect our partners to be there for us the way we need 60% or 90% of the time, allowing only a slim margin for human error?

Sometimes we all need a little grace. Not as a license to harm, but as a healing salve necessary for our human predicament. If our parents disappointed us on occasion (and for some, on many occasions), surely our partners will as well.

Myth-Busting Truth: Even the Enlightened Would Disappoint

I've noodled over this thought experiment more times than I can count: what if someone ended up dating the likes of Jesus, Buddha, or Mother Teresa? At first blush, it'd be downright enchanting—being swept off your feet by their boundless compassion, sterling character, and almost magical abilities (I mean, Jesus raising the dead is pretty epic!).

But let's fast-forward past that starry-eyed beginning. Imagine you feel the need for a hug or a pep talk, only to find Jesus and Mother Teresa perpetually busy with their gigs of miracle-working or doling out loaves, fishes, or bandages. Or picture yourself as the Buddha's plus-one, initially in awe of his Zen-like presence and his uncanny ability to tune into your every existential and emotional whim. Fast-forward a bit, and there you are, drumming your fingers, searching for the Buddha only to find him in his meditation room again. Or you might find yourself feeling overwhelmed by his intense desire for intimacy, to the point where you just need to escape and watch some mindless TV. Even the most enlightened among us would disappoint their partners occasionally. And if they would, certainly our partners will too.

Myth-Busting Truth: We Don't Show Up for Ourselves Perfectly

Let's shift our focus from the relationship we have with our partner to our relationship with ourselves. If we often fail to support ourselves in ways that are kind, loving, and healthy, why then do we expect such high, almost perfectionistic, standards from our partners?

For instance, the mere thought of our partners gaslighting us—making us question our own memory, perception, feeling state, or sanity—can elicit intense anger. While it's crucial to stand up for ourselves and communicate our feelings about what is acceptable and what isn't, we must also consider how we might be gaslighting ourselves.

How does this happen?

We gaslight ourselves when we invalidate our own feelings of rage, anger, sadness, shame, and sometimes even joy, effectively alienating those tender parts of ourselves as if they are irrational. This occurs when we tell the wounded parts of ourselves that they are being overly dramatic or emotional, or are making too much of a situation. We gaslight ourselves when we silence a part of us that desperately seeks to be acknowledged by insisting there's no problem and proceeding as usual. We also gaslight ourselves when we harshly criticize the vulnerable parts of us that yearn to be expressed, thereby making them feel invalidated simply for existing.

There are other situations where, instead of being kind to ourselves, we let the Inner Critic take over, tearing us down without our even realizing what's happening. While we abandon and gaslight ourselves, we expect our partners to be super understanding and empathetic. Not only do we expect more from our partners than we are often willing to give ourselves, but we become upset with them when they fall short. In these moments, we forget that we're all just trying to do our best to be kind and loving.

And then there's that whole "They should just know what I need" thing. Sure, it feels amazing when our partners just get us and do things that make us feel loved without our having to spell it out. But let's be real; do we always know exactly what we're feeling or what we need? Not really. Given that, maybe it's fair to relax our perfectionistic standards for our partners a bit.

Myth-Busting Truth: Our Partners Can't Fill a Community-Shaped Hole

As you reflect on what we've discussed so far, you will probably realize that relying solely on our partner to fulfill all our needs and desires is like expecting a single favorite food to satisfy every culinary craving—it's unrealistic. However, for some of us, the fantasy of our partner being our everything is perpetuated by the loss of community and belonging, which creates such a significant ache and void that we unknowingly expect our partner to fill it. Yet we know, at least on some level, that our partner cannot provide what a community is supposed to.

Sadly, the days when community life naturally fulfilled many of our social needs are now behind us. Many find themselves reminiscing about spending time on porches for casual hangouts, participating in block parties, or enjoying those spontaneous evenings when wacky aunts and uncles dropped by for a chat. Others recall frequent church gatherings, neighborhood watch meetings where local issues were amicably debated, or Sunday dinners that felt like mini family reunions. The camaraderie of local sports leagues and the shared responsibility of community gardens also fostered a strong sense of belonging. However, especially after COVID, many of us are navigating life in our individual lanes as our society advances along an increasingly individualistic trajectory.

"But, Mark, we have social media. Isn't that enough?"

Technology, which promised to connect us, offers quick hits of dopamine with every like and share. However, social media fails to fulfill our deeper human needs. While some have found pockets of solace online, for many, the immediate reinforcement from our online activities often provides only a shallow fix. Our virtual worlds cannot replace the depth of face-to-face interactions. And let's not forget the endless stream of polarizing, painful, and downright nasty posts (usually born from unprocessed trauma). Instead of feeling more connected, we often end up feeling more depressed, wondering if we'd have been better off steering clear of social media in the first place.

As we age, the challenge of making new friends doesn't get any easier. The reasonable precautions many of us take in this post-pandemic society, combined with media portrayals that continually emphasize the dangers of our world, result in even more isolation. The polarization of politics makes trusting your differently affiliated neighbor, friend, or family member fraught with challenges. Additionally, some individuals find that their long-cherished religious communities no longer provide a safe space for authenticity and growth, leaving them facing the loss of yet another source of community. These situations can make the task of bridging the gaps that divide us and forming new friendships even more daunting. With loneliness on the rise, it's clear that we're all feeling the effects of the past few years.

Due to recent societal challenges, we've found ourselves expecting our partners to fulfill an array of roles without even realizing it. As the fabric of communal life thins, relational voids become more pronounced, compelling us to look to our partners for solutions. Consequently, partners are articulating their needs more explicitly and, at times, critically. I find that statements like "I need you to be more than just a co-provider and co-parent; I need you to be my intimate, emotionally intelligent best friend" are becoming more common. In my experience in the therapy room, I observe this more frequently in women than men. However, for many of us, we unknowingly expect our partners to be our spouse, protector, consoler, encourager, nurse, therapist, healer, adventure companion, sounding board, and coach, among other roles. This places an immense burden on them, one that a single person cannot sustainably bear, as these are roles traditionally filled by a community.

Sometimes when we find ourselves unhappy in our relationship, it isn't just our partner's fault. It could be that we're longing for more varied, intimate connections in general. When we're without a tribe, feeling disconnected from others, there are consequences. Recent neuro-science findings tell us that humans have a basic need to belong, to feel safe, and to be loved.[4] This need is so deep that our nervous systems see loneliness, isolation, and rejection as primal threats. Loneliness and isolation make anxiety and stress hormones flood our brains and bodies, taking a toll on our immune system and overall well-being.[5] Mother Teresa once said, "The most terrible poverty is loneliness, and the feeling of being unloved." We're not meant to travel life alone.

We need a village—a community or tribe where we feel we belong. We need people in our lives who have strengths, gifts, and abilities that our partners may not possess. Maybe some of the dissatisfaction we feel in our relationships actually comes from being disconnected from friends and family. Are we unintentionally expecting our partners to fill roles that are better suited for a supportive community? Are we blaming our partners, using them as scapegoats for pain and aches they didn't cause?

While much of this book is about deepening the connection within your romantic relationship, finding greater happiness might also mean nurturing relationships outside that partnership.

Embracing Our Humanness

Look at us fascinating creatures, us mammals, who evolved from billions of years of evolution, floating in outer space on an orb called planet Earth. Ours is but one of many planets, within many solar systems. And here we are, in this vastness, trying to engage in life together, while keeping a loving relationship alive and ourselves sane. It is quite remarkable. Sometimes when life is moving so fast, we forget our stories, our courage, our fragility amidst our resilience.

As we wrap up this exploration of myths, truths, and the intricate dance of our wonderfully messy relationships—so distinct from the fairy tales we've grown up with—I want to pause and acknowledge the possibility that reading this chapter might stir up feelings of grief. This grief stems from a profound sense of loss—the shattering of illusions about who we thought our partner was, the longing for perfect re-parenting that we will never receive, and the slow dissolving of fairy-tale fantasies.

Grief is that gnawing unease we often find residing in our chest. It often carries with it a chorus of anger, hurt, defiance, and sadness. Our grief may ride within us like an uneasy wolf that walks around in aimless circles, not quite sure of where to go or what to do next. Our array of heavy emotions can thrust us into a fog-laden, liminal space, leaving us grappling for stability as we navigate an uncertain path in what feels like a shoddy caravan with four balding tires and two that are low on air. When we choose to face the truth about the relationship myths that bind us, we can overcome that grief and begin a new journey. This journey will be one that traverses many rocky patches, leads us through the briars lurking in the untrodden woods we find ourselves in, and guides us through the creeks life's storms create. It is only by taking the joint journey down this wild path that we can move toward a more authentic, mature form of love.

Acknowledging the existential dilemma created by life's challenges and giving up our propensity for fantasy isn't about lowering our standards. It's about bravely confronting reality in its rawest form. Only through our willingness to work to dispel the illusions of our youth can we attain a deeper, more mature understanding of what it means to be in a genuine relationship. If you are willing to walk this rough path, you will be rewarded by reality as it truly is. If you are ready to awaken from Sleeping Beauty's slumber, you will find that romance isn't the fantasy you wished it to be. However, you will discover a richness and depth that can never exist in a fairy tale. Now you can begin experiencing life in the flesh, without it being cloaked in fancy and ornate disguises and without substances to numb your existence. The journey to deeper intimacy, stronger connection, and a feeling of safety in our own skin in the presence of our partner (aka "secure attachment") begins with honesty. Echoing the wisdom of the ages, "The truth will set us free." I might whisper in addition, "But freedom's gate swings on the hinges of change's poignant pain."

Seeing clearly who our amazing yet imperfect partners are—and recognizing our imperfect and courageous selves in the process—allows us to embrace the beautiful, the chaotic, the mundane. It gives us the ability to work through hurt and complicated feelings and messy mood states with greater empathy and equanimity. These elements are fundamental to a love that's richly colorful, deeply felt, and truly meaningful. From the ashes of our fantasies, there will arise a new strength that can help us persevere.

Chapter One Wrap-Up

Instead of pursuing an elusive fairy tale, you have the opportunity to cultivate a genuine, enduring bond and friendship with your partner. This true relationship will have a depth enabling you to navigate the fleeting and flailing journey through the perplexing maze known as life. By working with your partner in your true reality, you can overcome what you believed to be unbearable, work toward a realistic destination, and find what is possible with more aliveness. You will hold each other in a mirror of true wonder where neither of you is weighed down by constant judgment, accusations, or shaming.

My wish for you is that through the ups and downs, bliss and betrayals, hurts and hopes, you find yourselves able to say to one another: "Our eyes have been unveiled. I see you, my beloved, and you see me. We stand naked, battered, and tattered—not broken but brave, secure with one another, and unashamed."

Key Takeaways

1. Beyond the Honeymoon: Mature love begins where the fairy tale ends, as the initial excitement of our relationship fades and both partners' quirks and past traumas emerge. It is in this moment that we're invited to navigate the complex reality of a mature relationship, transforming challenges into deeper connection and understanding.

2. Love's Tough Road: Who said love was going to be easy? Certainly not me. It requires work, patience, and a profound level of understanding. Life is challenging, and so is love. Navigating through differences and accepting that our partners can't complete us or be the sole source of our happiness are essential parts of this journey.

3. Understand Each Other's Wiring: Everyone's brain works differently, and that's okay. Understanding how your partner ticks—especially when it comes to emotions—can make a world of difference. It's all about talking and listening in ways that connect, not clash. This means we need to suspend our judgments and enter into a period of mutual curiosity.

4. Rethink Relationship Expectations: If we accept the concept of "good enough" parenting, which suggests that children can thrive with parents being attuned to their needs about 30% of the time, then expecting our partners to meet our needs almost perfectly sets an unrealistic standard. Try redefining what you require of your romantic relationship. Allow your partner to be a "good enough" partner, and leave the idea of perfection behind.

5. Beyond Just Us: A good relationship isn't just about two people; it's also about having friends and a community that supports you. Spreading your social wings can take the heat off your relationship and bring more joy into your life.

6. Navigate Grief Together: Grief challenges us to confront the loss of our fairy-tale expectations and embrace the reality of our relationships. Being willing to go on this tough but transformative journey can deepen your connection into a more genuine and mature love.

Chapter 2
Discovering Each Other's Operating Manual

"We get to know our partner fully in order to become competent as managers of our partners in the best way. By competent managers, I mean partners who are experts on one another and know how to move, shift, motivate, influence, soothe, and inspire one another."

— Stan Tatkin, *Wired for Love*

What if, instead of navigating your relationship as if you were trying to pilot a spacecraft with no training, struggling to comprehend who your partner is and how they function within the relationship, you had access to their well-worn user guide? Imagine a guide that reveals their relational blueprint, illuminating how they view both themself and you, detailing their deepest needs and fears, along with their strategies for managing the complexities of your relationship. This guidebook would explain the "hot buttons" you've inadvertently pressed and point out other crucial levers in the relationship that you may have overlooked—levers essential for maintaining a secure connection. This manual would replace the guesswork and assumptions with a more grounded and informed understanding of the raw realities driving your partner's behavior, which might otherwise remain a mystery. It would enable you to find clarity and allow each of you to navigate your shared journey more smoothly, flying confidently without the risk of crashing.

If such a manual existed, would you want to read it? If you're nodding yes, you're in the right chapter. In the journey of love and companionship, understanding your partner's manual is more than just helpful; it's essential to building and maintaining a meaningful bond.

I want to tread lightly here. I admit, I have a slight aversion to being labeled and to folks claiming they offer the holy grail of understanding oneself and others. When horoscopes, astrologists, personality tests, Enneagram gurus, and spiritual leaders categorize us and tell us what we care about and how we view and navigate the world, I wince. Instantly, I'm skeptical and start questioning their interpretations and motivations. We should have the agency to define who we are. We should be the ones to share our owner's manual and explain how our operating systems work, rather than letting others do it for us.

There is a conundrum here, however. For many of us, our neurobiology has a manual of its own, which is difficult to understand. Not everyone has a degree in psychology or neuroscience. And this is where we need a village. And within that village, we need those who have worked hard to decode our intricate internal landscape and patterns of thinking and relating. Enter the realm of *attachment theory*, a domain where psychologists have charted the terrain of our relationships, offering a map to better understand not only ourselves but the underlying dynamics that have produced our unique styles of relating to one another.

Attachment theory offers a perspective for interpreting how our early relationships with primary caregivers have significantly shaped our sense of self and our place in the world in a way that profoundly influences every interaction we have with others into adulthood. We'll explore the different attachment styles (or "relationship tendencies")—*secure, anxious, avoidant,* and *disorganized*—and how they manifest in relationships. This theory has been beneficial not only in my personal life but also in my work with numerous couples from diverse ethnic and cultural backgrounds, where I'm always considering how the prism of attachment is viewed through their lived experiences.

A big game changer with the couples that I work with occurs when partners start looking at the big picture of who they are to each other and why they respond the way they do during conflicts. Instead of assuming in those rough moments of disconnection that their partner is just cold and distant or too reactive and critical, they start to understand the deeper forces at play.

For instance, this change in perspective can be liberating for some partners to comprehend why it's challenging for their significant other to handle intense emotions—or any emotions—when they understand the dynamics their significant other experienced growing up that shaped their way of relating. It might also be enlightening for others to recognize why their partners tend to pursue and provoke them, driven by a fundamental question: "Do you love and care about me?"—a query they have been anxiously posing to important people in their lives for quite some time. Recognizing the historical reasons behind their own or their partner's struggles with understanding or regulating emotions, low self-worth, and feeling trapped in a relentless cycle of chaotic drama can also be freeing.

I'm hoping that by the time you turn the last page of this chapter, you'll view your relationship with your partner through a new lens and will better understand why you and your partner relate to each other the way you do. By getting the lowdown on each other's attachment tendencies, as laid out in your personal manuals, you'll be better equipped to form a connection that is not just healthier but also filled with more understanding and empathy for each other.

Attachment Theory Basics

Attachment theory, first proposed by psychiatrist and psychoanalyst John Bowlby, suggested that a warm, caring emotional bond between an infant and their mother is paramount for the healthy psychological development of the child. For people today, attachment theories' principles may seem like a no-brainer that emotional bonds are important for healthy growth and development, but in Bowlby's time, during the early to mid-1900s, this was not unanimously the case. Back then, of course there was an emphasis on being good parents (though what "good" meant has evolved over time). However, the idea that a primary caregiver's lack of attunement, warmth, and a loving emotional bond with a child, especially during their early years, could be detrimental to an infant's development was an emerging idea.

From the moment we are born, our brains begin to log what can best be described as experimental data. When a baby cries, their nervous system, operating in its own preverbal language, signals, "I am uncomfortable and in pain." The baby's nervous system then observes, "What happens when I cry?" It is anticipating a response, hoping for a superb outcome of being attuned to and cared for. Meanwhile, it keeps watch on the outcome. This initial mapping of our world relies almost entirely on our first caregivers—most often our mothers. Back in Bowlby's day, it might not have been immediately obvious that our psychological, emotional, and relational health is deeply connected to how responsive our mothers were to our needs as infants.

Attachment theory highlights the crucial role our caregivers, as our primary attachment figures, play in our early lives. Beyond our genetic makeup and temperament, our relationship with our primary caregivers shapes the course of our lives more profoundly than any other factors, including peer and cultural experiences. Studies on attachment styles in human relationships consistently demonstrate that the ways our caregivers interact with us during our early years—particularly the first eighteen months—lay the foundation for what attachment theorists refer to as *internal working models*.[1] These models deeply influence our ability to develop stable, healthy, and secure relationships in the future, both with ourselves and with others.

Internal Working Models

From the moment we're thrust into this world, our brains get busy sketching out the landscape of relationships, figuring out who we are and who everyone else is. This grand adventure unfolds over time, through countless little moments with our primary caregivers. These experiences shape our internal mental and emotional maps, which we can think of as

our internal working models. These models, crafted from our early interactions, become the blueprints for all future relationships, guiding our
expectations about whether others will be there for us when we need
them most.

Attachment theory tells us that if our caregivers consistently meet our
physical, emotional, and nurturing needs, we usually develop a *secure
attachment style*. This means our internal model expects others to be
supportive and trustworthy, and we see ourselves in a positive light. On
the flip side, if our caregivers are unreliable, we might end up with an
insecure attachment style. This results in a model filled with mistrust and
doubts about our own worthiness of love and support.

Take infants, for example. When they have primary caregivers who
are consistently available, attentive, and fully engaged, they develop
implicit beliefs and expectations about themselves and these key figures.
Even though they can't yet voice complex thoughts, if their nervous
system could speak, it would whisper: "Ah, my parents are reliable. I feel
taken care of. I can trust that if I need something, my parents will be
there. The world, including myself and others, is good." This realization
grows into a deep-seated belief system of secure attachment, painting
their worldview with optimism.

As the child grows, they carry this foundation of positivity and trust
into other relationships. In adulthood, this manifests as a profound sense
of self-assurance and ease within their connections. It's a beautiful thing,
really, how those early moments shape us, coloring our lives with the
hues of love and trust we received when we were just beginning to navigate this wild, wonderful world.

Unfortunately, not everyone grows up with a consistent set of the
ABCs of attachment: *Acceptance*, *Belonging*, *Comfort*, and *Safety*.[2] Sure,
some folks have a secure attachment style—supposedly around 50% of
us—but many of us end up with what the researchers call an *insecure
attachment style*. Maybe we grew up in homes where our parents were
distant, preoccupied, disconnected, juggling a child with special needs,
abusive, controlling, battling addictions, or drowning in their own grief
during our formative years. These complex family dynamics create environments lacking safety and consistency, breeding internal insecurities

and a nervous system perpetually on edge. This wreaks havoc on our internal working models of ourselves and others, leading to insecure styles of relating—like *anxious*, *avoidant*, and *disorganized* (which we will discuss shortly).

Originally, attachment theory zeroed in on the bond between kids and their primary caregivers (mostly mothers). But almost half a century later, it's expanded to include the dynamics of adult romantic relationships. Attachment theory shows us that emotional bonds with primary attachment figures—those relationships where we feel acceptance, belonging, protection, comfort, nurturing, and emotional safety—are crucial from the cradle to the grave, from our first cry to our last goodbye. When we find ourselves in securely functioning relationships with these vital ingredients, we flourish—not just as children, but as adults too.

Where Did Attachment Styles Originate?

In 1969, Mary Ainsworth, working closely with Bowlby, began exploring the intricate ways babies bond with their mothers. She was driven by a deep curiosity about the different patterns of *attachment security*—the felt sense of safety within a relationship. Ainsworth's research laid the foundation, but it was the contributions of her collaborator, Mary Main, that were crucial in defining the attachment styles we recognize today. They hypothesized that distinct attachment styles—those habitual ways of being in relationships—could already be identified at the infant stage. To delve into these dynamics, Ainsworth devised an innovative laboratory experiment known as the Strange Situation. This experiment allowed her to peek into, and record, the complex dance of infant-parent attachment and observe what relationship styles would emerge.[3]

So, let's break down the experiment in a nutshell. It was set up in eight parts, each lasting three minutes. Picture this: a young child, aged twelve to eighteen months, and their mom walk into a new room loaded with toys. The mom allows the kid to explore and play freely. Then, a stranger enters and makes small talk with the mom before the mom discreetly exits. Now, the kiddo is left alone with this new person they've never interacted with before. If the little one remains calm and doesn't throw a fit, the stranger stays in the room.

After a bit, the mom reappears, pausing at the entrance. The researchers are taking notes as they question, "What's the kid's move when mom steps back in?" Next up, the stranger bows out, followed by the mom, leaving the precious little one solo. If the tot doesn't hit peak meltdown, they remain solo until the stranger pops back in. The grand finale? The mom returns for a reunion, and the stranger dips out. Meanwhile, there's an observer jotting down every behavior of the child during the experiment. They note the child's willingness to explore, separation anxiety when the mom leaves, anxiety in response to the stranger, and the pivotal reaction upon the mom's return (a key moment of observation).

Ainsworth zeroed in on the infant's responses when the mother returned. She identified three distinct styles of relating: one where the baby cried upon the mother's entrance but was soothed once the mother embraced them; the second where the baby sought connection with the mother but was upset, visibly angry, and had difficulty being soothed; and the third where the baby was indifferent upon the mother's return. Later on, reviewing the tapes again, they noticed a fourth pattern where the baby seemed erratic, simultaneously pulling for connection and wanting to pull away. This research led to Ainsworth and Main's categorization of four infant attachment styles—secure, anxious, avoidant, and disorganized.

The Use of Terms

Following Bowlby's and Ainsworth and Main's seminal work, other psychologists coined terms for corresponding adult attachment styles. However, many educators of attachment theory in romantic relationships, myself included, continue to use the early infant categories to describe adult relational tendencies. Why? For the sake of simplicity, and because these terms effectively capture distinct ways of interacting with others that resonate with many people's experiences.

For instance, some of us may be more inclined to *avoid* and shy away from emotions, conflicts, intimacy, and vulnerability. Others might be more prone to anxiety within our relationships, frequently fearing the loss of connection and love. This anxiety can manifest in a tendency to anxiously pursue and cling to partners, rather than distancing from them. Therefore, to simplify our terminology, I'll use the categories of secure, anxious, avoidant, and disorganized to refer to adult attachment styles.

Furthermore, to avoid the rigidity of the term "attachment style," which often suggests fixed ways of being, I prefer to use "relationship tendencies" moving forward. This contrasts with the concept of a singular "style," which can imply a static state of being across all relationships. Each set of tendencies represents unique ways of being in our relationships and exists on a spectrum; for example, one person may tend to be more avoidant than another, while another might be less anxious than another. Then, stating that a person can *tend* to behave in a certain manner opens up the possibility that they can express different behaviors.

For example, think of someone who tends to have avoidant tendencies but who, in a moment of calm, demonstrates a secure, loving presence. This is why, especially with insecure attachments, I discourage people from making statements like "my partner is disorganized" or referring to someone as "my anxious partner." The language we use is crucial; using such fixed descriptors suggests these traits define their identity. For example, instead of describing your partner as my "avoidant partner," it's more accurate to say "my partner who has avoidant tendencies."

While "attachment tendencies" is fine with me, and I do use the term "attachment" occasionally in this book, I find "relationship tendencies" more relatable and down-to-earth. When I think of *attachment*, it conjures images of email attachments or vacuum cleaners. People typically ask, "How is your *relationship* going with your partner?" rather than asking, "How is your *attachment* with your partner going?"

Relationship tendencies manifest as behavioral patterns and emotional responses that primarily serve to keep us feeling safe, sane, and loved. It is fascinating to consider that the way we interacted with our caregivers in the first few years of life could vastly shape how we relate to our partners decades later. If we developed insecure tendencies, the good news is that we can learn new principles and practices that help us connect with our partners, allowing our secure tendencies to emerge organically. However, before we can transition to a more secure way of being in our relationships, we must fully understand the current relationship tendencies we exhibit with our partners.

Quiz: Discover Your Primary Relationship Tendency

Let's take a simple quiz designed to help you uncover your relationship tendencies (to fill out manually, see the PDF workbook). When you're going through this quiz, remember that it's not about getting an A+ or finding the right answer. There actually are no wrong answers. It's simply a means of illuminating your behavioral and emotional tendencies in relationships. Just pick the answer that feels accurate; there's no need to overthink it. The results will give you a general idea of your dominant tendency. Then, as we discuss these tendencies in more detail, you can keep your primary relationship tendency in mind.

Additionally, you can retake the quiz while considering your partner's tendencies. Remember, this is merely a well-informed guess. It's crucial for your partner to identify which tendency best represents them. If you're comfortable doing so, you might ask your partner if they would be willing to take the quiz; who knows, maybe this would spur them to want to read more.

Let's Begin the Quiz

1. **How comfortable are you opening up emotionally to someone in a close relationship?**

A. I find it easy to share my feelings and be vulnerable.

B. I worry about rejection if I open up too much.

C. I prefer to keep my emotions private.

D. I struggle to understand my own emotions, making it hard to share them.

2. When there's a disagreement with your partner, do you express your concerns directly or avoid conflict altogether?

A. I believe in open communication and work toward a solution together.

B. I worry about upsetting my partner, so I might hold back my feelings.

C. I tend to withdraw and avoid confrontation.

D. Disagreements confuse me, and I might react unpredictably.

3. How would you describe your comfort level when asking for help from your partner?

A. I feel comfortable asking for help when I need it.

B. I worry they'll judge me or think I'm weak if I ask for help.

C. I prefer to handle things myself and rarely ask for help.

D. My comfort level with asking for help varies depending on the situation.

4. Do you enjoy spending time alone, or do you crave constant companionship?

A. I enjoy my own company but also value spending time with loved ones.

B. The thought of being alone makes me anxious.

C. I generally prefer solitude and feel more at ease when alone.

D. I feel torn. Sometimes I crave being alone, other times I don't.

5. Imagine your partner wants to spend more quality time with you. How do you feel?

A. I'd be happy to spend more time together.

B. I might worry that they're clingy or insecure.

C. I might feel a need for some personal space.

D. My feelings would be mixed, depending on my mood.

6. How important is physical and emotional intimacy to you in a relationship?

A. Intimacy is a vital part of a healthy relationship for me.
B. I crave intimacy but might be afraid of rejection.
C. I don't see intimacy as a necessity and might avoid it.
D. My views on intimacy are inconsistent and confusing.

7. Do you generally feel secure and worthy of love in your relationships?

A. Yes, I have a positive self-image within relationships.
B. I often question my value as a partner.
C. My sense of worth doesn't depend heavily on relationships.
D. My feelings of self-worth fluctuate greatly in relationships.

8. How easily do you trust your partner?

A. I trust easily and openly in my relationships.
B. I find it challenging to trust fully and fear betrayal.
C. Trusting someone deeply takes a long time for me.
D. Trust is a complex issue for me, and my feelings can change quickly.

9. Imagine your partner expresses a desire for more independence in the relationship. How would you react?

A. I'd be supportive, understanding the need for space.
B. I might feel insecure and worried about losing them.
C. I'd feel relieved and happy they value their independence.
D. I'd have mixed emotions, unsure how to respond.

10. When your partner is upset, what's your natural instinct?

A. I want to offer comfort and understanding.

B. I might feel overwhelmed by their emotions and become anxious.

C. I might withdraw or feel uncomfortable with their distress.

D. I'm unsure how to react and might feel confused by their emotions.

11. How would you describe your ideal communication style in a relationship?

A. I am open, honest, and comfortable discussing anything.

B. Frequent reassurance and check-ins are important to me.

C. I prefer clear communication but avoid overly emotional conversations.

D. Communication can be confusing; sometimes I crave it, sometimes I withdraw.

12. Imagine seeing your partner talking to someone attractive. What's your first thought?

A. I trust my partner and wouldn't be worried.

B. I might feel insecure and wonder if they're attracted to someone else.

C. It wouldn't bother me; I trust my partner to maintain boundaries.

D. I might experience a mix of jealousy and confusion.

13. How do you handle disagreements with friends?

A. I can express my perspective calmly and work toward a resolution.

B. I might worry about damaging the friendship and avoid conflict.

C. I tend to dismiss disagreements or withdraw from the situation.

D. Disagreements with friends can be emotionally unpredictable for me.

14. Do you find it easy to forgive your partner after a fight?

A. Yes, I believe in forgiveness and moving forward.

B. I might struggle to forgive if I feel hurt or insecure.

C. Forgiveness comes easily; I don't hold onto grudges.

D. My ability to forgive depends on the situation and my mood.

15. How comfortable are you introducing your partner to your close friends and family?

A. I'd be happy to introduce them and share them with loved ones.

B. I might feel anxious about how they'll be perceived.

C. I might prefer to keep my personal life separate for a while.

D. My comfort level with introductions would depend on the circumstances.

16. Imagine your partner cancels plans last minute. How do you react?

A. I can understand and would try to reschedule.

B. I might feel hurt or rejected and wonder if they don't care about my feelings.

C. It wouldn't bother me much; I'm flexible with plans.

D. My reaction would depend on the reason and my mood at the time.

17. Ending a relationship is difficult for you because:

A. I value commitment, and I invested time in the relationship.

B. I fear being alone and worry about finding someone else.

C. I prefer to avoid messy situations and prolonged goodbyes.

D. My emotions are conflicted, and I might feel a mix of relief and sadness.

18. How would you describe your past romantic relationships overall?

    A. Generally positive with healthy communication and trust.
    B. Often characterized by insecurity and a fear of abandonment.
    C. Mostly independent with limited emotional intimacy.
    D. Inconsistent and confusing with mixed experiences.

19. Imagine your partner is going on a work trip for a week. How do you feel?

    A. Supportive and understanding; I enjoy some alone time too.
    B. I might feel anxious about missing them and worry about the distance.
    C. I wouldn't mind; I value my own space and independence.
    D. My feelings would be mixed; I might crave their presence but also enjoy the time alone.

20. In your opinion, the most important qualities in a relationship are:

    A. Mutual respect, trust, and open communication.
    B. Constant reassurance, affection, and emotional security.
    C. Independence, personal space, and clear boundaries.
    D. A balance of closeness and independence, but it can vary over time.

What Tendencies Emerged?

Now, to understand your relationship tendencies, let's look at how you answered the questions. If *A*'s were popping up everywhere, it indicates a *secure* way of being in relationships. People with this tendency generally have a solid and positive view of themselves and tend to connect smoothly with others. They're comfortable with intimacy and place a lot of trust in their partners, believing the best about them. If you found yourself circling a lot of *B*'s, that suggests an *anxious* tendency, characterized by worries about lovability and fears of rejection and abandonment. Individuals with this style may seek constant reassurance and feel anxious about their partner's commitment. When their finely tuned radar perceives signs of disconnection or rejection, they will definitely let their partners know. A heap of *C*'s points to an *avoidant* relationship tendency. Those with an avoidant tendency value space and independence in relationships. Closeness and all that "emotional stuff" can feel overwhelming. And if *D*'s were in the majority, it hints at a *disorganized* way of being in relationships, marked by a high alert for danger and less predictability in relationships, often (but not always) resulting from histories of abuse and neglect.

Applaud yourself for taking this quiz. Although questions like these can feel disquieting to uncover your relationship tendencies, having this awareness will be a major help to you as you move through this book and work toward developing a healthier connection with your partner.

General Considerations
About Relationship Tendencies

Now that you have an idea about your own—and possibly your partner's—tendencies, we'll turn to some important considerations before diving into the four different relationship tendencies.

Relationship Tendencies Can Change

Each of us has a primary relationship tendency, which exists on a spectrum where traits can be more or less pronounced. These tendencies are not set in stone; they can vary depending on the individuals we are in a relationship with and can evolve over time. For instance, it's possible to exhibit a secure relationship with a partner but an anxious tendency with a sibling. We might start with a secure relational tendency with our partner, but after experiencing several painful relationship injuries over time, we may develop an anxious or avoidant way of being with them. In contrast, years of trusting interactions between partners—one with an anxious tendency and one with avoidant leanings—can eventually lead each to achieve a more secure way of being with one other.

These concepts should serve as springboards for "aha" moments and deeper conversations. They're also meant to inform us and provide insights to help us move toward a secure relationship with each other, particularly when we consider both of our blueprints. Take what resonates and discard the rest. We often exhibit a primary tendency in our romantic relationships, but it's not uncommon to identify traits from various attachment styles in your current partnership. Consider discussing with your partner which characteristics they perceive you as having, as we often have blind spots. Although we can learn a lot from experts and others, ultimately, you are the expert of your own story and how you want to be perceived.

Relationship Tendencies Should Not Be Weaponized

Before we explore relationship tendencies further, it's important to remember that these classifications should not be weaponized to use against each other. Too often, we "otherize" and pathologize one another. Phrases like "You are a gaslighter," "You are co-dependent," "You are a narcissist," "You're a borderline," and "You're an abuser" are increasingly thrown around, even in relatively healthy relationships, without a clear or consistent pattern of abuse being present.

I encourage you to exercise caution and care when discussing your primary but changeable modes of being. As you will soon see, these are tendencies that were once extremely adaptive and developed for good reasons. Please avoid using these insights as sharp barbs—for example, by saying, "You are such an avoidant. Go seek therapy," or "You have an anxious tendency, just like your mother! Get some help already!" Instead, let's use our understanding of our relationship tendencies as tools for growth and connection, not as means to criticize or humiliate.

Empathy for Primary Caregivers

Exploring relationship tendencies invites us to cultivate empathy, recognizing that we did not choose or craft these tendencies. They were shaped by early childhood experiences intersecting with our temperament, both beyond our control. Additionally, they might have been reinforced or primarily shaped by traumatic events unrelated to our parents, such as sexual abuse, racial trauma, or peer abuse. Despite the various factors that can contribute to our relationship tendencies, they often originate from our relationships with our primary caregivers.

Since we are about to talk about parental (or primary caregiver) dynamics and how those dynamics shaped us, know that I do not do so with a gavel in hand. The paths our parents walked were often carved out without their say, shaped by forces beyond their grasp.

Consider this: parents who couldn't provide the emotional warmth we needed likely grew up in a home where warmth and emotional sharing were rare commodities. Then, there's the anxious, critical parent who probably faced their own set of dragons, perhaps sharp criticism from their own perfectionistic parents or hidden battles with addiction, without the solace of therapy or supportive others to turn to. Consider the overworked parent, sacrificially holding down multiple jobs to make ends meet. What about the war veteran whose persistent PTSD made it very challenging for them to be consistently present, warm, and nonreactive? Our parents, shaped by their beautiful and tragic experiences, became who they are—just as we are shaped by ours. How can we judge them harshly, knowing that if we had lived their lives, with their genetics, temperament, upbringing, neurobiology, and cultural milieu, we would have acted similarly?

Acknowledging the ways our parents have shaped our relationship tendencies doesn't mean we're throwing them under the bus. It also doesn't have to mean we are going to ignore the past. Sure, my invitation is to not hastily brand them as the villains of our story without a second thought to the bigger picture—their own histories, the cultural tides they swam against, and the family legacies and burdens they carried. But understanding their struggles doesn't mean we give them a free pass and live in denial.

Whether it's due to abuse, their own overwhelming issues, or realities that would make us weep, it's okay to acknowledge that when we were younger, we didn't receive the nurturance, guidance, love, and protection we needed. For some of us, it's crucial to explicitly name abuse as abuse. These are realities and wounds we have the right to deeply feel and acknowledge. We have the right to speak our truths, name our deprivations or traumas, and courageously seek to leave a healthier legacy behind—while humbly noting that we may also need to save for our children's therapy fund.

Now, let's explore the four relationship tendencies in more detail.

The Four Relationship Tendencies

When discussing the origins associated with different tendencies, it is common to focus on early childhood experiences, as these are the ones most often remembered. It's crucial to understand that our relationship tendencies are initially established during infancy and further shaped and reinforced by ongoing interactions with our parents and others as we grow. We will start with the insecure relationship tendencies: anxious, avoidant, and disorganized, and then move on to the secure relationship tendency. For each, I'll give an example of how the tendency developed and then discuss how it manifests in romantic relationships.

Anxious Tendencies

My Personal Story

I remember it with striking clarity. The meal our mother had lovingly prepared was hurled to the kitchen floor by my father in a fit of anger. In response, our mother, consumed by fury, brandished a large knife from a drawer and aimed the blade at my father. A storm of words erupted between them, their harsh accusations and curses further tearing at the fragile fabric of their relationship. They viewed each other not as partners but as adversaries, oblivious to the lasting scars their battles would inflict on those caught in the crossfire.

Prompted by the sight of our mom wielding a knife, my two brothers and I seized the chance to escape the chaos and fled outside. It was a moment for swift action, not questions. Outside, we could still hear the echoes of their conflict, sharing glances of mute horror. Fear gripped us, uncertain of what might unfold next. That image of our mother, knife still in hand, driving our father from our home is a vivid memory, though I was only six years old. That episode stands as a stark memory of my parents together—if such turmoil could even be called togetherness. Tragically, this was but a prelude to further loss.

The incident with the knife was a breaking point; divorce was inevitable. Overcoming such deep-seated animosity seemed insurmountable for my parents. Marrying young and quickly expanding their family presented its own challenges. Their six-year union was surprisingly long under the circumstances, yet their separation was anything but amicable. It's astonishing how quickly love can curdle into hatred.

Children often bear the brunt of such domestic strife. Although my brothers and I have our own narratives of those times (one tragically resulting in schizophrenia and imprisonment), my story is mine to tell. At six, my understanding was limited, but fear dominated my experiences. I was torn, caught between two people I loved, navigating a minefield of loyalty and betrayal. The weekends with my dad were tainted by his bitter words about my mom. In turn, my mom would spitefully withhold our visits with Dad to punish him. I lived in a state of fear and confusion, forced to suppress my feelings and conform to the expectations of whichever parent I was with, lest I lose their love entirely. My life was further complicated by a violent stepfather who, while he loved my mom in some ways, was demeaning and physically abusive toward her on a consistent basis.

The turmoil with my parents, which also occurred during my first couple of years as an infant, while stark, wasn't the darkest part of my childhood. My mother, despite her best efforts, battled a drug addiction that I witnessed for as long as I can remember, leading to her untimely death from an overdose. My father's presence was marked by mental, emotional, and physical cruelty. Affection or words of love and pride were foreign concepts to him. Instead, I grew up hearing harsh criticisms that echoed his disdain. I might be called a "fucking loser just like your mother," a "lazy piece of shit," "weak," and "clueless," among other damaging remarks on any given day.

The lack of relational nutrients when I was younger reinforced an internal working model with a rocky and frightening terrain. I looked out at the world through dark-tinted lenses. I had acute abandonment issues, along with powerful, ingrained, shame-based beliefs about myself and my worth etched upon my body and nervous system. Sure, there were times when I felt my mother's love and to some degree, my father's love. However, I never knew what state they would be in. I couldn't trust that love, warmth, and care would be right around the corner if I needed it. Therefore, growing up, I believed, mostly on an unconscious level, that I couldn't count on anyone—that no one would ever really love me for who I was. I grew up with an anxious tendency, desperate to be loved, yet never feeling that I was lovable.

Remember the anxiously attached infants in the Strange Situation? When faced with entering a strange room they had never been in, they clung to their mothers, became distressed when mom separated from them, and were visibly anxious when meeting the stranger. Then, when the mother returned, they were able to receive some comfort, yet for some, it took a while to feel calm and safe. That is very common for anxiously attached children. They tend to have a heightened attachment alarm system, monitoring their environment and cues from their primary caregivers, wanting, hoping, and wishing to be loved in the ways they are desperately seeking. Then, when they are loved, it is hard to let that moment of connection go, fearing it won't be found again.

Certainly, not everyone with an anxious tendency has a dramatic family origin story like mine. Their parents didn't have to be drug addicts or abusive; during their formative years, their parents could have been navigating through stressful life events, grappling with depression, career stress, their own parental loss, or their own anxieties, which prevented them from being adequately present. Alternatively, they might have been so overwhelmed by their own anxiety that it overshadowed their child's needs, smothering them with what they thought was love yet creating a fear-based environment. As a result, these children might have found it difficult to feel calm and soothed, always aware that a state of unpredictability could be just around the corner, potentially disrupting the warm and secure connection with their parent.

Regardless of the specific circumstances, those of us who developed anxious tendencies as children did so as an adaptation to our environment. We were uncertain when our emotional needs would be met. In every case, love and care became a hit-or-miss experience. We didn't know whether our cries would be met with care and attention to our needs or be ignored. Upon encountering our primary caregivers, we were unsure if we would be met with love or how transient that love might be. It's crucial to note that someone with an anxious tendency might have experienced numerous loving moments with their parents; the core issue remains the inconsistency of that love.

Having an Anxious Tendency in Romantic Relationships

Although everyone needs acceptance, belonging, and love, those of us with an anxious tendency are more prone to have these needs constantly at the forefront of our experience. More often than not, our hypervigilant relationship radar is constantly asking questions such as "Do you really love me?" "Am I important to you?" "Will you be there for me if I need you?" This behavior is partly because we often have a negative self-view and doubt our own lovability. Because we struggle to see ourselves as worthy of love, we are hoping to find our lovableness in the gaze of the other. Romantic partners might describe us as "clingy," "needy," "overly anxious," "oversensitive," or "in need of too much reassurance." They often feel frustrated, thinking, "No amount of love I give them will ever be enough."

Individuals with an anxious attachment tendency often initiate couples therapy for themselves and their partners. They diligently read the assigned materials, desperate for change, and eagerly await the therapist's intervention to "fix" their partner—though to be fair, both partners typically hope the therapist will fix the other. They often harbor thoughts like "I wish my partner was as emotionally healthy as I am" and "I deserve to be loved by someone with the amazing love I am able to provide." The partner of someone with an anxious tendency can frequently feel criticized or even controlled, placing them in a subordinate position, perpetually feeling judged. If the individual with anxious tendencies is high on the anxious spectrum, their partner might feel smothered. This dynamic intensifies their negative cycle: the more the partner with an anxious tendency presses for love, attention, and affection, the more overwhelmed the other feels and wants to withdraw, perpetuating a relentless cycle of disconnection.

Reflecting on the past, I realize that my wife and I were caught in a tenacious tango, with her being more avoidant (which we will get to in a moment) and me being more anxious in my tendencies. In those days, her saying, "I need space," was interpreted by my nervous system as "I want a divorce." Of course, she wasn't suggesting divorce. She merely wanted some space to process a conflict in her own way, in her own time.

Yet, my nervous system, always fearing separation and a loss of love, would perceive her words as a signal of primal panic. Then, I would become clingy, desperately seeking her attention and affection. Sadly, this emotional intensity acted like the opposite poles of a magnet—just as opposing poles push each other away, my attempts to pull her closer only made her withdraw further. Thus, the very warmth, kindness, and care I hoped to receive were pushed even further from my grasp.

People with anxious tendencies display a wide range of behaviors, with their anxiety and hypervigilance about the potential loss of love varying across a spectrum. Some with this attachment proclivity tend to be people pleasers, always aiming to satisfy others and make them happy at the expense of their own needs. Some can verbally poke with a searing hot poker just to get their partner's attention, while others can prod with a velvet hammer, which is less painful initially. Some playfully inquire, "Do you love me?" seeking reassurance. Meanwhile, others may express jealousy, accusing their partner of dedicating more time to colleagues or friends than to the relationship. Over the long run, these behaviors can be exhausting to the other partner.

I have immense compassion for those like myself with an anxious tendency. We simply yearn to be loved with the same intensity and commitment as we offer to those we cherish. We desire for our nervous systems to be continually embraced by our partners' reassurance. We react strongly to invalidating comments because deep inside we yearn to feel we are worthy of being validated. We long for what we never had—a secure, consistent, loving emotional bond with a partner who we know has our back and will honor and care for us. We long for a partner to deem us just right, instead of feeling like we are too much.

As an aside, there's wisdom to be appreciated in understanding the part of us that often feels so insecure. A tenet of internal family systems (IFS) therapy, an evidence-based approach to psychotherapy, is that we host multiple sub-personalities, or an *internal family system*, within us. These various sub-personalities, or *parts*, have their own points of view, emotions, impulses, motivations, and unique personalities. Among these is the wounded and anxious young child, yearning for acknowledgment, visibility, and acceptance—often referred to as our "inner child" (we will discuss this further in chapter nine). This is just one of the numerous sub-personalities residing within us.

This concept of an inner child (or *exile* in IFS language) is just a single aspect of the complex mosaic that constitutes our inner selves. My intention in highlighting this is to challenge the misconception that we are defined solely by our vulnerabilities—such as anxiety, neediness, or emotional disarray. Within us also lie incredibly vibrant and dynamic parts. These facets of our personalities are not only capable of engaging with the world in playful and creative ways but also embody resilience and determination. They enable us to tackle challenges head-on, innovate, and find joy in our endeavors. Furthermore, we possess the capacity for profound empathy and wisdom, allowing us to extend a helping hand to those around us with compassion and understanding.

I've learned from experience not to shame and judge our anxious tendencies and longings. Part of our healing journey is to mourn the fantasy of a perfect partner—someone who could become our most loving and perfectly imperfect advocate, friend, and lover—instead striving for a securely functioning relationship with the imperfect beloved before us.

Avoidant Tendencies

David's Story

David's path to an avoidant tendency was shaped within the structure of a deeply religious home, a place where emotions and free expression were not merely devalued but treated with outright suspicion and punishment. Here, the firm grip of biblical doctrines took precedence over personal feelings, encapsulated in the maxim "Spare the rod, spoil the child." These dynamics, established during David's first eighteen months of life, helped to solidify his relationship tendency, and similar experiences further reinforced it as he grew.

David's mother was a stern disciplinarian. Although moments of warmth and kindness were present, they were primarily contingent on David's performance. Academic achievements and adherence to Christian virtues earned parental approval. However, low grades (anything less than an A) and failure to comply with instructions were met with criticism, sometimes framed by threatening religious admonitions suggesting that God was always watching. The implied message was that God would be displeased. So, for a young boy's mind, it's not a stretch to imagine that if the most powerful being in the universe is angered, then punishment by that wrathful deity could be imminent.

David's father, an engineer of few words and even fewer displays of affection, remained distant. Therapy would later reveal David's unmet desire for a closer bond with his father, a man whose aloofness was compounded by a hidden struggle with alcohol.

David's early childhood was marked by solitude. He perceived himself as disconnected from his parents, unable to confide in them about his fears, desires, or true identity. This sense of isolation ingrained in him the painful belief that he was essentially on his own—that depending on others would only lead to disappointment and hurt. Consequently, the dynamics from his infancy reinforced throughout his early childhood shaped his relationship tendency to evolve into one of avoidance. He came to value independence above all else and shunned emotional intimacy as a potential threat.

Additionally, in such a rigid family framework, David harbored a secret that further distanced him from his family's values. Being gay meant risking the loss of the precarious acceptance he had managed to secure. This led him to a life of concealment, hiding not just his sexuality but also his genuine thoughts and emotions. He suppressed his anger, sadness, shame, and fear, masking these emotions by a veneer of compliance and a façade necessitated by the constant pressure to smile and embody "the joy of the Lord." The mere thought of expressing other emotions or different ways of thinking felt like an invitation to scrutiny and punishment. Thus, David learned to meticulously conceal his inner world.

Recall the avoidantly attached infants observed in the Strange Situation experiment? When the mother left, the infant remained calm, showing no visible signs of anxiety or distress. Upon her return, the infant displayed a notable lack of enthusiasm for reconnection or seeking her comforting embrace. Similarly, interaction with the stranger didn't pique their interest either. These infants seemed content in their own space, embodying a sense of independence and composure, as serene as a cool cat in its quiet fortress of solitude.

Within the narrative of a partner with an avoidant tendency lies a story steeped in sorrow and fear, resembling a kind of trauma or learned helplessness. Lacking any real sense of attunement from their parents, children conditioned to adopt this attachment style often come to the realization, mostly implicit, that their needs must be repressed. The roots of an avoidant tendency sprout from diverse grounds. Some children are raised in environments where parents are emotionally unavailable, failing both to model healthy emotional expression and to create spaces where their children can freely express their feelings. This dynamic often begins in infancy and continues into childhood.

Alternatively, children may be confronted with messages, either stated outright or implied through lack of response, that sadly communicate, "Be strong. Get over it." Such messages signal to the child that their palate of emotions is only partially acceptable, leading them to suppress feelings deemed unwelcome and to face them alone.

In some families, the overwhelming emotional states or needs of the parents overshadow the child's own experiences, leaving little room for the child's individuality. This dynamic is sometimes exacerbated by parental expectations that the child reflect the parent's values, feelings, and aspirations, disregarding the child's distinct personality and desires. There are also scenarios where the family's focus is consumed by a sibling's medical, psychological, or behavioral condition, relegating the developing child's needs to the background. In these situations, the child might suppress their own needs and feelings, either from a sense of being overshadowed or from guilt, considering their sibling's more visible struggles.

Understanding that most parents aren't purposely inflicting pain is important. The complexities of life, intertwined with parental trauma and ingrained family traditions and societal norms, make altering deep-seated behaviors a daunting task. When looking at the background and challenges faced by the parents of children who grow up with avoidant tendencies, it's tough to be harsh and judgmental. However, I always want people to be congruent—in other words, for their actions to align with their thoughts and feelings. In the healing journey, if you find yourself coming to grips with family dynamics that had detrimental effects lasting into adulthood, then feel what you feel, and be where you are.

Those who develop an avoidant tendency essentially master the art of self-reliance, teaching themselves to tough it out solo. They adopt a strategy of emotional suppression and independence, viewing the concealment of their emotions as a shield. Expressing or listening to emotional disclosures sits uncomfortably with them. This approach, akin to a Lone Ranger attitude, logically stems from their survival instincts— it's their way of coping. Venturing beyond this would mean confronting a realm of pain, reflecting back on times of isolation without anyone to offer comfort or understanding.

Having an Avoidant Tendency in Romantic Relationships

Relationship educator Stan Tatkin captures the essence of avoidant tendencies with a brilliant one-liner, which he uses as a subheading in his book *Wired for Love*. Hitting the nail on the head he writes, "I Want You in the House, Just Not in My Room...Unless I Ask You."[4] This is in contrast to someone with an anxious tendency, whose mantra is "I Want You in My Room...And don't go until I feel like you love me."

Adults with avoidant tendencies guard their personal space vigilantly. Establishing trust takes significant time before someone can enter the sacred room of their mental and emotional life. Of course, it is different in the beginning. In the honeymoon phase, things often feel less risky for those with an avoidant tendency, and they're much more likely to have you in their room, chatting for hours. They are often charming and know exactly what to say to woo you. Despite their longing for connection, the risk that comes with letting their person get too close or stay in their room too long becomes unbearable, and their previously suppressed tendency to keep partners at an emotional distance becomes the status quo.

Individuals with an avoidant tendency lean toward logic and left-brained processes, rather than embracing the demonstratively emotional. They are emotional beings, precisely because they are human; however, they often lack awareness of their feelings and do not readily share them with others. This behavior often stems from a deep-seated belief that others are untrustworthy and uncaring. They also have a significant aversion to conflict. Why? Because conflict poses a major threat to their nervous system. Of course, they may not perceive themselves as being "scared" or "fearful" when pressed by their partner to discuss weighty matters. They likely think they are calm, cool, and collected. Yet their body tells a different story. If they could measure their heart rate and stress hormone levels in those moments, they would find them off the charts. Under a functional magnetic resonance imaging (fMRI) scan, the threat-response areas in their brains might activate as intensely as if they were facing a rabid dog emerging from the bushes. The emotionally distant and conflict-averse tendencies can be quite frustrating for their more emotionally expressive partners.

For the partner of someone with an avoidant tendency, particularly on the far end of the spectrum, moments when they need emotional availability, deep discussions, and working through issues can be frustrating.

They might feel as if their partner is acting like a robot, or as an uncaring, stoic figure who appears selfish and indifferent to their needs.

Sadly, the avoidant-leaning partner frequently struggles with expressing and responding with the emotional empathy their partner seeks, particularly when their limbic system—the part of the brain that responds to threat and stress—is activated. This often leads them to experience feelings of shame. When their partners point out instances of emotional disconnect or perceived missteps, those with avoidant tendencies may blame themselves and feel like a failure as a partner (of course, they would never share those feelings). Consequently, if their partner becomes hurt, then angry, and then pressures them to connect, they may feel overwhelmed and controlled, prompting a desire to withdraw.

It was hurt and fear that initially led the avoidant-leaning person to secure their emotions behind a metaphorical padlock within their psyche. This defensive mechanism was once adaptive and protected them from rejection and harm. Therefore, any hint of judgment, fear, withdrawal of love, or high emotional intensity—mirroring the early childhood dynamics that prompted them to repress their emotions in the first place—will only lead to increased defensiveness, further shutdown, and more pronounced withdrawal. When they do withdraw, they tend to turn to the person they trust the most—themselves.

Disorganized Tendencies

Tracy's Story

Tracy's childhood was filled with chaos and unpredictability. As the oldest of three kids, she felt nonexistent to her parents once her siblings started to arrive. To be truthful, her parents were not very present from the start. Her mother suffered from depression and often spent days high on drugs in her room with the door shut. In the early years, she emerged only out of necessity—to feed the kids, ensure they were alive, and eventually send them to school. The older Tracy got, the healthier her mom became. However, too much neglect in her earlier years had left its mark.

Her father was extremely emotionally volatile and could swing from being the life of the party to being a cold, distant figure, or even a tempest of anger, with little warning. Sometimes he would be in a good mood and would hug Tracy. Other times, in his fits of anger, he would beat her. To make matters worse, her dad sexually abused her from age five to age nine.

Tracy learned to fend for herself emotionally and sometimes physically. Growing up in this whirlwind of emotional inconsistency left her in a constant state of hypervigilance. With her dad, she was perpetually walking on eggshells, and with her mom, she often became the caretaker. This chaotic emotional landscape sowed the seeds for Tracy's disorganized attachment. She longed for closeness and security, yet the intimacy she sought also evoked deep-seated fears of abandonment, rejection, and shame.

Recall the disorganized attached infants observed in the Strange Situation experiment? The babies exhibited contradictory behaviors: sometimes they would be disoriented and unsure how to interact with the mom; sometimes they would express fear and anger; sometimes they would freeze when the mother entered the room. The babies would seemingly want the mom but then would push her away. There was not a predictable pattern of engaging the mom; this is where "disorganized" comes from. Despite the infants' desperately wanting their mother to be a safe and comforting attachment figure, their nervous system simultaneously encoded her as a threat.

Individuals with disorganized tendencies often come from backgrounds marked by trauma. Even as infants, they usually experienced some form of trauma, whether physical, sexual, or through extreme neglect. Due to their trauma, their adaptive response was to become distrustful and guarded, which is understandable. Take Tracy, for example: why would she open up and share her vulnerabilities with her parents if they were the source of her trauma? Naturally, Tracy would be vigilant, as danger could lurk around any corner. Those with disorganized strategies are torn between a natural desire for their parents' comfort and support and the reality that these caregivers are also their source of fear and pain. Understandably, it would make sense that

Tracy's internal working model is such that she perceives herself as broken and views people as potential threats.

Having A Disorganized Tendency in Romantic Relationships

Individuals with a disorganized tendency often navigate life with the unpredictability of a roller coaster. Lacking early models for self-soothing during tough times, on top of abusive environments, they struggle to find a sense of balance in life and relationships. Of course, they have moments of calm and can express intense love toward their partners. However, their nervous systems, always on alert for potential threats, make them prone to being easily triggered. This heightened state leads to a pattern of dramatic ups and downs in their relationships. They often exhibit push-and-pull behavior, craving love desperately but feeling threatened as soon as intimacy is offered, prompting them to push away in great force. Such individuals might also experience intense mood swings, including bouts of rage. Additionally, there's a side to disorganized behaviors that mirrors those with an avoidant tendency, characterized by a propensity to shut down and retreat from others.

How can we not be empathetic toward individuals with a disorganized tendency? Their behaviors, deeply rooted in their past traumatic experiences, once served as vital survival mechanisms. A heightened threat system, an inherent fear of caregivers, and a tendency to shut down or avoid close relationships were once necessary for their survival.

However, these once adaptive strategies often become counterproductive or even detrimental in their adult relationships. I feel a deep sadness when people with these tendencies express to me, "Mark, if I could just be calmer and less reactive, I truly would. But it feels impossible." I can't imagine that sense of helplessness. Yet not all is hopeless. I firmly believe that through dedicated trauma work with a trained mental health specialist, which is both challenging and transformative, they can foster fulfilling relationships. Achieving this, however, typically involves a long journey filled with numerous moments of genuine love, acceptance, empowerment, and encouragement from compassionate, safe, and healing others.

Secure Tendencies

Marina's Story

Marina did not have perfect parents. They had their issues and quirks. Her father possessed an unusual sense of humor, frequently causing embarrassment to Marina's mom, who was by nature more reserved. Despite this, he was loving, worked hard—sometimes too hard—and prioritized the family. Marina's mom was hardworking and an extrovert. She always loved having people over and had a knack for keeping the house spotless. Her dad joked that she had some form of obsessive-compulsive disorder (OCD). Yet Marina's mom would just laugh the joke off, ensuring everything was done decently and in order. Marina's parents had their flaws, but they made sure their home was filled with a sufficient amount of love, care, and connection.

When Marina was a baby, her parents demonstrated optimal attunement. They responded to her cries, tuned in to what she needed with a loving gaze, and provided the necessary care. When Marina was sick, they were there to take care of her. In moments of sadness, they were her sanctuary, providing listening ears, compassionate eyes, and warm cuddles. They met challenges with a balanced approach of calmness and firmness, instilling discipline where needed. When Marina faced complicated homework assignments, they were present and encouraging. This nurturing atmosphere enveloped Marina in a sense of support, safety, and security, shielding her from harm and complete overwhelm. It was in this beautifully flawed yet loving family atmosphere that Marina was able to explore her environment with calm curiosity, grow up with a strong sense of self, navigate life's challenges with greater ease, and trust others confidently.

Recall the securely attached infants observed in the Strange Situation experiment? These infants felt free to explore their environment. When the mom left, they still carried her loving presence with them, experiencing minimal separation anxiety. They showed some anxiety when the stranger appeared, but it was manageable. And, when the mom returned, they were ready to reconnect and receive her care and support. They also had a nervous system that allowed them to absorb their mother's love and feel soothed.

Having a Secure Tendency in Romantic Relationships

Those with a secure tendency have a mantra that goes, "I would love to have you in my room. However, if you're not in the mood to chill, no problem. We can connect later." If you have a secure tendency as an adult, you typically remain composed and unflappable. You excel at connecting with your partner and with people in general. You're able to keep it real, express your feelings, and be there for your partner when they're going through a tough time. You maintain a positive view of yourself, and when challenges arise, you have a healthy level of resilience and can face them without being overwhelmed. You also have a positive view of others, seeing them as trustworthy. You feel balanced and in control. You trust that your partner will be there for you when needed. However, if they're dealing with their own issues, you likely have a few other close connections to turn to for support.

Chapter Two Wrap-Up

It's essential to get a grip on each other's "owner's manual," the one that outlines our attachment tendencies. This can really help boost empathy when relationship troubles arise. In the heat of conflict, when our stress response is activated, empathy and compassion often take a backseat. Our bodies and nervous systems are keeping score, each with its own unique way of interpreting events. When we're triggered, our brains often perceive our partners as threats, even if our rational minds beg to differ.

We need to honor those warning signals. If there's repeated abuse, prioritizing our safety and possibly leaving the relationship is crucial. But in a healthy relationship where both people are striving to make things work, it's important not to view everything through the lens of our threat system and its negative narrative. That's why broadening our perspective to include each other's emotional and relational histories is so beneficial.

When we consider our partner's attachment styles, we see why one or both of us might, for example, have avoidance tendencies and struggle to discuss emotions and stay empathetic in the face of each other's pain. For those terrified of intimacy, it becomes clear why such fear exists: growing up in a home marked by neglect and abuse taught us that opening up to love often led to more pain. Viewing our interactions through an attachment lens also helps us understand the anxiety and reactivity that arise when our partner withdraws or distances themselves. This behavior mirrors the protest and clinging of a baby realizing their mother is about to leave the room. Conversely, some of us, by sheer luck, had decent childhoods and now possess high self-confidence, emotional regulation skills, and a solid trust in others.

Keeping both your and your partner's attachment styles in mind can nurture greater understanding and empathy when reflecting on past conflicts and those that may arise in the future. As empathy grows, reactive behavior in future conflicts doesn't vanish, but it does diminish. Why? Because we begin to see our partner's actions not as personal attacks but as reflections of their inner operating system at work. By turning down the volume on the reactive noise in our relationship, we create space for a more harmonious relational sonnet to unfold.

Key Takeaways

1. Foundations of Attachment Theory: Attachment theory, brought to light through the seminal contributions of Ainsworth and Bowlby, highlights how our earliest relationships with caregivers fundamentally shape our psychological development, internal working models, and perceptions of ourselves and others, influencing our capacity for resilience and forming healthy connections.

2. Origin of Attachment Styles: The Strange Situation experiment, developed by Mary Ainsworth in collaboration with John Bowlby and Mary Main, revealed the complex dynamics of infant-parent attachment, establishing a framework for identifying secure, anxious, avoidant, and disorganized attachment styles that profoundly affect our relational patterns throughout life.

3. Evolution of Attachment: Our attachment styles aren't fixed; they can change as we grow and learn, helping us build stronger, healthier relationships. This dynamic nature encourages us to view personal development and relational improvements as ongoing processes that enrich our connections and understanding of one another.

4. The Spectrum of Attachment: Attachment styles, formed in response to early relational experiences, significantly influence our interpersonal dynamics. Anxious, avoidant, and disorganized attachments arise from varying degrees of emotional inconsistency, neglect, or trauma and manifest in relationships through heightened vigilance, independence, or confusion. Conversely, secure attachment, nurtured by consistent care and attunement, fosters healthy relational patterns characterized by trust, balance, and resilience.

5. Empathy in Conflict: Recognizing our partner's attachment style can deepen our empathy in conflicts, where our instinctive brain often misinterprets actions as threats. Having this broader understanding transforms perceived hostility into opportunities for connection, enabling us to acknowledge reactions as reflections of underlying attachment dynamics.

Chapter 3
Awakening the Gift of Reflective Empathic Compassion

"Empathy is seeing with the eyes of another, listening with the ears of another, and feeling with the heart of another."

— Alfred Adler

In my journey through the heartlands of couples therapy, a common refrain echoes from the depths of wounded hearts: "I got duped. It was a bait and switch. The person standing before me now is a stranger compared to the one I fell in love with."

To them, I offer a feisty perspective, "Indeed, you both presented different versions of yourselves. You both were also high on drugs."

Their expressions of confusion often switch to annoyance, and typically, one partner asks, "What's that supposed to mean?"

I then delve into the concept of "the honeymoon phase," a term scholars use to describe the initial euphoria of a new romantic relationship. During this time, our bodies and minds are flooded with a neurochemical cocktail, casting us into a frenetic state akin to the fervent craving an addict feels for cocaine:

"I want you."

"I need you."

"I desire you."

"I can't live without you."

"I ache for you."

"You're all I think about."

"When will I get to experience you again?"

In this elevated state, our insecure relational tendencies—whether anxious, avoidant, or disorganized—often recede into the background. These tendencies usually surface during periods of perceived threat, which are less prevalent at the beginning of relationships, when they are overshadowed by our aspiration to present the best versions of ourselves. We meticulously groom our appearance and tuck away our less flattering traits into the dark corners of our psyche. This phase is an exhilarating adventure; we are filled with anticipation and eagerness to spend time with our partner, craving the sound of their voice. During this time, we morph into the living embodiment of our partner's idealized vision— becoming the epitome of perfection in their eyes.

The honeymoon phase is that magical time when "reflective empathic compassion" truly takes center stage. I define reflective empathic compassion as *exploring our partner's inner and outer experiences with a beginner's mind, sensitively tuning into their feelings on an embodied level, and thoughtfully offering care and comfort that truly align with their unique needs and desires.* The heart of this definition can be summarized by three key questions: "What is happening in your world?" "How are you feeling?" and "What do you need from me?" The degree to which we ask these questions in our hearts and minds and act accordingly will be the degree to which we feel connected in our relationships.

In the honeymoon phase, we continually reflect—almost obsessively —on our partner and the relationship. We deeply immerse ourselves in our partner's world: their dreams, fears, longings, struggles, and the intricate details of their lives.

"What types of music and movies do they enjoy?"

"Do they think about me as often as I think about them?"

"What are they up to right now?"

"When will they call next?"

"Do they still have feelings for me?"

"How did that situation at work pan out for them?"

We are also profoundly empathetic. Just as our partner's happiness becomes ours, their troubles cast a shadow over us. It's as if their emotions are contagious, resonating deeply within us. This empathy we experience is largely attributed to our *mirror neurons*. Mirror neurons allow us to "mirror" the emotional or physical experiences of others, providing a glimpse of what they might be feeling or doing without our engaging in the same actions. If we heard our partner's mom speaking harshly on a call, the parts of our brain that help with empathy would light up. It's like our brain feels what our partner feels during that conversation but doesn't realize we're not the mom's target. The upside is that we get where our partner is coming from and can share in what they're going through, even though it's not happening directly to us.

This amazing mirroring process is key to understanding and sharing the emotions of others, making it a vital aspect of human connection and empathy. Alongside oxytocin, a hormone known for fostering bonds and making us feel closer and more connected, mirror neurons contribute to the deep emotional resonance and understanding we can have with those around us. Together, these elements form a powerful duo, enhancing our ability to empathize, connect, and build strong, meaningful relationships.

In the honeymoon phase, witnessing our partner's struggles triggers a powerful reaction within us. Seeing them struggling or in pain ignites a surge of compassion, motivating us to do whatever we can to alleviate their suffering. Acting on compassion creates a profound connection, where we're not merely passive observers on the sidelines of each other's life—we're actively feeling, sharing, and living closely tied to each other's experiences, driven by a deep desire to bring comfort and joy to one another.

Shortly, we'll dive deeper into this concept of reflective empathic compassion. First, though, let's take a look at a relationship very much lacking in this ingredient, and the relationship tendencies that led to this.

Rebecca and Antonio

In the serene sanctuary of my office, I sit with Rebecca and Antonio, a couple entwined in the dance of their fifteen-year marriage, now standing at the precipice of change, yearning for liberation from their relentless discord. Their journey together, marked by a classic cycle of pursuit (by Rebecca) and withdrawal (by Antonio), is a testament to the invisible threads of their past hurts pulling at the fabric of their present.

The Origins of Rebecca and Antonio's Relationship Tendencies

From the very start of her precious young life, Rebecca faced inconsistencies in her emotional environment. Her mother, struggling with postpartum depression, was often overwhelmed by the demands of work, family drama, and managing the household mostly alone. Rebecca's father, though physically present, was frequently absorbed in work and disengaged from family life.

Despite her challenges, Rebecca's mother endeavored to be emotionally available and responsive, aiming to provide the comfort and nurturance Rebecca needed. However, life's demands and her own anxieties sometimes led to moments when she neglected Rebecca's needs for attention and comfort. This inconsistency in care and emotional availability became the foundation for Rebecca's anxious relational tendencies.

Growing up, Rebecca perceived that love had to be earned. Good grades were met with praise and extra attention, while poor performance resulted in disappointment and a palpable withdrawal of affection. Moreover, her mother's focus on Rebecca's appearance, coupled with mixed messages about her weight, added to the confusion. Despite the presence of celebratory moments, big hugs, and times of connection—even with her father—the inconsistent expressions of love, the prevailing performance mentality, and her father's emotional absence taught Rebecca that attention and love were conditional, needed to be earned and potentially fleeting. Combined with Rebecca's sensitive temperament, this resulted in her developing a hypervigilant nervous system and an inner child who longed for consistent love.

Antonio's development of avoidant tendencies and accompanying strategies of self-protection can be traced back to the ethos of his family life, where emotional stoicism was not merely a trait but a valued hallmark of masculinity. Antonio shared that he grew up surrounded by "machismo"—a culture where it wasn't acceptable for boys to cry. Showing vulnerability was considered shameful, and those who did were ridiculed. In an environment where expressions of vulnerability were viewed as a weakness, Antonio learned to mask his feelings and rely solely on himself, mirroring his father's silent resilience. In this way, masculinity became synonymous with emotional suppression.

His mother, embodying a different kind of strength, ran their home with an iron will. Juggling her career and household duties, she enforced strict discipline, leaving little room for emotional flexibility. There was one way: her way. Given the turmoil of her own upbringing, her need for order was understandable. She equated strength with hard work and high morals and instilled a profound fear of God in her children. Antonio's parents did their best with the available knowledge, tools, and resources they had.

Present-Day Struggles

In the early stages, Rebecca and Antonio's relationship epitomized the honeymoon phase: exhilarated by their love and desire for one another, they were deeply compassionate and connected. Over the years, however, they became entangled in a classic cycle of withdrawal and pursuit. Molded by a stoic interpretation of machismo, Antonio felt estranged from his emotions, often retreating from Rebecca's attempts to connect, seeking solace elsewhere (usually in busyness and socializing with friends). His lack of presence and avoidant tendencies spurred Rebecca's deep-seated desperation for any sign of care and affection. Her yearning for connection often triggered Rebecca's anxious tendencies, leading her to persistently prod and poke. Her pleas occasionally transformed into critical and nagging remarks. The more Antonio withdrew into his own world, the more Rebecca sought to connect, inadvertently triggering his fear of emotional vulnerability and feelings of inadequacy.

Their attachment systems were fully engaged, with their internal working models and responses to perceived threats exacerbating the cycle. Rebecca harbored a profound fear of being perpetually alone, a worry that her needs for closeness and affection would forever go unmet. On the other hand, Antonio was plagued by a sense of inadequacy, fearing that no matter what he did, he could never truly satisfy Rebecca or meet her emotional needs. This dynamic, steeped in fear and misunderstanding, kept them locked in a dance of distance and pursuit. Each longed for connection, yet they could not bridge the gap created by their fears.

Rebecca and Antonio's relational dance of disconnection is marked by struggles stemming from accumulated hurts and unmet attachment needs—primal needs to be loved, accepted, valued, and taken care of. The toll of their dance became evident in Rebecca's weariness, a burnout so profound that its depth only truly revealed itself to me upon witnessing her reaction to Antonio's heartfelt confessions.

During our eighth session, I attempted to peel back the layers of Antonio's defenses. With a softened voice, I asked, "Antonio, can you share what emotion arises when you perceive that Rebecca, the woman you cherish, says she wants to connect with you, yet seems to criticize you frequently?"

His response was a whisper of exhaustion. He shared, "I am tired. Weary from her endless nagging. I feel like I can't succeed at anything lately. I can never seem to satisfy her. I feel like I am always letting her down. My weeks are forty-five hours of stressful work, leaving me drained, with nothing left to give—"

"—as if I'm not tired too!" Rebecca's frustration sliced through the room before Antonio could finish.

At this point I interjected, "Rebecca, I understand your hurt, your own profound fatigue. But, if it's okay, I want to ask that hurt part of you to step aside just for a moment. Let's just linger with Antonio's feelings a bit longer, okay?" She hesitated and gave an annoyed nod, so we continued.

Turning to Antonio, I gently said, "Tell me, what's it like feeling as though you can never get it right with the woman you love?"

"All I wish for is to make her proud, to show her I care, and that I'm really trying to make her happy." Tears breached his defenses as he continued, "I'm just so sad. I long for the normalcy of our early days when love seemed easy."

Turning to Rebecca, hoping to bridge their chasm of disconnect, I said, "When you hear Antonio speak of his sadness, with tears in his eyes, and his yearning for the connection you once shared, what happens within you?"

"Nothing. I feel nothing for him."

In that moment, reflective empathic compassion seemed a relic of the past.

How can Rebecca and Antonio, and any couple experiencing such a chasm, find their way back to a pattern of reflective empathic compassion?

Reflective Empathic Compassion
Broken Down

Though reflective empathic compassion seems to flow naturally during the blissful days of the honeymoon phase, it can seem elusive amidst the backdrop of hurt, disconnect, and anger. Yet it's still possible to summon these responses and, through practice, to have them become natural once again. To understand how, we'll break reflective empathic compassion down into its components.

Be Reflective

In a relationship, the "reflective" part of reflective empathic compassion refers to truly grasping what's happening in your partner's mind and heart and thoughtfully considering their experiences and feelings as they navigate their world. This skill involves a keen, meditative capacity to tune into and contemplate your partner's thoughts, emotions, concerns, and specific situations. Here are several questions to ask yourself about your partner during a conflict, or if that feels too Zen-ish, afterward when you've had a chance to cool off:

- "What's happening in my partner's world right now?"
- "How might they be feeling about what's going on?"
- "They seem off today; what kind of day might they have had?"
- "Is there something stressing them out at work?"
- "How might my actions have impacted them?"
- "Have they been getting enough sleep lately?"
- "How could their past be playing into their feelings or reactions now?"
- "Are their needs or wants not being met?"
- "Is there anything coming up for us or our family that may be contributing to some anxiety?"

Going back to Rebecca, it's easy to hastily label her as cold and distant. Antonio has certainly expressed similar sentiments, probably using stronger and more colorful language: "You're such a _____ [rhymes with 'itch.']" However, if we adopt a stance of reflective curiosity—a stance I invited Antonio to take in future sessions—we might explore a deeper question:

What experiences does Rebecca believe she endured from Antonio that have led her to shut down her caregiving system, being unable to provide empathic concern?

With some understanding of the couple's history, we can begin to reflect on the relationship dynamics at play and ponder how Antonio's actions might have contributed to the emotional state he now finds so distressing:

- Could Rebecca feel angry at the perceived unfairness of trying to pursue a connection with him for years, and now, in this moment of vulnerability, he expects even more care from her?

- Maybe Antonio hasn't assumed enough emotional labor or responsibilities within their home, causing Rebecca to feel overwhelming resentment.
- Could Antonio's actions, such as texting other women early in their marriage, have hurt Rebecca and contributed to an emotional wound that now makes it challenging for her to fully open her heart to him?

Taking the time to reflect and ask deeper questions about Rebecca's apathetic reaction to my question in our therapy session reveals the complex mix of thoughts, feelings, and actions at play. This approach works just as well when we're trying to figure out what's going on with our partners amid their reactions that feel adverse. But remember, our expertise lies in our own lives only. So, we should ultimately check with our partners about any guesses we make about their feelings or experiences. We want to stay curious, recognizing that we don't have all the answers. It's about maintaining an open mind, tuning into our partner's experiences, acting with the data we have in the moment, and striving to understand them more completely over time.

Be Empathic

Following this, we can strive to be empathic. Our role as partners involves more than just reflecting on our partner's experiences, which tends to be on a more cognitive level; it's about being attuned partners, tuning into their emotional world and attempting to feel what they feel. While we can never fully grasp their subjective experience, this process invites us to empathize with their sadness, shame, pain, fears, and other emerging emotions.

Antonio might be running low on empathy, but I totally get where Rebecca is coming from. Seeing her so unaffected while her husband shares vulnerability, talking about how worn out and sad he is, underscores an illuminating truth: she is also suffering.

Rebecca didn't begin her journey with Antonio like this; she entered their relationship with an open heart, ready to do anything to support her man. This knowledge enables me to look beyond her defense of apathy and reflect on what's going on underneath. As I do, I feel her hurt within myself. I feel the tension in my chest as I think about her protest. I get a felt sense of her anger and the hurt and longing to be loved by Antonio. I know the feeling of loving, trying, begging for love to be reciprocated, and getting drips and drabs over time. It's a terrible feeling. It makes total sense that she would be on guard.

This situation brings to mind the wisdom of compassion teacher Michelle Becker:

> The truth is that we all struggle, and we all behave in ways that are unskillful when we are suffering, to one degree or another. Where did we ever learn that we should be perfect and our partner too? What a setup! When, with courage, we can see how "this could be me," it softens us, connects us, helps us to recognize that we are all human, no one above or below. We're in this thing together.[1]

If Antonio could summon empathy for Rebecca by tuning into what she might be feeling, she might begin to lower her guard.

Be Compassionate

Lastly, there is compassion. Compassion is defined as "being sensitive to the suffering of self and others with a deep commitment to try to prevent and relieve it."[2] Unfortunately, by the time folks get to couples therapy, their survival strategies are in full swing. Their hawk-like threat system maintains their protective strategies, which could include withdrawing, trying to stay out of sight and out of mind; pursuing through criticism or nagging; displaying apathy; or adopting a demeanor as cold as ice. When our threat systems are activated, the last thing we want to do is offer openhearted warmth and care toward our partners. However, for relationships to thrive, compassion—*healing and practical love in action*—is a necessity.

Both Antonio and Rebecca require compassion. They need it from me as their therapist, but more crucially, they need it from each other.

Imagine how impactful it would have been for Rebecca to show tenderness, to become attuned to Antonio's suffering amidst his tears, to turn toward him, place her hand on his leg, and express, "I understand it's difficult. It's challenging for me, too. Seeing your tears right now evokes feelings of sadness for your pain. I love you. I care about you. It pains me to see you in pain. I, too, yearn to return to how we felt about each other at the beginning."

Imagine Antonio, when hearing Rebecca state that she had nothing for him, tapping into his compassionate side, turning to Rebecca with empathy in his eyes and saying, "I get it. How could you possibly reassure me in this moment? I haven't been the husband I should have been for many years." Then, imagine him saying, from his heart, "I am genuinely sorry."

Reflective empathic compassion plays a significant role in fostering healthy relationships. Feeling seen, understood, and deeply known cultivates a sense of love, security, and vitality. When we perceive that our partner truly cares about us—about the real, unique individual we are, along with our authentic experiences and with a spirit of acceptance—this sense of connection acts as a catalyst. It empowers us to be the best version of ourselves, not only within the relationship but also in our professional lives, in parenting, and in friendships.

But how do we go from imagining these types of reflective, empathic, compassionate responses to actually feeling and expressing them? How do we break down the protective barriers we have erected over time to respond in these healthy ways? To get there, we first have to examine the obstacles in our way.

Obstacles to Reflective Empathic Compassion

In my therapy practice, the comments I hear most often from partners about why they don't show reflective empathic compassion sound something like this: "How can I do it if I don't feel it?" "I can't get over how you hurt me," and "I'm exhausted and just don't have the time or energy!" Do any of these sound familiar? Let's take a closer look at what underlies these statements.

How can I do it if I don't feel it?

"Well, Mark, you don't know what my partner did! You don't know what I've been through. They don't deserve reflective empathic—whatever the hell it is—that you're trying to convince me to give to them."

I know. I get it. You make a good point. This way of caring, this kind of empathy and compassion, is challenging. While resuscitating love takes work, I don't expect you to immediately explore your partner's experiences with curiosity, tune into their feelings on a deeply personal level, and provide care and comfort based on their needs and desires. This process takes time and involves navigating challenges that hinder our ability to love effectively. In my experience with couples, two primary obstacles typically arise that can prevent us from loving our partners in this meaningful way: being in a threat state and a stressed state. Let's explore these challenges in more detail.

I can't get over how you hurt me.

Recent neuroscientific research has revealed that the human brain has three major systems that work together to manage and regulate our emotions.[3] The *threat system* helps us detect danger and avoid harm, producing emotions such as anger, anxiety, and disgust in order to move us toward safety. In relationships, this can pop up during tense arguments or when something just feels off, causing us to get snippy or defensive.

Then there's the *drive system*, which is all about getting us moving to achieve stuff, like finding food or learning cool facts, and making us feel pumped with joy or excitement. When it comes to relationships, this is the buzz we get from planning our future together, diving into new hobbies, or cheering on each other's wins.

The third is the *soothing system*, which encourages us to rest and relax. It kicks in when we're kind to others and ourselves, helping us to calm down and feel close to the people in our lives. It's the warm hugs, the "I've got your back, baby" moments, and those peaceful, quiet times that bring us closer. These built-in systems shape the dance of our relationships, protecting us and guiding how we connect, have fun, confront challenges, and care for each other.

One of the major obstacles to engaging in reflective empathic compassion is that, more often than not, in relationships that are in distress, one or both partners' threat systems are overactivated, overriding the soothing system. That makes sense. We are not going to willingly hug a porcupine. If our nervous system encodes our partner predominantly as a threat (often outside our awareness), we will not be openhearted, ready to give them a big hug or a listening ear. We will be in fight, flight, freeze, or fawn mode (the latter meaning doing whatever our partner wants to make them happy to get them off our back). Remember Maslow's hierarchy of needs? Safety comes before love and belonging. The powerful threat system has to be turned off before our soothing system can fully engage.

Suppose one partner has a relational history that includes attachment injuries, a lack of positive care over time, and a negative cycle of disconnection. This can lead to a pattern of "negative sentiment override," in which negative emotions supersede and often nullify positive ones. This almost guarantees that entering their partner's world with empathy and helping them feel loved and cared for will be difficult.

Let's break this down. An attachment injury is "a sense of betrayal and/or abandonment at a key moment of need that, if not addressed and healed, undermines trust and connection and triggers or fuels relationship distress and partner insecurity."[4] If you ever felt let down by your partner during a critical time of need, such as a health crisis, childbirth, parental loss, job loss, or accident, or discovered infidelity, leading you to view your partner negatively and eroding your trust, that could be an attachment injury. They act as poisoned arrows to the heart, a form of insidious trauma that lingers in the mind, body, and nervous system, often resurfacing with potency during conflicts.

When unresolved attachment injuries and broken trust intersect with ongoing missteps, misattunements, missed opportunities, and a cyclical pattern of disconnection, negative sentiment override begins to set in. This shift marks the transition from viewing our partner through rose-tinted "you are amazingly wonderful" glasses to donning dark-tinted ones, fostering hypervigilance and a predisposition to see our partner in a negative light. This dynamic exists on a spectrum: the more relational hurts remain unprocessed and accumulate, the more we are inclined to perceive our partner through these dark lenses. When negative sentiment override is at full capacity, every action and word seem to carry a sharp edge, triggering negativity and pain and casting a lurking shadow over their positive actions. If we find ourselves wearing dark-tinted glasses much of the time, it clearly affects our ability to engage with reflective empathy and compassion.

I'm exhausted and just don't have the time or energy!

The pressure we're all under in this fast-paced, perfection-chasing, and anxiety-soaked society is through the roof. A common theme I hear from couples, especially the ones juggling dual careers and kids, is, "There's just no time to connect. And when the rare moments arise, we're too wiped out to make it count." Sure, now and then, one partner might dig deep, willing to trade a bit of sleep for some quality time. But let's be honest, carving out moments during the week to truly bond feels like an uphill battle.

From our morning microdosing of social media, prepping the kids and ourselves for the day, and tending to pets … to surviving the work grind, dodging bullets from bosses and coworkers, chasing deadlines, keeping on top of bills, squeezing in a workout, managing doctor's visits, feeding the family, and shuttling kids around … to dipping back into the social media well, tucking everyone into bed, and handling life's curve-balls, often the last thing on our minds is diving deep into emotional connection with our partner. Why? Because reflecting and connecting requires energy. And, by evening, we are running on fumes. Kicking back to watch Netflix for a quick half-hour together (if we're lucky enough to get even that) feels like a win.

So, if you're struggling to find the time and feel too exhausted to regularly ponder, "What's *really* going on in my partner's world?" "How are they feeling?" and "What do they need from me?" I totally get it. However, failing to prioritize our relationships comes at a cost.

Flexing Your Reflecting,
Attuning, and Caring Muscles

I just spent some time reflecting on how difficult it can be to engage in reflective empathic compassion with your partner. *And*—not *but* (see me here trying to avoid a typical communication mistake)—we have a clear call to action for the health of our relationships. Waiting around for all the hurt they've dished out to somehow vanish before we make an effort to really understand them, to genuinely get curious about their feelings, and to actually ask those crucial questions, all while showing them love in the ways they truly feel it, just keeps us stuck in that relational rut we're all tired of. Allowing time to fly by due to the tyranny of the "should" ("I should do this. I should do that") without dedicating time to nurture the plant of our relationships carries a hefty price. When both of you emerge from your own corners of pain, tiredness, and exhaustion and make time for each other, you'll start seeing a brand-new cycle of connection gradually sprout up between you. So where do you start?

Schedule a Scuba Diving Encounter

Here's a practice that might just change the way you and your partner connect: embark on a weekly scuba diving expedition into the depths of each other's emotional, physical, and mental landscapes. Picture this adventure as setting aside sacred time each week (or more frequently, if you can) to put on your metaphorical diving gear and explore the undercurrents of your partner's experiences with three golden connective questions:

"What is happening in your world?"

"How are you feeling?"

"What do you need from me?"

This isn't a time for arguments or battles of ego. It's not about going tit for tat or trying to outdo each other with past grievances. Instead, it's about navigating the deeper waters of each other's lives. It's about intimacy—"into-me-see."

As you connect, take turns. Reflect back what you hear the other person saying. Remember, "ear" is nestled within "heart," as a gentle reminder that empathic listening is a direct path to reaching someone's oceanic heart.

For a deeper way to communicate and connect, we can shake things up a bit. Instead of asking "How are you feeling?" try this: "What are you experiencing?" It's a subtle shift but it opens the door to richer, more meaningful conversations.

We often prioritize sharing certain parts of our experience and neglect others. Some of us are more comfortable talking about our feelings, while others lean toward discussing thoughts. But intimacy is enriched by exploring each other's different channels of experience. These channels offer a comprehensive understanding of the myriad ways we experience and express our inner worlds, creating a deeper and more nuanced connection.

Consider the seven channels of experiencing as developed by David Mars, the founder of Transformative Couples Therapy®.[5] Sharing your experiences along these channels to your partner, and listening empathically as your partner shares theirs, provides a holistic approach to understanding and connecting with your partner on a profound level:

1. **Sensation:** Tune into physical sensations in the body. Notice tension, relaxation, warmth, coolness, and other bodily experiences. Bridging the mind-body divide can bring awareness to how physical states influence emotions and thoughts. Recognizing muscle tension can sometimes speak louder than words.

> *Example:* "I notice that my shoulders tense up whenever I think about work. Just talking about it makes my neck feel tight. It's like my body is carrying the weight of my stress."

2. **Emotion:** Recognize core emotions such as anger, sadness, joy, fear, and disgust. Pay attention to how these feelings manifest physically. Allowing tears to flow when feeling sadness can create a moment of shared vulnerability.

Example: "I feel really sad when I think about how little time we've had together lately. It's like a heavy feeling in my chest, and sometimes I just need to cry about it."

3. **Energetic:** Observe the subtle energies in the body, like feelings of lightness or heaviness, and the overall energetic charge. Feeling into what you love about your partner and noticing how this energy touches you can enhance your emotional bond.

Example: "When I think about our last vacation, I feel this warm, light sensation in my chest. It's like my whole body relaxes and fills with happiness."

4. **Movement:** Pay attention to body movements, postural shifts, and nonverbal expressions. A shift in posture during a conversation can indicate deeper, perhaps unspoken, feelings.

Example: "I noticed I crossed my arms when we started talking about finances. I guess it's a sign that I'm feeling defensive or worried about it."

5. **Auditory:** Listen to the tone, pitch, and rhythm of speech. The sweetness of your partner's voice, for instance, can touch you deeply and communicate their affection.

Example: "When you told me about your day, I could hear the stress in your voice. It sounded strained, and I could tell you were overwhelmed."

6. **Visual:** Observe facial expressions, eye movements, and overall visual cues. Seeing your partner's bright eyes and soft smile can communicate warmth and love nonverbally.

Example: "I saw your eyes light up when you talked about your new project. Your whole face seemed to brighten, and it made me feel so proud of you."

7. **Imaginal:** Engage with spontaneous or intentionally invited internal images, whether literal or symbolic. Imagining holding your younger self in your mind's eye can bring past experiences into the present for healing and understanding.

> *Example:* "When I think about that argument we had, I picture myself as a kid, feeling scared and small. It helps me understand why I reacted so strongly."

You might be thinking, "Who talks like that?" I get it. It's not your everyday conversation style. We usually just share our thoughts, and when we do talk about emotions, it's often *about* our feelings rather than *from* our feelings—unless we're angry, of course. But just because it's uncommon doesn't mean we should shy away from these deeper ways of being known. By bringing these channels into your regular check-ins, you and your partner can cultivate a richer, more empathetic connection. This approach helps both partners feel truly seen, heard, and understood on multiple levels, strengthening your bond.

Diving into these questions about each other's world and exploring what you both notice through these different channels will likely open you up to offering empathy and compassion whenever the opportunity arises. Once we attune to each other's experiences, we can seek to love one another in ways that truly help us feel loved and cared for.

If turbulent currents or a whirlpool of negativity pull you off course, take a break. Come up for air on your respective sides of the boat and plan to dive back in when the waters are calm.

Craft Some *ART*

If your schedule is tight or the idea of sitting face-to-face, locking eyes, and delving into deep, heartfelt conversations causes palpitations and feels about as unpleasant as biting into a sour lemon—then maybe you can try crafting some ART. ART stands for **A**ttachment-**R**elated **T**exts.

Never overlook the power of a text message to show your partner that you're tuned into their life and empathically understand their thoughts and emotions. Using attachment-based language aims to speak to the core of our partner's being, making them feel seen, heard, appreciated, respected, valued, and loved.

Here are some examples of ART:

1. Expressions of Love and Affection

- "I love you."
- "I miss you."
- "Hey, sexy! Thinking about you!"
- "I feel so connected to you, even when we're apart."
- "Just thinking about our last conversation brings a smile to my face."
- "I love how we can talk about anything and everything."
- "I miss your smile. Can't wait to see you and hold you again."

2. Appreciation and Gratitude

- "You are so important to me."
- "Thank you for being such a wonderful mom."
- "Just wanted to remind you how much I appreciate you."
- "Thank you for being my rock. I appreciate you more than words can say."
- "I'm so grateful to have you in my life. You make everything better."
- "Your kindness and love mean everything to me."

3. Support and Reassurance

- "I'm here for you, no matter what."

- "No matter what happens, I'm here with you."
- "You never have to face anything alone—I'm always by your side."
- "We're a team, and we can get through anything together."
- "Sorry you are feeling sad. I have a hug waiting for you when you come home."
- "I believe in you. You've got this!"
- "I'm so proud of everything you're doing. You inspire me."
- "I'm always cheering you on, even from afar."

4. Check-Ins and Thoughtfulness

- "Can't wait to hear about your day."
- "Just checking in—how are you doing today?"
- "Thinking of you and hoping your day is going well."

5. Empathic Apologies

- "Thank you for apologizing this morning. It meant a lot."
- "I'm sorry for how I handled things earlier. I realize now how it affected you."
- "I regret that my words hurt you, and I want to make things right."
- "I can see now that I wasn't fully listening to you, and I'm sorry for that."
- "I'm sorry for my part in our argument—I value our relationship too much to let this linger."
- "I understand now why you felt hurt, and I'm truly sorry."

Tom and Anna

In a busy office, Tom's mind wanders from his work to his wife, Anna. He begins to ask himself the three golden questions: "What is happening in her world?" "How might she be feeling?" and "What does she need from me?"

As Tom thinks about those questions, his thoughts drift back to their morning conversation over coffee, when Anna expressed how torn she is between working more hours and spending more time with their kids. Sitting at his desk, Tom feels a warmth in his chest and a desire to reach out to her. He knows a quick text can't solve everything, but a meaningful piece of ART might lift her spirits. After a moment of compassionate reflection, he sends her a thoughtful message:

"I know you are struggling to choose between more time at work or with the kids. I know how heavy this decision has been for you. Just know I'm here to listen whenever you need."

What was the outcome?

His wife felt understood, supported, and loved.

Now meet Allen and Ben, a couple navigating the tumultuous aftermath of a heated argument from the night before. Hurtful words were exchanged, and the couple ended up throwing the proverbial kitchen sink at each other in frustration. Unfortunately, they went to bed angry and hurt—a situation we all dread.

The next morning, Allen had to leave for work early, departing while Ben was still asleep, missing the opportunity for a face-to-face discussion about what happened. The weight of their unresolved conflict hung heavily on Allen throughout the morning, prompting him to consider sending Ben some ART.

Mid-morning, amidst the bustle of work, Allen took a deep breath and typed a heartfelt message: "Ben, I've been thinking about last night, and I realize my words hurt you deeply. For that, I am genuinely sorry. It was never my intention to cause you pain. Let's chat later about it. I hope you have a good day, my love."

Ben received the message as a compassionate gesture of love. Since Allen seldom apologizes, this act of acknowledging fault and expressing regret was particularly meaningful and appreciated.

Do you want a relationship with depth? Continue exploring your partner's inner and outer experiences by sensitively tuning into their feelings and thoughtfully offering care and comfort that truly connects with their unique needs and desires.

Practice Priority Compassion

Vulnerability, curiosity, deep listening, empathy, and compassion are foundational elements that enrich the depth of a relationship, especially within heartfelt conversations. There is also what I call *priority compassion*: being genuinely sensitive to our partner's aches and longings with a dedicated effort to alleviate and address their *primary* concerns.

Some partners crave priority compassion through activities like weekly "scuba diving" sessions, seeking a partner who intentionally sets aside time for in-depth conversations. They are ecstatic when their significant other shows care, explores their inner and outer worlds, provides validation and interest, and shares moments of happiness together. Yet, for some, these gestures are just the beginning. Feeling listened to is important, but they seek a deeper level of compassion—one that actively seeks to resolve their biggest grievances. In this context, it is common to hear, "I'm done with words. I just need action." Without addressing a partner's core issues, a gap persists, hindering a deeper connection between partners.

Sage and Quinn, both in their early thirties and juggling dual careers alongside raising three children, thrived on travel and weekend adventures. However, the arrival of COVID forced a new normal upon them: working from home while their children adapted to virtual learning and limited outdoor interactions. This sudden shift brought mounting pressures and stressors, revealing the strain that constant proximity placed on their relationship. The daily grind of being together without respite led to increased irritation with each other, and the challenges of parenting under these conditions tested their patience. Even as the world began to move beyond COVID, they noticed a profound change within themselves and an unwelcome shift in their relationship dynamics.

Once they didn't have to work from home any longer, they both relished the idea of going back to work. Things started to feel semi-normal again. However, Sage and Quinn felt very disconnected from one another. Then, an issue that Sage had pre-pandemic magnified the mounting space between them: the equity of responsibilities in the home and with the children.

Sage was the overfunctioner in the family, handling everything from the children's educational responsibilities and doctor's appointments to birthday parties and necessary paperwork, in addition to most household tasks like cooking and cleaning. She also assumed the role of emotional and relationship manager, tuning in to the family's emotional needs and organizing weekend social activities. Despite working full-time like Sage, Quinn contributed by occasionally doing dishes, bringing home food a few times a week, maintaining the lawn, spending time with the kids after work, and then saying goodnight to them. Despite his efforts, there was a clear disparity in their contributions, reflecting lingering patriarchal norms.

The mental, emotional, and physical resources each parent invested in the family, coupled with the uneven expectations placed on Sage, underscored an unfair balance. While I support leveraging each partner's strengths and recognize that not everything can be divided into a perfect 50/50 split, it's clear that Sage is frustrated, unhappy, and feels alone within the dysfunctional system established between them.

Priority compassion for Quinn would involve not just being curious and empathic toward Sage's concerns but also taking proactive steps. Occasionally saying, "I'm sorry" isn't going to cut it. By intentionally prioritizing Sage's primary concerns, Quinn could lessen her emotional and mental burden, reduce her frustration toward him, increase her sense of support, diminish her sense of aloneness, and enhance their connection. That would be a heck of a win!

Words without action toward our primary complaints diminish faith in the relationship. It's remarkable how many men I meet who express dissatisfaction with the lack of warmth and affection from their partners. However, upon examining their lack of emotional intimacy, empathy, and efforts to engage in priority compassion and address their partner's main concerns, the reason for their partner's attitude becomes clear. If we ignore the explicit keys our partners give us to the door of their hearts and affection, how can we expect lightness and love to flow toward us?

What is your primary complaint in the relationship? How can you turn that complaint into an invitation? For example, instead of "You don't even care. You never show me affection. We haven't had sex in a month." Maybe you could share, "I am feeling a bit alone lately. Would you be open to connecting this evening and possibly being physically intimate?" While there is no guarantee the invitation will be accepted, you can rest assured that the complaint will go nowhere.

What is your partner's most pressing need? Do they repeatedly highlight a specific concern during conflicts? Are they seeking more intimacy, help around the house, meal preparation, quality time together, deeper conversations, more fun activities, encouragement, completion of a particular project, more effective co-parenting, or additional dates?

As you keep their main complaint in mind, as long as it aligns with your values, I hope you can flex your reflecting, attuning, and caring muscles. By taking your partner's longings seriously and hoping that they, in turn, seriously consider yours, you can initiate a snowball effect toward achieving a healthier and happier relationship you both have longed for.

Chapter Three Wrap-Up

Research shows that reflective, empathic, and compassionate principles and practices are key to the health and longevity of romantic relationships. That's why these aspects are game-changers for couples. However, if feeling empathetic toward your partner, having the internal space to warmly reflect on their experiences, and engaging in compassionate activities like scuba diving, ART, or primary compassion feel too challenging, it might indicate that the negative cycle—the real enemy of connection—is deeply entrenched between you both.

But don't lose hope. Recognizing this challenge is the first step toward breaking free from the patterns that block a deep sense of connection. The next chapter will be invaluable, offering insights to uncover and address these destructive cycles. Together, you can reclaim the love and connection you both deserve.

Key Takeaways

1. The Honeymoon Phase and Reflective Empathic Compassion: Initially, couples experience a heightened state of connection and understanding powered by neurochemicals and an innate desire to bond deeply. Reflective empathic compassion—exploring your partner's experiences, tuning into their feelings, and meeting their needs—is at its peak during this phase.

2. The Role of Mirror Neurons and Oxytocin in Empathy and Connection: These biological factors underpin our ability to empathize and feel connected, illustrating the natural basis for sharing and understanding our partner's emotions.

3. Understand and Navigate Attachment Injuries and Trust Issues: Deep-seated wounds from past experiences can lead to a "negative sentiment override," where we interpret actions through a lens of hurt and skepticism, highlighting the importance of addressing these issues for a healthy relationship.

4. The Challenge of Time and Exhaustion: Modern life's demands can significantly hinder couples' ability to maintain empathic connection, underscoring the need for intentional effort to overcome these barriers.

5. Foster a New Cycle of Connection: To break free from relational ruts, it's crucial to actively engage in practices that foster understanding, curiosity, and empathy toward our partners. Committing to regular, meaningful conversations centered on the three golden connective questions—"What is happening in your world?" "How are you feeling?" and "What do you need from me?"—can transform your relationship.

6. Priority Compassion: Priority compassion, characterized by actively addressing and alleviating each other's core concerns, stands as a cornerstone in deepening relationships. Use this approach to transform complaints into opportunities for connection, emphasizing the significance of shared responsibility and proactive engagement in nurturing and sustaining your partnership.

Part Two
Mapping Negative Patterns

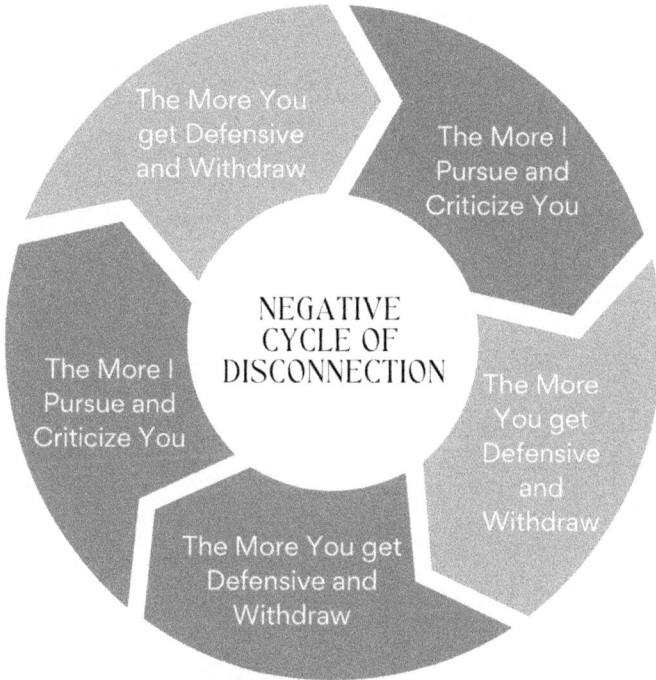

NEGATIVE CYCLE OF DISCONNECTION

The More You get Defensive and Withdraw

The More I Pursue and Criticize You

The More I Pursue and Criticize You

The More You get Defensive and Withdraw

The More You get Defensive and Withdraw

Chapter 4
What Is Your Negative Cycle?

"The pattern, not the partner, is the enemy. They have both unwittingly created this enemy that is taking over their relationship, and they must work together to wrest their relationship from its clutches."

— Sue Johnson, *Love Sense*

I magine you and your partner, at the beginning of your relationship, like two dancers in a dimly lit room. The steps you take aren't choreographed; they arise spontaneously, each one delicately attuned to the other. Your dance moves are guided by the music of your intuition and your unfolding desires and emotions. After some time, your nervous systems and internal rhythms finally begin pulsating in sync. Your connection is secure, and your internal worlds are at peace, allowing your intricate dance to flow smoothly and harmoniously. Each movement draws you closer; each step in your tango is a testament to the trust and attraction you share. Toes may occasionally be stepped on, but this doesn't disrupt the overall sensual and smooth synergy. Instead, it leads to another risk taken together, another step in your intimate, improvised, ever-evolving connection.

However, when toes are stepped on too often, discord strikes. Then, your threat systems kick in, shifting the music to a cacophony of sounds. Instead of a felt sense of love guiding you both, with your gazes gently fixed upon one another, you now find yourselves more focused on yourselves. Protection at all costs. The slow erosion of trust is taking its toll. Suddenly, one of you may start moving to a faster, more frantic beat, driven by a melody of anxiety and fear. The other might slow down, pulling back to avoid missteps, overwhelmed by the sudden, jolting changes. The more one partner moves toward, the more the other tries to create distance. This pattern becomes more frequent, leading both of you out of sync.

At this point, instead of toes being stepped on, whole feet are unwittingly bruised. As the music of your emotions grows more dissonant and constricting, you find yourselves trapped in a threatening loop. The faster one moves to regain the connection, the more the other retreats, and the greater their retreat, the more desperate the pursuit becomes. The tension-filled music becomes unbearable, causing the withdrawer to let go of the other's hands and run away in frustration and defeat, leaving the other feeling alone and abandoned.

Just as this dance routine dissolves into a disaster on the dance floor, so do the negative cycles that we engage in as partners, harming our relationships. It is these negative cycles that are the focus of this chapter.

The Negative Cycle as an Empathy and Connection Killer

Have you ever noticed that even though the day and the topics change, when disagreements or arguments arise, you and your partner seem caught in the same predictable pattern of disconnection? Couple therapists refer to this pattern as the "negative cycle." Negative cycles are entrenched patterns that result from wired-in relational tendencies interacting with each other, along with the cumulative effects of unmet relational longings, unclear signals, reactive emotions, and often unprocessed pain. After manifesting numerous times, these patterns become like a powerful snowball rolling down a hill, gaining a life of their own and harming the relationship.

The negative cycle is an empathy killer and an avid promoter of disconnection. Why? Because when couples are caught in it, they often enter self-protection mode and become *me-centric* instead of *we-centric*. When we are trapped in this cycle, we are not emotionally accessible to our partner and instead are drawn into our feeling state. Here, our relationship insecurities are activated, and we focus on our version of events or being right and what we need in that moment, rather than responding to our partner's perspectives and unmet desires.

When we are in a full-blown negative cycle, we become trapped in a threat state and our fight, flight, freeze, or fawn mode kicks in. In this state, it becomes nearly impossible to suppress our hurt, anger, and pain in order to turn to our partner with warmth and empathy. Saying, "My love, I am so sorry you are in pain. How can I support you in this moment?" becomes exceedingly difficult. Instead, when we are in the negative cycle, our responses, at least what we say to ourselves, are more likely to be full of hostility, and may sound more like "I'm glad you're in pain—you can kiss my ass if you think I'm going to support you right now."

It's important to remember that when our threat system is activated, our capacity to experience and provide feelings of warmth, positivity, and comfort is significantly reduced. Although someone engaging in a fawn response might seek to appease their partner, this is a survival strategy designed to avoid further escalation or harm and does not contribute to creating a positive cycle of loving connection and mutual reciprocity.

The Negative Cycle, Not Your Partner, Is the Enemy

Imagine a scenario where, as a couple, you find items repeatedly stolen from your home by a mischievous thief. This thief lurks in the shadows, always ready to disrupt the harmony and felt sense of security that you have built over the years. Surely, you would not turn against each other in blame but would decide to unite with a common purpose: to fortify your home against this joy-stealing intruder. Together, I am sure you would reinforce doors, secure windows, and install new locks to safeguard your home from this cruel and selfish crook.

This powerful metaphor illustrates the crucial shift in perspective required in relationships—viewing the negative cycle as the true enemy, not each other. The negative cycle is flammable, ready to combust at any moment, and it causes significant harm to your relationship. By jointly recognizing and combating this threat, you protect and strengthen your relationship, turning adversities into opportunities for growth and deeper connection. As Sun Tzu said in *The Art of War*, "If you know the enemy and know yourself, you need not fear the result of a hundred battles."[1] Identifying your negative cycle is crucial so that you and your partner can overcome it together and create a stronger, more resilient bond in the process.

The Four Dances of Disconnection

Couple experts have identified four main negative cycles that adversely affect relationships.[2] I refer to these negative cycles, or dances, as Blame and Bash; Fracture and Fortify; Wend, Whirl, and Withdraw; and Pull Back and Protest. The most common dance, illustrated by Rebecca and Antonio in the previous chapter, is Pull Back and Protest, in which one partner withdraws and the other pursues. As you explore these distinct patterns, notice whether one reflects your relationship when in conflict more than the others. Think about which partner in the following stories sounds most like you. Remember, you may have experienced more than one pattern throughout your relationship. Pay attention to the dance you currently find yourself in with your romantic partner.

Blame and Bash

Greg and Stacy, both in their forties, have been together for twenty-five years. They have three older children, all in college. Both of them harbor unresolved attachment injuries and are filled with hurt and anger toward each other. Greg's early affair was never properly addressed, and Stacy's solo trip following Greg's major surgery left unresolved resentment. At this stage in their marriage, they find themselves ensnared in a Blame and Bash cycle. The following exchange illustrates this cycle.

After Greg came home from hanging out with "the boys" without telling Stacy where he was going, Stacy remarked in a critical tone, "Oh, you were out with your friends tonight. Did you meet some slut?"

Greg rolls his eyes, and with his veins pumping with adrenaline, retorts, "Stop it. I just hung out with friends. What about you? Did you drink all night?"

"No, I didn't actually. I went to yoga with Cheryl, and we just talked about how much of an asshole you are," Stacy replies.

"I'm fed up with this. I'm so sick of you. Can't we get divorced already?" Greg declares.

"Yeah, well, you act like you're already divorced, anyhow!" Stacy yells. "Anyway, I don't have time for this."

"Good!" Greg exclaims. "I don't need to hear your crazy rants anyways."

This is just one of many similar interactions that Greg and Stacy experience. Their exchanges, like those of many caught up in this Blame and Bash dance, are tension filled, predominantly negative, and laden with contempt, blame, and criticism. They can escalate from zero to one hundred in milliseconds. Over time, their voices grow louder and their anger fiercer as blame and verbal attacks escalate in a vicious cycle. Both perceive the other as mean, cruel, and selfish, using the "D" word and other verbal arrows to swiftly erode trust and ignite further anger. While occasional avoidance or moments of amicability occur, they mostly operate in attack mode. Vulnerability is rare; protecting their hearts and softer emotions at all costs is the modus operandi. The more one blames and bashes, the more the other does the same, perpetuating a destructive pattern of mutual blame and bashing.

Fracture and Fortify

Mia and Luna, both in their mid-fifties, started their relationship over thirty years ago, drawn together during their vibrant graduate school days by shared passions for art and nature. Their early years were rich with

mutual support and joy, characterized by long hikes and creative collabo-
rations. However, as time passed, their paths began to diverge sharply.
Mia's career in environmental research demanded extensive travel and
long hours, while Luna experienced fluctuating success in the music
industry. This professional disparity started to create rifts, with Mia, with
a predominant avoidant tendency, becoming increasingly withdrawn and
distant, particularly when her work took her away from home. At the
same time, Luna, with a propensity toward anxious tendencies, felt more
isolated and unsupported, turning more frequently to social outings with
friends as a way to cope.

Attempts to address these growing tensions often led to confronta-
tions. Mia would shut down or dismiss Luna's concerns with logical but
emotionally detached responses, leaving Luna feeling increasingly
unheard and resentful. Their home, once a sanctuary of shared dreams,
gradually turned into a silent battleground of unspoken grievances and
misunderstandings. Over the decades, their interactions dwindled to
functional, surface-level exchanges, designed to avoid any deep
emotional engagement that could spark conflict. An example of one of
their exchanges illustrates this dynamic:

As Mia entered the kitchen after a long day at work, she found Luna
absorbed in sorting bills and emails. Luna glanced up and, her tone
subdued, said, "The water bill's gone up again. Have you seen it?"

Mia, weary and distracted, shrugged slightly. "Yeah, I glanced at it.
We should probably cut back on using so much water."

Luna returned her gaze to the papers, her voice quiet but distant. "It's
not just about the water, Mia. It feels like you're never really here."

Mia set her bag down, her voice tired. "I'm here now, Luna. I'm just
really tired, that's all."

Luna sighed, focusing on her documents rather than Mia. "You're
here, but it's like you're not. We barely talk. It's like we're strangers."

Mia began slicing vegetables, her movements slow. "I don't know
what you want me to say. I've had a long day. Can we not do this now?"

Luna nodded, her voice cool. "Sure, we can talk some other time."
Her tone suggested resignation, a deep fatigue with the recurring theme.

They ate their dinner in separate rooms that evening, fortified in their own worlds, each wrapped in a defensive silence thick with unspoken words and lingering frustrations. The distance between them felt vast, as they each dwelled on the pain, fractures, and disconnection that had come to define their relationship, reflecting on what once was and might never be again.

In this second pattern of the negative cycle, relationships between partners show deep fractures. The foundation of love, respect, empathy, and compassion becomes riddled with cracks. Without the necessary love-saturated ingredients that bolster their relationship and mend the cracks of hurt, pain, deprivation, and anger, they are on the verge of crumbling altogether. Couples caught in this dance are no longer shaking it up on the dance floor. They tend to feel like distant roommates and get their emotional needs met elsewhere. Conversations typically revolve around mundane, practical matters, such as tasks that need to be completed, where each partner spends their time, or discussions about their children.

Sadly, the partners are fortified in their interactions as well, meaning that, as I like to say, "they each have more defenses than the Pentagon." Of course, their defenses are understandable. Guided by protective inner wisdom, individuals build walls to shield themselves, primarily to side-step conflict and the sting of rejection. This guardedness also includes shielding themselves from the pain of sharing without receiving any genuine caring. Why share, "I feel lonely in the relationship and desperately need to feel your touch again," if it would be easily dismissed? Why tell your partner, "I feel so hurt. I am scared of losing you and don't know what to do," when the response might be criticism, or the other partner would quickly make it about themself? Even with pain in their eyes, they can feel numb and hopeless. The more one shuts down and avoids, the more the other does the same, further fortifying the cycle.

Couples caught in the Fracture and Fortify cycle have love stories just like the rest of us. They were once in love and enjoyed a more secure relationship. With these couples, though, after the honeymoon phase ends, a negative cycle emerges. One partner—typically with anxious tendencies—begins pursuing the partner with avoidant tendencies. They send countless signals, expressing a desire to feel more connected and yearning for greater love and presence, only to be repeatedly rebuffed.

At some point, the pursuer begins to feel burnt out. When they start to pull back, it can trigger a sense of panic in the more avoidant-prone partner, who fears losing them. This fear can turn the tables, leading *them* to start becoming the pursuer. Sometimes, the hurt partner with anxious tendencies recognizes this bid for connection and returns to the dance floor. At other times, they might be so burnt out—a mix of calcified hurt, anger, resentment, and emotional exhaustion—that they shift toward a more avoidant spectrum, becoming distant and protective of themself. Consequently, the avoidantly attached partner may give up and start to harbor resentment and protect themself by becoming more distant. Over time, both partners remain in a protective and avoidant mode, uncertain of how to regain a more secure footing, and unsure if they even want to.

Wend, Whirl, and Withdraw

Both in their late twenties, Ainsley and Casey have been together for five years, each carrying their own emotional wounds into the relation-ship. Ainsley, a college student with a creative soul and a whimsical flair, bears the scars of a traumatic childhood that included sexual abuse and neglect. These experiences led her to develop disorganized tendencies. On the other hand, Casey, a real estate agent, often exhibits avoidant tendencies. His parents divorced when he was just five years old, and his mother raised him. After moving to another state and remarrying, his father's visits became infrequent.

One evening, Ainsley returned home after a particularly grueling day filled with back-to-back classes. The moment she stepped into their cozy apartment, she was greeted by the smells of dinner and the sounds of a TV show coming from the living room. There, she found Casey watching their favorite reality show and "stuffing his face." This scene unexpect-edly ignited a surge of abandonment fear and anger in Ainsley.

"Why didn't you wait for me to eat and watch our show?" she blurted out.

Casey, visibly startled by the confrontation, muted the television and turned to face Ainsley. "I didn't realize what time you'd be home," he explained calmly. "I thought it was going to be much later because you had a project meeting for class, and I was really hungry."

"Of course, you didn't wait," Ainsley snapped, her frustration spilling over. "You don't care about me. It's always just about you!"

Casey's expression softened as he stood up, his response tinged with regret. "I'm really sorry. Let me fix you something to eat. I know today was tough," he offered, attempting to bring some calm to the situation. Even though his nervous system was revved up, he moved toward her to give her a comforting hug.

But Ainsley wasn't ready to let down her guard. "I don't want you to touch me right now. I can't trust you to look out for me," she said sharply, tears forming in her eyes as the words tumbled out.

Attempting to soothe the rising tension, Casey reached out to embrace Ainsley again. For a moment, with his hands on her shoulders, it seemed like Ainsley might soften, but the peace was fleeting. Suddenly, Ainsley hit his arm and pulled away sharply. "I'm fed up with feeling this way. I don't think I can do this anymore. If I am not around in the morning, you will know why," she declared. Without waiting for a response, she turned and walked swiftly into their bedroom, slamming the door behind her.

Casey followed. Filled with frustration, he began persistently knocking on the door in a desperate attempt to get Ainsley to calm down. "Can we just talk about this? Please, let's try to calm down and have dinner together," he pleaded.

Exasperated, Casey retreated to the living room to reconsider the reasons for staying in the relationship. It took another hour for Ainsley to calm down and then she was ready to reconnect. However, all Casey could manage was to say he loved her and that he needed to sleep for work the next day. Casey's inadequate response led to another round of arguing. Ultimately, both went to bed frustrated and exhausted. Sadly, getting caught in the Wend, Whirl, and Withdraw cycle, as they did that evening, was all too common for them.

Let's examine the three *W*s of this cycle. *Wending* refers to the act of moving in a specific direction but taking an indirect path to get there.

This often occurs in individuals with disorganized tendencies. They desperately crave love, but with their heightened nervous system perceiving threats everywhere, they find it daunting to trust anyone. As a result, their approach to love is often on a winding road, marked by unclear and often contradictory signals. Because it's challenging for them to regulate their emotions and vulnerability feels perilous, they struggle to communicate directly. For example, instead of saying, "I feel hurt that you ate without me and watched a show that I thought was ours," their feelings manifest through reactivity, biting criticism, and blame.

Being with someone who has a disorganized tendency often resembles being caught in a *whirlwind*. The nature of the relationship is unpredictable and marked by swift changes. The partner with a disorganized tendency—let's call them partner A—may demonstrate conflicting behaviors. They might deeply desire closeness and intimacy, reflecting an intense need for connection; yet almost as soon as they draw near, they might suddenly pull back, viewing the intimacy they sought as a potential threat. This back-and-forth creates a relationship environment rife with instability and upheaval. If soothing Partner A becomes too challenging, Partner B may *withdraw*, thereby confirming partner A's fears of being unlovable or uncared for. This can lead Partner A to either withdraw as well or to anxiously pursue connection in a reactive manner, perpetuating the wend, whirl, withdraw cycle.

Pull Back and Protest

Jenson and Laurie, both in their mid-thirties, have been together for fifteen years. For many of those years, they've been locked in a long-standing Pull Back and Protest cycle that, as we'll see shortly, reflects their attachment tendencies.

Let's examine a conversation that typifies their Pull Back and Protest dance. The incident occurred the night before a typical workday. Laurie had hoped that Jenson would join her in bed at the same time. Jenson had even promised to do so but became engrossed in preparing for work the next morning. By the time he finished, Laurie was already asleep.

The next morning, just as Jenson was about to leave for work, Laurie, filled with exasperation, confronted him. "Can we talk about last night?"

Jenson, distracted and slightly annoyed, replied, "Not right now. I am getting ready for work."

Anxiously, Laurie said, "I waited for you to come to bed last night, but as usual, you didn't even bother to say goodnight."

Jenson retorted sharply, feeling the tension from Laurie's tone, "What the heck! I was busy. You know how much work I've had lately. Why do you always have to complain?"

"Yep. I knew it. Defensive as usual," Laurie snapped back.

With his anger now palpable, Jenson didn't reply. He simply grabbed his lunch, walked out the door, and coldly said, "Have a great day."

As Jenson approached his car, Laurie, now in tears, called out to him, "Why do you do this? I just want us to spend more time together."

This type of negative cycle is common for Laurie and Jenson—and for many other couples caught up in the Pull Back and Protest dance. The trigger might be something as simple as undone dishes, Jenson not coming home for dinner on time, or even the toilet paper roll not being put on correctly. Regardless of the trigger, the pattern of disconnection remains similar. Jenson, who has an avoidant tendency, tends to do his own thing, having more of a "me" mindset than a "we" mindset. As Jenson pulls back into his own world, Laurie, who has an anxious tendency, feels increasingly hurt and alone and protests in an attempt to communicate her feelings. When Jenson turns to logic and reasoning, invalidating her experience, Laurie's response is to pursue him more assertively, sometimes with criticism. This, in turn, triggers Jenson to pull back even further and shut her out. The more he retreats, the more she protests the disconnection, and the more she protests, the more he retreats, perpetuating the Pull Back and Protest cycle. The end result is both of them feeling exhausted, with Jenson feeling frustrated and inadequate, and Laurie feeling hurt, abandoned, and alone.

Now that we've covered the four most common negative cycles, which one do you feel most closely resembles your relationship, particularly during moments of conflict?

- Blame and Bash
- Fracture and Fortify
- Wend, Whirl, and Withdraw
- Pull Back and Protest

If you're not exactly sure, the following exercise should help you figure it out.

Negative Cycle Worksheet

Fill in the blanks below to better understand your and your partner's predominant communication pattern and recognize its cyclical elements.

Basic Moves

The more I _____ [describe your action], the more my partner _____ [describe their action], and then the more I _____ [describe your action], and around we go in circles.

Now, reverse the pattern. Start with your partner's typical action, followed by your response. This helps illustrate that the cycle can begin with either person, underscoring the shared dynamics in the relationship.

Reversing the Order

The more my partner _____ [describe their action], the more I _____ [describe your reaction], and then the more they _____ [describe their action], and around we go in circles.

While we will explore the negative cycle in rich detail in the next chapter, let's take a look at an example of the very basic moves with a couple caught in the Pull Back and Protest cycle:

Basic Moves

The more I **pursue and protest**, the more my partner **pulls back and withdraws**, and then the more I **pursue and protest**, and around we go in circles.

Reversing the Order

The more my partner **pulls back and withdraws**, the more I **pursue and protest**, and then the more they **pull back and withdraw**, and around we go in circles.

Chapter Four Wrap-Up

The negative cycle, a formidable force, thrives on blame, defensiveness, and a lack of empathy, and it can erode even the strongest relationships. This cycle is a common challenge, not a unique failure of your relationship. It arises from natural human impulses to connect and feel loved, as well as to protect oneself and the relationship. Understanding its dynamics empowers you to break free from its tenacious grip. Remember, the cycle—not your partner—is the enemy. Viewing the cycle as the adversary enables you both to unite against it, rather than against each other, leveraging this understanding to forge a stronger, more resilient bond.

So, don't lose hope. Recognizing this challenge is like finally spotting that piece of spinach in your teeth—it's embarrassing, sure, but it's also the first step to removing it. This recognition is your lifeline, your golden ticket to break free from those suffocating patterns that choke the life out of connection.

The next chapter will provide a detailed analysis of the negative cycle, serving as your treasure map through the dark forest of misunderstanding and hurt. We'll navigate through the tangled roots of your negative cycle, uncovering the hidden triggers and emotions that trip you up. By the end, you won't just see the dance; you'll see the threads that weave it together. So, let's roll up our sleeves, face the real enemy, dissect its anatomy, rob it of its sting, and reclaim the love and connection you both so richly deserve.

Key Takeaways

1. Understand the Dance of Connection and Disconnection: Relationships often start with a harmonious, intuitive connection, but they can devolve into dissonant patterns due to unmet needs, miscommunication, and emotional wounds. Recognizing these shifts is crucial to understanding and addressing negative cycles.

2. Identify the Negative Cycle: The negative cycle is an entrenched pattern of disconnection that stems from relational tendencies, unmet needs, and unprocessed emotions. This cycle is a significant barrier to empathy and connection, often leading to self-protective and self-focused behavior.

3. The Negative Cycle as the Enemy: It's essential to view the negative cycle, not your partner, as the true enemy. By uniting against this cycle, you can protect and strengthen your relationship, transforming adversities into opportunities for growth.

4. Four Common Negative Cycles: Couples often fall into one of four negative cycles—Blame and Bash; Fracture and Fortify; Wend, Whirl, and Withdraw; and Pull Back and Protest. Understanding these patterns helps you recognize your specific cycle and address it more effectively.

5. The Impact of Negative Cycles on Empathy and Connection: When caught in a negative cycle, couples struggle to maintain empathy and connection, as their threat systems activate, leading to reactive emotions and self-protection. Recognizing this can help you focus on reconnecting rather than blaming.

6. Break the Cycle: You and your partner can then work together to change your pattern of interaction, fostering a more resilient and loving relationship.

Chapter 5
What Is the Anatomy of Your Negative Cycle?

"One partner may have "started it"—they may have done or said some-thing, or not done or said something, that created potential for the nega-tive communication cycle to set into motion—but it takes two to engage and keep it going."

— Julie Menanno, *Secure Love*

B y now, you should have a clearer understanding of which negative cycle mirrors the dynamics of your relationship—be it Blame and Bash; Fracture and Fortify; Wend, Whirl and With-draw; or Pull Back and Protest. We will now delve deeper into the anatomy of the negative cycle by exploring its essential components. By the end of this chapter, you will be equipped to map, or dissect, your own negative cycle, understanding its unique anatomy. Once you understand what is happening in your dance of disconnection, you can start to make different choices for the sake of love and connection.

Components of the Negative Cycle

All negative cycles, no matter the form, contain the following essential components: the inner threat detector, triggers, emotions, behaviors, relationship-based negative narratives, and contextual factors. Although we'll examine each element separately, it's crucial to recognize that they form an interconnected whole. Let's get started.

Our Inner Threat Detector

Today, for most of us, going outside is unlikely to be a death sentence. However, for our primeval ancestors, leaving the cave or wandering too far from the tribe could mean encountering threats behind every tree. Wherever they traveled, there was likely some animal slithering or sneaking in the shadows, looking for a scrumptious human snack, or another Neanderthal seeking an enemy to slaughter!

Of course, the brain has evolved over millions of years, but it still prioritizes its primary motivation: keeping us safe. It does whatever it can to help us stay alive. If the brain had a motto, it would likely be akin to the words of Star Trek character Mr. Spock, who famously greeted and took leave of others with the salutation, "Live long and prosper!"

Since the brain's main objective is to protect us, it maintains a particularly sensitive monitoring system that is constantly on alert, scanning for threats. This threat detection system is an important piece of the anatomy of the negative cycle. It is largely subconscious, operating outside of our awareness. Stephen Porges, a well-known neuroscientist, refers to this latent subconscious monitoring as neuroception.[1] The process involves our nervous system being responsive to what is happening both in our environment and within ourselves, as it looks for cues of safety or danger and responds accordingly.

Neuroception activates the physiological changes needed for us to connect with others, engage in fight-or-flight responses to danger, attempt to appease or pacify a threat, or shut down for survival.

Our romantic relationships are deeply influenced by our brain's internal threat detection system. This system is perpetually active, scanning for cues that might signal danger, including threats to our attachment security—the felt sense of whether we are in harmony with one another or not. It continuously evaluates our interactions, questioning, "Is what I am seeing, hearing, and experiencing with you a threat to our connection?" It signals to us whether we should draw closer with an open heart; freeze up, not knowing what to say or do; just appease our partner to get the conversation over with; or pull away in defensiveness. For those with insecure relationship tendencies, this threat detection system may be finely tuned, sometimes to the point of triggering false alarms.

Triggers

Once our inner threat detection system, or "connection-disconnection radar" as I refer to it in the context of relationships, gets a blip on the scanner, you know you have been triggered. A trigger is any behavior, word, sound, image, event, or situation that ignites a jolt of energy in your body, causing an immediate emotional reaction. The reaction can be big or small and can last for a short time or a while. It is often the moments we get triggered that allow the snowball of the negative cycle to start rolling down the hill.

Triggers happen very quickly and are largely beyond our initial control. This is because they activate the older part of our brain, the limbic system, which is closely linked to our visceral emotional responses, rather than the rational command and control center known as the prefrontal cortex. Given this neurobiological reality, despite the often-heard statement, "No one can make you feel a certain way," that is simply not the case. It's like saying that no one can make you catch a cold. That is plainly not true. Just as our partners can transmit a cold to us, they can also trigger a cascade of stress hormones and emotions within us. While it's essential for our partners to take responsibility for their actions, it's equally important for us to own our triggers and how we respond to them. Just as we are responsible for hydrating, resting, and caring for ourselves when we're sick, it is also our duty to manage the aftereffects of our triggers. In order to do this, we need to understand the various types of triggers—situational, historical relational, and internal— and how they affect us in different ways.

Situational Triggers

Navigating triggers within relationships is a nuanced process. Some triggers are situational; they come with little historical baggage and carry a lighter emotional weight. For instance, our partner might forget to pick up the special dessert we wanted from the store. When we realize that fantasizing about biting into that favorite delicacy has been for nothing, this can trigger an emotional response, such as feeling hurt. We can then communicate our disappointment to our partner. There's no need to read deeply into this trigger; there are no deeper Freudian or parental wounds to consider here. Sometimes, an apple is just an apple. However, other triggers can evoke more intense reactions, often tapping into deeper neural pathways associated with past relational pain.

Historical Relational Triggers

When something reminds us (either consciously or subconsciously) of a past relationship wound, whether from within or outside the current relationship, we call this a historical relational trigger. These triggers are like echoes from past experiences that resurface in the present, often catching us off guard. For instance, a partner's inattentiveness during a conversation might evoke a deep-seated fear of being ignored, rooted in a past relationship where dismissiveness was common. Another example could be anxiety triggered by a partner's financial spending habits, stemming from childhood memories of financial instability. Or consider the partner who becomes overly suspicious after a minor misunderstanding, a response shaped by previous betrayal. Similarly, a person who felt controlled in a prior relationship might react defensively or feel suffocated when their current partner offers well-intended advice on how to handle a situation. These triggers, which carry baggage ranging from a small carry-on to a truckload, often relate to our feelings of autonomy (i.e., that it is being threatened) or connection (i.e., that it is lacking). The following chart depicts specific triggers that fall within these categories. As you view the chart, think about which of these might be triggers within your relationship.

Triggers

Triggers Related to Autonomy	Triggers Related to Connection
Perceived control or domination	Feeling neglected or ignored
Invasion of privacy	Lack of emotional intimacy
Being overly criticized	Inconsistent or absent communication
Excessive demands	Perceived lack of support
Pressure to conform	Use of a harsh tone
Disrespect for personal boundaries	Withdrawal of affection
Making unilateral decisions	Not feeling prioritized

Historical relational triggers can stem from wounds in your current relationship, previous romantic relationships, relationships with parents or primary caregivers, and cultural, religious, or societal traumas. In any case, these triggers invariably have the power to prompt a negative cycle.

Partner wounds. When the negative cycle is triggered and the battle begins, the memory networks associated with narratives like "my partner is a jerk" or "my partner is mean and nagging" are activated, along with common accompanying emotions such as frustration and anger. In this case, a situational trigger can also trigger the past associated relational pain.

Let's consider the case of Emma and Roger, a couple frequently caught in the Pull Back and Protest dynamic. Roger has historically neglected Emma's emotional needs and dismissed and invalidated her concerns, a pattern exacerbated by his past excessive drinking. Emma, who has shown considerable patience for quite some time, now finds herself reacting swiftly and sharply to perceived slights.

Let's revisit the special dessert situation, but this time with Emma and Roger as the main characters. Imagine Roger returning home without the dessert Emma had anticipated and notice what happens.

As we watch the playback, we see that Emma's immediate response was one of anger—a clear trigger reaction. This incident activated neural pathways linked to Roger's past hurtful and neglectful behaviors, prompting her to confront Roger aggressively: "I asked you to pick up that dessert I wanted! Why don't you ever listen to me?" Feeling attacked, Roger defensively responded, "I forgot, okay? You don't have to get so freakin' angry," before suggesting in a harsh tone, "Do you want me to go back and get it?" This exchange quickly escalated into a typical cycle of mutual triggering and a blame/blame cycle, culminating in Roger disengaging and retreating into his own world, scrolling through social media. At the same time, Emma felt hurt but distracted herself by making dinner.

Parent wounds. Adding more nuance to an already complicated situation, situational triggers can also activate past relational pain, stimulating neural networks linked to childhood wounds. A classic question in couples therapy to a partner experiencing intense emotions toward their significant other is "Who is the face behind the face?" In other words, "Yes, you are feeling hurt by your partner, and that pain feels familiar because your partner has previously hurt you in similar ways. But if we look back further in your life, before you met your partner, when have you felt something like this before?" Nine times out of ten, they recall a memory where they felt similarly toward one of their parents.

Sometimes, when we find ourselves entangled in a negative cycle, our partner's current actions not only trigger immediate reactions but also awaken deep-seated parental wounds, reviving familiar emotions from our childhood. Take the story of Emma and Roger, for example. Roger triggered Emma by forgetting her dessert, thus rekindling historical themes and pain between them. Another facet of the story is that the event also activated emotions from deeper wounds stemming from her relationship with her father. Emma's father, who struggled with alcoholism, had a history of breaking promises, leaving her to grapple with feelings of mistrust and unresolved emotions of hurt, anger, sadness, and shame throughout her adulthood. In this way, the face behind Roger's face was her father's, and although her feelings toward Roger were justified, they were amplified by her past childhood trauma.

Internal Triggers

To add further complexity to the discussion about triggers, we can also trigger ourselves. Our thoughts, impulses, feelings, and behaviors can all be triggers. For example, someone might think, "I hate my partner. I wish I was with _____ instead." That thought may trigger anxiety, provoke feelings of shame, and lead them to distract themself by eating some ice cream. Another example would be ruminating on a past incident where we felt hurt by our partner. Continually replaying the incident can trigger increasing anxiety and anger and potentially lead to more distancing behaviors toward them.

Feelings of lust toward another person can serve as another complex example. Instead of acknowledging our attraction and managing it effectively, this thought can trigger anxiety, leading us to employ defense mechanisms to distance ourselves from our feelings. However, the problem with defenses is that they can negatively impact our partners.

Imagine a husband with lustful thoughts and desires for a woman at work. Because he sees himself as a good Christian man, he cannot tolerate what he considers unacceptable sexual thoughts, feelings, and desires. As the internal cauldron of those feelings boils and bubbles, his anxiety increases, although he may not be conscious of this. Once the anxiety reaches a given threshold, the husband's defenses will kick in.

One evening he sees his wife on her phone. He doesn't know to whom she is talking, but her laughing and free-spirited conversation catches his attention. After the call, she walks by, and he says, "Who was that on the phone? Are you cheating on me?" Her astonishment and hurt are profound, pained that he would entertain such a thought. Both of them get caught in a negative cycle of distress. Feeling hurt and frustrated, each withdraws from the other, and they go to bed feeling alone and angry.

In this instance, the husband projected his unbearable thoughts, feelings, and sexual desires for another woman onto his wife as if she, too, was having lustful thoughts for another person. His projection reduced his anxiety momentarily, so rather than him being the "cheater" in the relationship, she was the one having the same wandering thoughts. In this way, he avoided being upset with himself by becoming upset with his wife for feelings he thinks she has. However, like many defenses in adulthood, there was a cost. The connection with the person he loved most—his wife—ruptured.

Emotions

When our inner threat detector senses danger, it triggers an array of emotions. These emotions are the fuel that propels the negative cycle to take off, like that of a rocket. One partner's anger can trigger the other partner's anger. One person's shame can trigger the other partner's sadness. One partner's fear can create anxiety in the other. One partner's joy can trigger the other partner's happiness. Our emotions profoundly impact each other. Understanding how emotions function in our relationships, particularly in moments of disconnection, is eye-opening and crucial to understanding ourselves and our partners. Most importantly, this understanding will be key to shaping new interactions, which we will discuss in the next chapter.

What Is the Purpose of Emotions?

Our emotions serve as a built-in GPS, guiding us to understand our current situation, where we want to go, and how to get there. Each primary emotion conveys essential information that leads to adaptive action. For example, sadness signals a loss and prompts us to seek comfort and support, while fear alerts us to danger and propels us to take action to protect ourselves. Disgust warns us of something harmful and drives us to avoid it, while joy signals a successful outcome or pleasurable experience and moves us to share this with others. Anger indicates that something is unfair or unjust and compels us to take action to correct it.

Although emotions may not always convey accurate, objective, truthful information, they always point to an individual's valuable subjective truth. This is particularly important in the context of relationships. It is common for the negative cycle to escalate because one partner deems another's experience as "ridiculous" or "irrational." When a partner completely invalidates their partner's experience, it fuels more hurt and what they might deem as "negative" emotions. And, around and around they go. However, a person feels how they feel. Our subjective worlds should be taken seriously. Emotions don't have to lead to ultimate conclusions or definitively determine one's course of action, but they are trying to tell us something important. When we listen mindfully to our own feelings and those of our partners, our emotions can help us navigate the beautifully chaotic and wondrous world of relationships with greater skill and awareness.

The following chart details the wisdom that our basic emotions can bring into our lives. Generally speaking, emotions serve to communicate information and stimulate us to act in some way. As you read through the chart, note the emotions you have experienced in your relationship lately.

The Wisdom of Your Emotions

	Communicates Information	Prompts Action
Sadness	Tells us there has been a loss	Moves us to seek solace, nurturing, and care from others
Fear	Tells us there is danger	Moves us to fight, take flight, freeze, or fawn
Disgust	Tells us something is toxic or foul	Moves us to turn away from and avoid it
Joy	Tells us an experience felt very good and rewarding	Moves us to open up, stay engaged, or share with others

Wisdom of Emotions (*continued*)

	Communicates Information	Prompts Action
Anger	Tells us a goal has been frustrated or something is unjust or unfair	Moves us to right the wrong and make a change
Guilt	Tells us our behaviors or thoughts are contrary to our values or those of our community	Moves us to reconcile, make amends, and restore relationships
Unhealthy Shame	Tells us *we* are wrong for our behaviors or thoughts, which are contrary to our values or those of our community	Moves us to hide, attack ourselves or others, or engage in run-and-numb activities such as defenses or addictions

Primary, Secondary, and Instrumental Emotions

Primary emotions are our core emotions, namely anger, sadness, shame/disgust, fear, surprise, and joy. These emotions arise naturally from the situations we encounter. When someone recognizes and validates these primary emotions, it is as if they have truly crossed the bridge into our experience, leaving us feeling deeply understood. Examples of primary emotions include sadness from missing a partner, fear in response to a partner's shouting, surprise when receiving a gift, or anger in reaction to being gaslighted.

There are primary *emotions*, and then there are primary *emotional experiences*. Primary emotional experiences are actually reactions to stimuli, rather than the core emotions themselves. They often involve a combination of primary emotions and can be influenced by an individual's thoughts, memories, and context. When mapping the negative cycle of communication, it's crucial to honor and express what genuinely feels true. If something feels authentic to our core self, it should be considered part of the cycle. The aim is to vulnerably share with our partners both primary emotions and core emotional experiences, rather than secondary or instrumental emotions, which we will discuss in a moment. Here are several primary emotional experiences we can have during and after our conflicts:[2]

Core Primary Emotional Experiences		
Fearful	Insecure	Powerless
Rejected	Alone	Unwelcome
Exposed	Unvalued	Distressed
Ignored	Threatened	Confused
Shamed	Insignificant	Solitary
Despondent	Ashamed	Wounded
Sorrowful	Disappointed	Overcome
Defeated	Insecure	Powerless

Secondary emotions, or secondary emotional experiences, on the other hand, act as responses to these primary emotions and primary emotional experiences, often masking or hiding them. For example, the intense and fiery emotion of anger might merely be a facade for the underlying, more vulnerable feelings of sadness, shame, or fear. Jealousy or envy might cover deep-seated fears of inadequacy or abandonment. Shame could be disguising sadness or regret. Indifference or disinterest might protect against showing hurt or disappointment. Arrogance or contempt can shield a person from feeling vulnerable or exposed. Additional examples of secondary emotional experiences can include feeling controlled, resentful, shut down, tense, frustrated, or frozen. Each of these reflects a complex response often masking deeper primary emotions.

Instrumental emotions are strategically expressed to achieve specific outcomes, often to manipulate or influence a situation. For instance, a man might cry to elicit sympathy from his partner, effectively sidestepping responsibility for his actions. Similarly, someone might feign surprise to deflect blame, show exaggerated happiness to gain social approval, or display undue anger to intimidate others into compliance.

Each of these examples highlights how instrumental emotions can be used as tools to shift dynamics or evade genuine accountability in interpersonal interactions.

Relationship Longings

Behind the array of emotions lies our relationship longings. For example, if we felt sad because our partner was spending more time at work and less with us, it signals a longing for our partner to want to spend more time with us. If we felt shame because our partner pointed out how neglectful we had been in our parenting duties, this indicates a longing to not feel judged, to be accepted, and to be reassured that we are good parents. If we felt angry that our boundaries were not respected when we expressed the need for space, it points to the obvious—we need our space respected. If we felt fear about the future, unsure if our job was secure, we might long for a hug or a word of encouragement. If we feel joy, we long for our partner to share in our joyful experience and celebrate with us.

Emotions and Our Physiology

Emotions first manifest in the body, profoundly influencing our physiology and neurobiology even before we cognitively process them. Joy, for example, can release endorphins and dopamine, causing us to feel energized and expansive, with increased heart rate and a sense of lightness. Feelings of love may trigger the release of oxytocin, lightening our spirits and making us feel freer and more open, often accompanied by a warm sensation and relaxed muscles.

However, these experiences can be complex for individuals with insecure tendencies or early childhood trauma. For them, joy might unexpectedly trigger the release of stress hormones like cortisol, leading to feelings of guilt, a sense of heaviness, energy depletion, and a reluctance to share accomplishments. Similarly, genuine love from a partner might evoke fear, prompting a fight-or-flight response that leads to withdrawal.

This could involve increased heart rate, muscle tension, and the activation of the amygdala, the brain's fear center.

Thus, our personal histories deeply influence how we interpret and react to our emotions, affecting our physiological responses and neurobiological processes.

When we are triggered and feel constrictive emotions such as shame, anger, disgust, and fear, these feelings act as signals that often fuel the negative cycle. Such emotions are termed "constrictive" because they shut us off from feelings of love, presence, and openheartedness, instead directing our internal energy toward protecting ourselves.

When our feelings arise, we can observe their profound impacts throughout our bodies. Here are a few examples of how our emotions may manifest physically:

- **In our hearts**, we might feel a rapid or heavy heartbeat, a common response when we encounter fear or excitement.
- **In our chests**, there might be a tightness or pressure, which is often associated with anxiety or grief.
- **In our throats**, we may experience a lump or constriction, especially when we feel sad or scared, hindering our ability to speak. That may also occur when anger is suppressed.
- **In our heads**, emotional stress and a rise in anxiety can lead to headaches or a feeling of heaviness, making it hard to concentrate or think clearly.
- **In our hands**, nervousness or anxiety can cause sweating or trembling, while anger might lead to clenched fists.
- **Throughout our whole bodies**, emotions can trigger a range of sensations such as fatigue, shaking, or an adrenaline rush that prepares us for a fight-or-flight response. Alternatively, we might attempt to avoid conflict by submitting or aiming to please an aggressor, or we might feel a sense of bodily collapse, accompanied by an inability or unwillingness to move.

Let's go back to Emma and Roger. Imagine if we could pause the tape the moment Emma discovers that Roger forgot her dessert. Anger, a natural emotion deeply rooted in our tribal evolution signaling an experience of wrongdoing or injustice, would have surged through her and fueled her with energy to express her grievances. This anger, with its strong physiological component, would have tensed her muscles, elevated her heart rate, and boosted her adrenaline levels. Angry energy would likely have pulsated in her chest and hands, priming her to confront a pattern of invalidation and neglect.

One could argue that Emma's primary emotion was sadness, accompanied by feelings of being unheard, unimportant, and alone, and that her anger was merely a secondary response. Sensing the injustice of yet another act of neglect, her initial hurt may have morphed into secondary anger, serving as a protective layer that shielded her from directly communicating her sadness and disappointment. This secondary response might have obscured her underlying feelings, making it harder for Roger to perceive the true depth of her emotional pain. In either case, Emma's emotions would manifest physiologically in a similar manner.

Behaviors

When we find ourselves caught in the negative cycle, we are not just experiencing feelings; we are also acting from them. Remember, each emotion has associated action tendencies that typically prompt us to act in particular ways, likely perpetuating the negative cycle. For instance, some people move toward conflict while others move away. Some may express disdain with an eye roll, raise their voices, or air every grievance at once—effectively throwing in the proverbial kitchen sink. Others may speak softly, attempt to placate, or resort to crying, begging, or repeating themselves until they feel acknowledged. A few might even resort to physical expressions like smashing objects or abruptly leaving the scene. There are many different behaviors we might engage in during the heat of battle.

Going back to Emma and Roger, their story isn't just about feelings; it's also about actions. When Emma's internal threat detector sensed a relationship threat, it wasn't just any alert. It was a painful reminder that

Roger had once again forgotten her needs, stirring up a storm of anger and hurt within her. This emotional turmoil didn't stay inside. Instead, it propelled Emma to walk toward Roger. With each step, her emotions turned into reactive energy, culminating in sharp words of criticism as she confronted him. Roger's eye roll only escalated the situation. His subsequent invalidating remarks, attempts at problem-solving, and rationalizations further exacerbated the tension. Finally, his decision to retreat without setting a time to continue their discussion inflicted even more pain. Below are examples of behaviors and actions we might engage in at the start of or during the negative communication cycle:[3]

Behaviors/Actions

Blaming or pointing out mistakes	Yelling	Ignoring or withdrawing
Expressing frustration or anger	Getting angry	Giving the silent treatment
Seeking information	Asking questions	Withholding information
Becoming critical	Expressing disapproval	Overreacting to feedback
Advising our partner how to change	Not listening and numbing out	Avoiding responsibility
Suggesting improvements	Problem solving	Being dismissive
Labeling our partner as the problem	Freezing or not responding	Jumping to conclusions
Demanding attention	Staying calm and reasoning with our partner	Overanalyzing situations

Relationship-Based Negative Narratives

So far, in dissecting the negative cycle, we have explored the threat system, triggers, emotions, and behaviors. If we could press the pause button during our tenacious tangos, we would notice that our thoughts or beliefs about ourselves and our partners also contribute to the persistence of the negative cycle. Now, we will examine the *relationship-based negative narrative* that arises during our conflicts.

We can think of the relationship-based negative narrative as a hit song that plays on the radio in our minds when we are in a threat state and feel harmed by our partner. It doesn't matter what day it is or what you are arguing about; if it's a full-blown negative cycle, the same radio station is dialed in, with the same hit song on repeat.

Here are some examples of lyrics (thoughts) about our partners when we are getting caught in the negative cycle:

- They are selfish and don't care about me.
- They will never change, and I have to live with this for the rest of my life.
- They are crazy and so emotional.
- I better just stop saying anything because it never goes well.
- Screw them. They are such an abusive gaslighter.
- They're just using me; they don't care about my feelings.

Here are some examples of lyrics (thoughts) about ourselves when we are getting caught in the negative cycle:

- I'm always the one trying harder, and it's never enough for them.
- They must find me unattractive or unworthy; why else would they ignore me?
- Every time I open up, I just get hurt. It's safer to keep to myself.
- Why am I always the problem in this relationship?

- I can't do anything right in their eyes; I'm always disappointing them.
- Uh-oh. What the heck did I do wrong now?
- No matter what I do, I'm never going to be good enough in their eyes.
- I am too good for them. I deserve way better.
- I am so low on their importance list. Screw them.

Here are some examples of lyrics (thoughts) about our relationship future when we are getting caught in the negative cycle:

- This is too hard. We're never going to find a way to get past this.
- We're stuck in a loop, and there's no way out. Why bother trying?
- They don't really love me. It's only a matter of time before they find someone else.
- I can't make them happy no matter how hard I try. I'm always going to disappoint them.
- I feel trapped. There's no future for us if things stay like this.
- We're too different and don't have enough in common. It's unrealistic to think we can bridge this gap.

Just as certain songs can get stuck in our heads, these negative narratives often play on repeat in our minds. Being aware of this is crucial in order to break the negative cycle. Let's now turn to the final essential component of the negative cycle.

Contextual Factors

Sometimes, reality is like a scene from *The Transformers*: there is more than meets the eye. We may think we are arguing over one specific issue, yet often, it's the unseen dynamics that maintain or trigger our negative cycles. These include power dynamics, financial stress, cultural and parental expectations, medical issues, racial trauma, existential questions, the impacts of patriarchy and gender norms, past trauma, chronic pain, unresolved grief, work pressures, and complex family relationships. Allow me to illustrate a few of these dynamics through the lives of Nora and James.

Nora and James, once deeply in love, found their relationship fundamentally altered by the arrival of twins. Last year, they welcomed their little ones, bringing them immense joy but also a dramatic shift in their lifestyle. The leisurely mornings with warm cuddles they once cherished disappeared, along with the relaxed evenings spent watching favorite shows over a glass of wine. Now, their nights are consumed by unpredictable bottle feedings and soothing restless infants, which has led to considerable sleep deprivation. This lack of rest has left both feeling depleted, increasing irritability and snappiness toward each other. As a result, they've grown more disconnected, with mounting complaints and criticisms fueling their negative cycle of Pull Back and Protest—James pulling back and withdrawing, and Nora pursuing and protesting. While their struggles may seem typical for new parents dealing with the intense demands of twin babies, other significant contextual factors also play a crucial role in their evolving relationship dynamics.

Nora harbored an undercurrent of resentment toward James. Since he worked part-time, he could spend significantly more time with their children. She feared that her children might bond more with James than with her, a concern exacerbated by the burdens of cultural pressures and patriarchy. Nora felt a relentless pressure to counter the pervasive stereotype that women are merely decorative, a notion stemming from early career experiences where she was demeaned and not taken seriously by male colleagues. She also grappled with the dual burden of career and motherhood, convinced that she must be exceptionally present with her children to avoid causing them emotional harm. Conversely, if the roles were reversed and James worked full-time, she believed that he wouldn't face the same unique burden. In his case, the mere presence of the children's mother's love was deemed sufficient, leaving him free from similar anxieties.

James was also grappling with his own contextual dynamics. About a year and a half ago, he lost his father to cancer, a loss that deeply affected him. His father was his role model, mentor, and confidant, especially during tough times. In his father's later years, James often helped support his mother in caring for him. However, after his father's death, James didn't have time to grieve properly; the twins were almost due, and both his and Nora's attention was focused on them. It was also the cultural dynamics of the "man code" that kept him from taking his own grief seriously and feeling the importance of sharing it with someone. It wasn't until couples therapy that James realized he was still grieving the loss of his father and recognized how cultural and familial dynamics had contributed to his holding those feelings in. Between his grief, the stress of becoming a new parent, and the strains on his marriage, he turned to alcohol as a coping mechanism.

Unspoken between them, these complex contextual dynamics simmered beneath their day-to-day interactions. Nora blamed their deteriorating relationship on James' perceived lack of involvement at home, convinced that if he contributed more, their situation would improve. Yet, she struggled to express her deeper fears and vulnerabilities, hindered by a culture that had always discouraged such openness, both in her family and professional life. Meanwhile, James was dealing with the loss of his father, which he rarely discussed, yet it significantly depleted his energy and emotional bandwidth on some days.

The stark truth remains: unless Nora and James can confront and articulate these underlying contextual issues, they will continue to fuel their negative cycle with devastating potency, putting the very foundation of their relationship at risk.

Examining Your Unique Anatomy of the Negative Cycle

Now that we have explored the generic anatomy of the negative cycle, including the threat system, triggers, primary and secondary emotions, behaviors, relationship-based negative narratives, and contextual dynamics, it's your turn to detail your own experiences within the negative communication cycle you and your partner encounter. If you need help completing the exercise, refer back to the charts earlier in the chapter. First, we will examine the unique anatomy of Nora and James' negative communication cycle.

Nora's Anatomy of the Negative Cycle
Relationship Tendency: *Anxious*
Type of Cycle: *Pull Back and Protest*

The contextual issues we are dealing with are **parenting, existential, roles and responsibilities, and effects of cultural expectations and patriarchy concerns**. When I encounter certain triggers, whether internally or from my partner, such as **minimizing and invalidating my feelings**, my partner often experiences my secondary emotions, such as **frustration and anger**. Then, they see me engage in certain behaviors, such as **blaming, attacking, and demeaning**. Often, during these moments, I can feel physiological reactions within my body, such as **a racing heart, tightening in my jaw, and flushed cheeks**. When we are in conflict, I often have negative thoughts about myself, my partner, or our futures, such as **"You don't care about me," "You don't do anything around here,"** and **"It is not fair you get to spend more time with the kids."** As my partner persists in their reactive thoughts, feelings, and behaviors, this further triggers me, and around and around we go. What my partner doesn't hear about is that deep down, I'm really feeling primary emotions/core emotional experiences, such as **sadness, guilt, and shame**. Behind my big feelings and reactive behaviors, there are more vulnerable needs and longings, such as **"I need you to hold me, tell me you love me, and reassure me I am not a bad mom."**

James's Anatomy of the Negative Cycle
Relationship Tendency: *Avoidant*
Type of Cycle: *Pull Back and Protest*

The contextual issues we are dealing with are **parental grief, alcohol use, cultural expectations, and roles and responsibilities**. When I encounter certain triggers, whether internally or from my partner, such as **blaming, attacking, and demeaning me**, my partner often experiences my secondary emotions, such as **frustration and anger**. Then, they see me engage in certain behaviors, such as **denying, intellectualizing, and withdrawing**. Often, during these moments, I can feel physiological reactions within my body, such as **a racing heart, upset stomach, and feeling hot in the face**. When we are in conflicts, I often have negative thoughts about myself, my partner, or our futures, such as **"Here we go again,"** and **"Why is she such a nag,"** and **"I just need to get away,"** and **"I can't do anything right with her."** As my partner persists in their reactive thoughts, feelings, and behaviors, this further triggers me, and around and around we go. What my partner doesn't hear about is that deep down, I'm really feeling primary emotions/core emotional experiences, such as **sadness, fearful and unvalued**. Behind my big feelings and reactive behaviors, there are more vulnerable needs and longings, such as **"I need to feel her warmth and love toward me, and a felt sense that she actually likes me."**

Now it's your turn…

What Is the Anatomy of Your Negative Cycle?
Relationship Tendency:
Type of Cycle:

The contextual issues we are dealing with are _____. When I encounter certain triggers, whether internally or from my partner, such as _____, my partner often experiences my secondary emotions, such as _____. Then, they see me engage in certain behaviors, such as _____. Often, during these moments, I can feel physiological reactions within my body, such as _____. When we are in conflicts, I often have negative thoughts about myself, my partner, or our futures, such as _____. As my partner persists in their reactive thoughts, feelings, and behaviors, this further triggers me, and around and around we go. What my partner doesn't hear about is that deep down, I'm really feeling primary emotions/core emotional experiences, such as _____. Behind my big feelings and reactive behaviors, there are more vulnerable needs and longings, such as _____.

Chapter Five Wrap-Up

Now that you've mapped out your negative cycle of communication, you have a firmer grasp on the real enemy harming your relationship. Recognizing this challenge is the first step toward breaking free from the patterns that block a deep sense of connection. With this newfound understanding, you are beginning to have the necessary awareness to gain the upper hand, prepare for battle (with the negative cycle, *not* your partner), and move toward a more secure bond. Let's move to the next chapter, where we will explore transformative principles and effective practices that foster connection, help you avoid getting sucked into the negative cycle, and guide you on how to escape if you do. Together, let's roll up our sleeves, face the real enemy, dissect its anatomy, rob it of its sting, and reclaim the love and connection you both so richly deserve.

Key Takeaways

1. Inner Threat Detector: Our brain's internal threat detection system, or "connection-disconnection radar," constantly scans for cues that might signal danger to our attachment security. This system, often operating subconsciously, can trigger emotional reactions that propel the negative cycle.

2. Triggers: Triggers can be situational or deeply rooted in past relational pain and childhood wounds. These triggers ignite immediate emotional responses that contribute to the snowball effect of the negative cycle. Recognizing these triggers helps you to identify, and possibly head off the cycle.

3. Emotions and Physiology:
Emotions act as the fuel for the negative cycle, with each emotion affecting our physiological state. Understanding the role of primary, secondary, and instrumental emotions helps you distinguish authentic feelings from reactive responses.

4. Behaviors: Emotional reactions lead to specific behaviors, such as blaming, withdrawing, or attacking, which perpetuate the negative cycle. Recognizing these behaviors and their impact on the cycle is crucial for changing the interaction pattern.

5. Negative Narratives: Relationship-based negative narratives are the repetitive thoughts and beliefs about ourselves, our partners, and our relationship future that emerge during conflicts. These narratives reinforce the cycle and hinder empathy and connection.

6. Contextual Factors: External factors like power dynamics, cultural expectations, financial stress, and past traumas significantly influence the negative cycle. Acknowledging these factors in your relationship helps you to understand the deeper layers of the negative cycle and address the root causes of your disconnection.

7. Relationship Longings: Behind the array of emotions and reactive behaviors lie deeper relationship longings, such as the need for connection, validation, and reassurance. Identifying and addressing these underlying needs can help transform negative cycles into opportunities for growth and deeper intimacy.

Part Three
Deepening the Bond

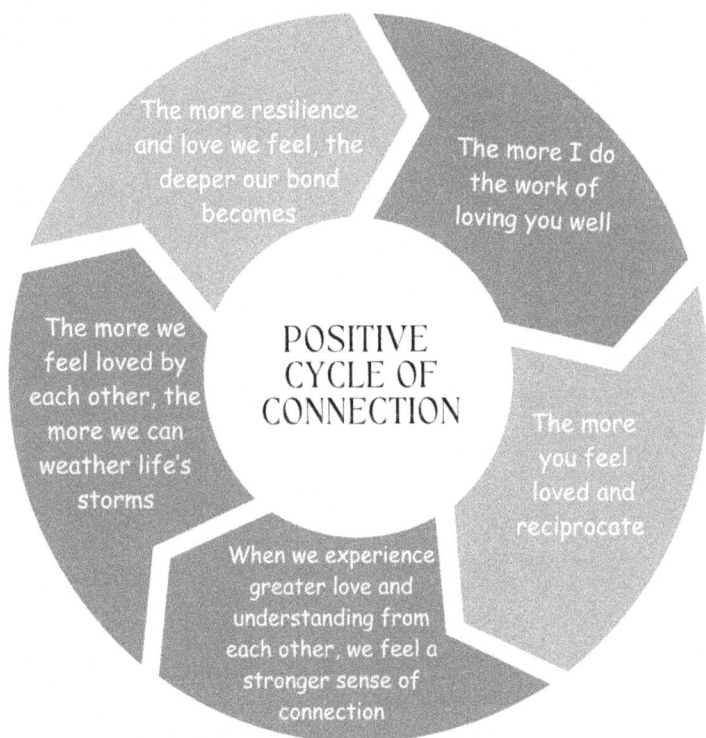

The more resilience and love we feel, the deeper our bond becomes

The more I do the work of loving you well

The more we feel loved by each other, the more we can weather life's storms

POSITIVE CYCLE OF CONNECTION

The more you feel loved and reciprocate

When we experience greater love and understanding from each other, we feel a stronger sense of connection

Chapter 6
Strengthening Your Connection

"Love is a byproduct of the relationship rather than the sole foundation, something that grows slowly, over time, and is built every single day in a thousand small and specific interactions."

— Sara Nasserzadeh, *Love by Design*

In your journey of deepening the awareness of your own and your partner's relational tendencies and understanding the anatomy of your negative cycle, it's now time to delve into practical principles and strategies. These strategies are here to help you steer clear of those detrimental patterns and enhance your connection.

Healthy relationship dynamics don't just fall into our laps by some cosmic accident. If we only follow our immediate desires and impulses —especially those cooked up by our threat system—we can find ourselves hopelessly adrift. Those emotionally driven, fear-based reactions shove us into a me-centric protection mode, instead of allowing us to be the rational, wise, and collaborative beings we aspire to be.

Protection mode can be a healthy response when we need to guard against pain, but if we're not careful, we can hurt our partner in that state, leading to more disconnection. By equipping ourselves with a broader array of tools specifically tailored to our unique relationship blueprints, we can significantly increase our chances of keeping our care-giving instincts actively engaged. This helps us sustain a more harmo-nious and connected relationship with the one we love.

So, let's roll up our sleeves and explore four key principles and prac-tices for connection in this chapter!

Connection Through Maintaining and Protecting Your Emotional Contact

Many of us seldom discuss and clarify with our partners what our nonnegotiables are and what agreements we are committed to sustaining throughout our relationship. Indeed, we exchange vows and proclaim "for better, for worse, for richer, for poorer, in sickness and in health" at our weddings. But over time, those sacred promises tend to drift into the background of our daily lives.

What we're left with are these implicit, unspoken agreements that sort of guide us. But if we want our relationships to really flourish, it's so important to bring our relationship vision out into the open and keep it front and center, guarding it against the many stressors that inevitably come our way. This includes the roaring lion of the negative cycle just waiting to pounce on our joy and connection.

To build a resilient relationship as a couple, especially in the whirl-wind of everyday life, we need to make a pact to maintain and protect our emotional contact. In simpler terms, we need to promise to be good and kind companions to each other, no matter what.

Through John Gottman's fifty years of marital research, he has made his message very clear that friendship is the key to relationship longevity. He writes, "The determining factor in whether wives feel satisfied with the sex, romance, and passion in their marriage is, by 70 percent, the quality of the couple's friendship."[1] Gottman goes on to write, "For men, the determining factor is, by 70 percent, the quality of the couple's friendship. So, men and women come from the same planet, after all."[2] While friendship has many components, one element is clear: we must "proact," meaning plan ahead and make a pact (an agreement) to elevate emotional intimacy and connection in our relationships to prevent that consistent contact from dissolving.

Stan Tatkin writes, "Agreements are to secure-functioning relationships what beams and supports are to a house structure. Without agreements, which are based on shared interests, a relationship, like a house, won't hold up."[3] We can make many agreements in our relationships, such as staying faithful, partnering fairly with bills, taking care of each other when sick, not cursing at each other, and protecting each other's honor in social situations. These are all excellent ideas and are important in friendships.

It's also vital for us to prioritize our friendship and carve out moments throughout the week to explore our partner's inner and outer experiences with a "beginner's mind." This means sensitively tuning into their feelings on an embodied level and thoughtfully offering care and comfort that truly connects with their unique needs and desires.

A wonderful and important question to ask is "Have my partner and I made an explicit, firm commitment to prioritize our connection during the week?" By proactively making a pact to maintain and protect our emotional connection, we signal to our partner their immense importance in our universe. When we feel that love and intentionality reciprocated, it fuels us to love in return, creating a positive cycle of connectivity. This is one of the most effective preventative measures for reducing the negative cycles in our relationships. Friendship is a buffer that keeps at bay the tenacious tango in which we get caught. And when we do inevitably get caught, it helps us escape with far fewer battle scars.

Speaking about the inevitability of conflict, I'd like to share a secret from the fascinating world of couples therapists' relationships. Even the healthiest couples have quarrels, and yes, that includes us— your savvy and put-together couples therapists. Countless times, I've engaged in discussions with bona fide relationship experts who recount occasions when they were ensnared by their own negative cycles with their partners. I, too, am no exception. So, don't let anyone fool you.

Indeed, all couples will experience moments of discord. It's a universal truth: healthy couples fight. We are all human, all striving for more love, belonging, respect, equity, safety, and connection. Yet, whether it is due to our differences, a lack of sleep, unprocessed trauma, bad food we ate from the fridge, job stress, existential or spiritual dilemmas, etc., riding on the fluffy clouds of connection can be fleeting. Occasionally, the negative cycle will get the best of us, and our mental radio will tune into the top-charting negative narrative, blaring obnoxiously loud.

However, we hold the power to decide to fight for our relationship, to cherish and nurture our moments of connection, and to manage our conflicts with greater skill. By embracing preventative strategies—like safeguarding and nurturing our emotional bond—we can not only lessen the frequency of disputes but also shorten the recovery time needed to restore harmony. This proactive approach reshapes the landscape of our relationships, fostering peace and reinforcing the belief that this whole relationship endeavor is undeniably worth it.

Putting It into Practice

I find it profoundly rewarding when couples I work with experience a stark revelation: the root of their disconnection often stems from simply not making time for each other. They have allowed work, children, friends, and endless scrolling through social media to take precedence, relegating their relationship to nothing more than emotional leftovers. This neglect leads to a gradual but inevitable erosion of their bond.

Had a friend asked them, "What do you think is the most challenging experience your partner is currently facing?'" their response might have been a puzzled, "I'm not sure." Inquiring further, "What brings your partner the most joy lately?" might yield, "I have no idea." Or even more telling, "What is the biggest obstacle preventing your partner from feeling loved by you?" would likely be met with, "I just don't know." How can we feel connected with our partners if we are merely skimming the surface of our relationship, neglecting to nurture it with presence, empathy, and curiosity?

How can we feel close without the foundational elements of friendship: intimacy and emotional connection? We may manage to coast along in a "roommate-like" existence or live in parallel universes for a time, but such arrangements are ultimately unsustainable. A couple cannot thrive without actively maintaining and protecting the time dedicated to connecting deeply.

During a session, Jasmine, feeling the ache of the growing distance between her and her partner, turned to him and said, "Honey, I'm sorry for not making you and our relationship a priority." Instantly, Bailey responded, "We both haven't." Eager to continue, Jasmine proposed, "Let's commit to prioritizing our relationship. How about we set aside time, at least once a week, to connect and check in with each other?" Bailey, wrestling with his avoidant tendencies, admitted, "I'd like that. But I'm still learning how to connect emotionally, and I often don't know what to say. I'm also worried it might just become a criticism session." Jasmine reassured him, "I promise you won't be a piñata for my verbal blows. We'll figure it out together in a way that feels good to us both."

In that beautiful moment, they made a pact to maintain and protect their emotional connection. I then introduced them to the activity of scuba diving, as discussed in chapter three. I also encouraged them to use discussion starters if needed, such as "What's happening in your world?" "What is bringing you joy lately?" "What has been the most challenging?" "Is there anything I can do to help make life easier for you?" and "What are you looking forward to?"

Coming together as a couple to proactively make a pact to maintain and protect your emotional connection is a wonderful gift you can provide one another. This may involve readjusting schedules to go scuba diving or engaging in daily ART (attachment-related texts) and quick check-ins to share feelings and experiences. It could also mean quickly repairing relational ruptures and injuries that have not been addressed to protect the bond between you both, making the negative cycle less likely to occur.

To deepen your emotional connection, I invite you and your partner to consider integrating a variety of enriching practices into your daily lives. This can include committing to regular date nights, participating in couples therapy or workshops, taking up shared hobbies, expressing gratitude, engaging in physical affection, practicing digital detox to enhance presence, and meditating together. If friendship is the adhesive that bonds couples for a lifetime and acts as negative cycles' kryptonite, then it's crucial to not only cultivate emotional connection through diverse practices but also to safeguard its sustaining power at all costs.

Connection Through Each Other's Operating System

I vividly recall a moment years ago when I felt utterly elated, six months into a relationship with someone I believed could be my lifelong partner. I was deeply in love and committed to demonstrating it in every way I could. In my mind, she was completely captivated by me, undoubtedly impressed by my steady affection and valiant efforts to love her well.

One day, after picking out some thoughtful additions for her apartment—imagining myself as her knight in shining armor—I noticed that she looked sad. Concerned, I gently asked, "What's wrong?" She paused, her eyes brimming with tears, and confessed, "I don't feel loved by you." That statement left me reeling; my heart sank. I thought to myself, "How could she feel unloved when I was going to such lengths to show my love?"

That day, I confronted a profound truth about relationships: *You can think you are loving your partner, but if your ways of loving aren't according to their "operating system" and filling their "love tank," then you aren't truly loving them.* Loving someone isn't merely about the actions you take or the love you think you're giving; effective love is love that is well received. The task is to love *them*; however, sometimes, if we are honest, when we think we are loving them, we are actually loving *ourselves*. In other words, we do not see the person before us. We love them as if they were ourselves, projecting our own needs and desires onto them. However, if our actions are not perceived as loving, they are ineffective. Loving well requires tuning into our partner's needs and desires and being aware of their relational tendencies, ensuring that our gestures of affection resonate with them personally.

One of the most common mistakes we can make in our relationships is assuming that our partners should think, feel, and act just as we do. It's a natural inclination—making assumptions and automating responses saves energy and mental effort. After all, who has the time to constantly consider their partner's preferences and feelings when there are conversations to be had, decisions to be made, and tasks to be completed? It's also easy to assume that if we feel loved in a particular way, our partners would, too.

Someone might think, "Why wouldn't my partner love soothing touch?" or "Why wouldn't my partner want to spend quality time with me?" This assumption makes sense if those are among their top three love languages. However, our preferred ways of feeling loved, which may come naturally to us, might not even appear on our partner's list, or they may rank as number four or five.

Putting It into Practice

So how do we find out what our partner's operating manual lists as preferred ways of feeling loved, and how do we make the shift to show them love in these preferred ways? Let's look at two important ways.

Fill Each Other's Love Tank

We all have relational needs, and our personal operating system includes a proverbial "love tank." A "love tank" is a metaphor for an individual's relational reservoir that requires love and affection in unique forms to maintain a felt sense of connectedness and happiness in a relationship. When a person's love tank is full, they experience love, acceptance, appreciation, and emotional fulfillment. Conversely, when the tank is empty or running low, they may feel neglected, unloved, or emotionally drained. This concept is linked to Gary Chapman's book *The Five Love Languages*, which highlights the importance of understanding and meeting each other's emotional needs to sustain a healthy and satisfying relationship.[4]

Chapman's five love languages include Words of Affirmation, Acts of Service, Receiving Gifts, Quality Time, and Physical Touch. Each individual tends to have one or two primary love languages that make them feel most loved and appreciated. *Words of Affirmation* involves expressing love through verbal compliments, appreciation, and encouragement. *Acts of Service* is about demonstrating love by performing helpful actions and chores. *Receiving Gifts* focuses on giving thoughtful presents as symbols of love and care. *Quality Time* emphasizes undivided attention and shared activities to nurture the relationship. *Physical Touch* includes affectionate physical contact like holding hands, hugging, and other forms of touch.

I will also include an *Other* category. This category is meant for you to step outside the box of the traditional concept of love languages and fill in what helps you or your partner feel loved. For example, it might include "Needing Space" as a category. There may be times when we need space to recharge, and having a partner who says, "I know you love me, and you know I love you. Take as much space as you need to take care of yourself right now" can be very affirming. If you had children before you met your partner, your love language could include "Loving My Child Well." Another possible "Other" category could be "Shared Goals." This involves working together toward common objectives, such as planning for the future, pursuing joint projects, or supporting each other's aspirations. Feeling supported and united in achieving shared goals can be a powerful way to feel loved and connected. Don't be boxed in by the traditional categories. Also, if you have four primary love languages rather than one or two, then trust your instincts and go with it.

Love languages are not set in stone, and their importance can vary depending on what season of the relationship you're in. Therefore, it's important to ask yourself, "What love languages resonate with me the most in this season of my relationship?" Another vital question is, "What do I think my partner's love language is in this season?" Even better, you could ask them directly and share what yours is. While love languages and filling each other's love tank are not the holy grail to successful relationships, they are healthy practices to keep in mind to love our partners well. By keeping our tanks close to full and avoiding running on fumes, we can ensure there is enough love to counteract the intensity of negative cycles or decrease their presence in our relationship.

Love Each Other with Your Relational Tendencies in Mind

As we keep one another's operating systems and love languages top of mind, another helpful practice is to love each other with a keen awareness of our relational tendencies. Since most couples I work with have anxious or avoidant tendencies, I will provide examples of how to love one another well with those tendencies in mind.

One of the ways to love our partners well in light of their relational tendencies is to think about their *core unconscious questions*. For example, the core questions of someone with an anxious relational tendency might be, "Am I truly loved and valued?" and "Will my partner be there for me when I need them?" If that's the case for our partner, we may need to be more intentional about avoiding stonewalling and withdrawing and providing consistent reliability, presence, and reassurance without pathologizing those needs.

Take Marissa, who has an anxious tendency, and Shelley, who has an avoidant tendency. They have been together for twelve years. After ten months of couples therapy, they have developed a good understanding of their relational tendencies and negative cycle. Shelley knows that when she's extremely busy at work, goes out with friends on a Saturday night, or needs to cool off from an argument, it's vital to keep Marissa's core questions in mind. In those moments, Shelley is extra intentional about reaffirming her love for Marissa, even in small ways.

For instance, when Shelley anticipates a busy week at work, she takes a moment to sit with Marissa and express how much she values their relationship. She might look her kindly in the eyes and say, "I know this week is going to be hectic, but I want you to know how much you mean to me. Just because I am away more doesn't mean I don't love you." This reassurance helps Marissa feel secure and valued, even during periods of physical absence.

When Shelley goes out with friends, she makes a point to check in with Marissa before she leaves. When she returns, she makes a small but meaningful gesture like a text or call saying, "I'm thinking about you and can't wait to see you later." This simple act of communication helps Marissa feel connected and reassured of Shelley's commitment, mitigating feelings of anxiety and insecurity. Marissa doesn't demand these actions from Shelley. However, after some work on Shelley's end, particularly moving past her initial knee-jerk reactions of feeling constricted or controlled, she realized it was all for the sake of love and helping Marissa feel secure. She saw it as a gift to give rather than a coercive demand. Additionally, Shelley recognized that if Marissa felt loved, it would reduce conflict in their relationship. This understanding was a significant motivator for Shelley to keep Marissa's core questions in mind and engage in these reassuring actions.

During conflicts, Shelley recognizes the importance of maintaining emotional availability, even when she needs a moment to cool off. Instead of abruptly withdrawing, she communicates her need for space while reassuring Marissa of her intentions. She might say, "I need some time to process my thoughts, but I love you, and we'll talk about this soon." This approach respects Shelley's need for space while acknowledging Marissa's need for emotional security.

Through these actions, Shelley demonstrates a deep understanding of Marissa's core questions and relational needs. By being mindful and intentional in her responses, Shelley not only alleviates Marissa's anxiety but also strengthens their bond and fosters a more secure, loving relationship. Over time, Marissa feels more secure in Shelley's love and trust in their relationship, leading to a more harmonious and fulfilling partnership.

With her avoidant relational tendencies, Shelley often harbors core questions that remain unspoken but significantly influence her interactions. These questions, typical for those with avoidant proclivities, include: "Will my independence be compromised?" "Can I trust others to meet my needs?" and "How can I avoid conflict, vulnerability, and intimacy?" Marissa is encouraged to accept Shelley for who she is, understanding that her need for space is an adaptive way to feel comfortable and safe. Instead of judging Shelley harshly for her core attachment questions and needs, Marissa can honor and respect them. Marissa, who prefers a lot of emotional intimacy and togetherness, can show love to Shelley by acknowledging her need for space and recognizing that

Shelley is simply different, not a robot, overly selfish, or broken in some way.

For example, consider when Shelley is busy at work and plans to go to a book club with her friends on Friday night. After Shelley reassures Marissa of her love and care, Marissa, keeping Shelley's relational tendencies in mind, could say something like "Shelley, you worked hard this week. And I know how much you like your small study group. You deserve some 'you' time. I love you and will see you when you get back." This reassurance relieves Shelley, knowing she can have some autonomy in peace without feeling guilty or fearing conflict.

We thrive in our relationships when we make an effort to truly understand each other's relational tendencies and love languages and love one another with them in mind. Accepting each other as we are, without harsh judgment or biting criticism, creates an environment where both partners feel loved, valued, and respected. However, when we project our preferences onto one another—assuming that our partners should feel loved in the same way we do—we often end up feeling disconnected and running on relational fumes. Add the pointy sticks and jagged stones of judgment toward each other's relational tendencies, and we create more harm and distance. This results in a dry, brittle environment where a tiny spark could set our negative cycles aflame.

Acceptance doesn't mean we're off the hook from changing or compromising; it means that before we courageously dive into making those changes for love, we feel seen and respected for who we are and the messy, beautiful, and often tragic stories that have shaped us. This kind of acceptance is the magic that gets us through tough times, keeps our love tanks full, and keeps those nasty, negative cycles from taking over more often than we would like.

Connection Through Launchings and Landings

Imagine you're a dog lover, and your dog eagerly greets you in the morning, jumping up with a lick and a bark (cat lovers, bear with me on this one). Sure, the dog's slobbering affection might be a bit annoying when you're still groggy and fumbling for your coffee, but there's something heartwarming about their sheer joy and excitement. That wild enthusiasm sets a positive tone for the day, whether we like it or not.

Now, picture coming home at the end of a long day. As you walk through the door, your dog practically smiles, its tail wagging like it might fly off. Your pet tries to jump up, showering you with unconditional love and making you feel like the most important person in the world—that kind of welcome lifts your spirits like nothing else can.

I'm not saying we need to act like dogs toward one another, though a little tail wagging upon arriving home would be pretty funny. But we can take a page from their best-selling canine book on how to make owners feel special (even if their behavior is just a clever strategy to score extra treats). We can create moments in our relationships that mirror this kind of love and enthusiasm. Whether when we wake up together, say goodnight, start the day with a loving gesture, greet each other warmly after time apart, or end the day with kindness and a kiss—these small rituals can transform our relationships. They can fill our love tanks and give us the emotional fuel to be our best selves, day in and day out.

The transition from a state of rest to a state of activity is called a *launching*. A launching occurs upon waking to start our day, head to work or school, or take the kids somewhere.[5] Launchings can provide positive energy that helps us be more effective at work and in our daily lives. *Landings* are the transitions from a state of activity back to a state of rest. These occur when we come home from work or school, return from an outing, or go to sleep at night.[6] Many of us struggle with anxiety and sleep issues. Even if we do not sleep in the same bed as our partner, which is an increasing phenomenon, cuddling just a few minutes before going to sleep in our separate beds can be a wonderful sleep aid. The romantic rituals surrounding these transitions can help soothe our nervous systems and reinforce our importance to each other. If you have children, by observing you both engaging in loving and supportive behaviors, they learn how to express and show love, creating a nurturing environment that fosters emotional intelligence and healthy relationships.

Putting It into Practice

Lily and Ethan, both in their late thirties, have been married for eight years and have two young children. Both have demanding careers, Lily as a corporate lawyer and Ethan as an architect. Their busy lives often left them feeling disconnected, especially with their different work schedules and the demands of parenting.

Lily's job required long hours and frequent travel, while Ethan's architectural projects often kept him busy late into the evening. Their differing schedules created a gap in their relationship. Lily often returned home late, exhausted from her day, while Ethan struggled to keep up with the household responsibilities and their children's bedtime routines.

After learning about "launchings and landings," Lily and Ethan prioritized them as something they'd practice daily. They discovered that consistent morning and evening rituals could help them stay connected despite their busy schedules. What they realized was that it didn't take much time to connect in this way, yet those small moments during launchings and landings had a significant impact.

Every evening, regardless of how late Lily returned, they made it a point to spend at least fifteen minutes together before bed. They would sit on the balcony, share a glass of wine, and chat about their day. Even on nights when Lily was particularly tired, Ethan waited up for her, providing a comforting presence as she unwound from her hectic schedule.

They developed a new morning ritual to help start their day together. Even though Lily often needed more sleep, she'd set her alarm to wake up briefly with Ethan. They called it "the morning power cuddle." During this time, they'd discuss their plan for taking care of the kids while enjoying a quick breakfast together—often just a smoothie or a cup of coffee—before Ethan headed to his office. This small effort helped them feel more connected and supported, giving them a sense of togetherness despite their busy schedules.

At night, they also adopted a practice of expressing gratitude. After turning out the lights, they'd take turns naming things they were grateful for that day. While there were nights when they were too exhausted to do it, they made an effort to pick up the ritual the next day. This practice not only helped them end the day on a positive note but also deepened their appreciation for each other and their life together.

Ethan noticed that these small but consistent rituals significantly improved their relationship. "It's incredible how just a few minutes together at the start and end of the day can make such a difference," he said. "We feel more in tune with each other and more capable of handling whatever comes our way."

Lily and Ethan's commitment to their launchings and landings strengthened their bond and improved their overall relationship satisfaction. These simple rituals helped them stay connected and supported, even when their schedules were hectic and demanding.

To incorporate launchings and landings into your own relationship, check out these ideas:

Morning Launchings

1. **Wake-Up Ritual:** Spend a few minutes cuddling or sharing a gentle wake-up kiss.
2. **Shared Breakfast:** Enjoy a quick breakfast together, even if it's just a smoothie or a cup of coffee.
3. **Positive Affirmations:** Share something you appreciate about each other or set a positive intention for the day.
4. **Morning Stretch:** Do a short stretching routine or yoga session together to start the day feeling energized and connected.
5. **Morning Playlist:** Create a playlist of your favorite upbeat songs to listen to together while getting ready.
6. **Goal Setting:** Take a few minutes to discuss your goals and plans for the day, offering support and encouragement to each other.

Evening Landings

1. **Evening Wind-Down:** Spend time together before bed, sharing a cup of tea or a glass of wine and discussing your day.
2. **Gratitude Practice:** Take turns naming things you are grateful for that day.
3. **Quiet Time:** Read to each other, listen to a podcast together, or simply lie quietly and hold hands.
4. **Bedtime Story:** Take turns reading a chapter from a favorite book to each other.
5. **Relaxation Routine:** Do a relaxation or meditation exercise together to help unwind and transition into sleep.
6. **Nightly Reflection:** Reflect on the day's events and discuss what went well and what you can improve on together.

Other Transitions

1. **Coming Home Ritual:** Make it a priority to greet each other warmly when one partner returns home. Share a hug, a kiss, or even a loving shout from the room if you are too preoccupied.
2. **Bedtime Routine:** Develop a routine that helps both of you transition into sleep. If you sleep separately or at different times, consider a quick snuggle, cuddle, or a kiss on the forehead before saying goodnight.
3. **Check-In Call:** If you are apart during the day, schedule a quick check-in call or text to touch base and show you're thinking of each other.
4. **Welcome Notes:** Leave a small note or message for your partner to find when they return home, expressing love and appreciation.
5. **Shared Activity:** Engage in a shared activity upon reuniting, such as cooking dinner together, taking a walk, or playing a game.

Great relationships aren't just accidental; they are co-created. Incorporating these simple rituals into your daily routine can enhance your connection, deepen your support for each other, and create a loving environment. These small, consistent efforts can transform your relationship, reduce the potential for negative cycles to take over, and help you navigate the challenges of daily life with greater ease and mutual support.

Connection Through Play and Novelty

In the sacred dance of love, staying connected amidst the mundane is a discipline of the heart. Our relational journeys aren't solely defined by grand moments of passion, soul-stirring conversations, elegant dinners, butterflies in our stomachs, and epic adventures. Often, love is found in the quiet repetition of daily life, where some weeks echo the feeling of Groundhog Day. It's here, in these ordinary moments, that we must actively choose to keep a positive mindset about our partners. We must resist the lure of negative narratives that whisper something is amiss in our relationship.

Consider this: why do we judge ourselves so harshly when a dinner together passes in comfortable silence, especially when we compare ourselves to other couples animatedly chatting away? If there's nothing new to discuss, that's perfectly fine. Let's savor the simple joy of being together and sharing a meal.

However, if our relationship perpetually feels mundane and monotonous, it risks becoming stagnant without the vibrant sparks of play and novelty. These are the vital ingredients that infuse our connection with vitality and protect us from the dreary cycle of festering aches and discontent.

Play and novelty are the lifeblood of relationships, infusing them with excitement and joy. Both require genuine connection or, at the least, enough safety to want to explore the adventurous unknown with one another. You can't truly dive into play or embrace novelty with your partner if you're guarded, barricaded, or walled off. Play and novelty involve risk, improvisation, and venturing into the unknown, breaking free from the restrictive script of fear, comfortability, and safety.

Research shows that couples who regularly engage in playful activities and seek new experiences together report higher levels of relationship satisfaction and emotional bonding.[7] Playfulness fosters intimacy, reduces stress, and enhances communication, making it a vital ingredient for a thriving relationship. Playfulness also has a physiological component; it increases neurochemicals that enhance our emotional connection. Dopamine, associated with pleasure and reward, enhances feelings of excitement and novelty, while oxytocin, known as the "love hormone," promotes bonding and trust.

Some partners tell me, "I don't feel connected to them. We feel like roommates. We've lost the spark." Connectedness and sparks don't materialize out of thin air. They are co-created events, born from intention, energy, and action. It's easy to fall into the trap of not engaging in connected moments because we don't feel connected.

However, there are times when we can adopt a behavior-first, feelings-later approach. This means that by engaging in the right behaviors, the feelings of connection often follow. Sometimes, we have to do the right thing to feel the right thing, leading to a genuine sense of connection If you think your relationship has become boring and lost its spark, it may be time to adopt the Nike approach—"Just do it!" Play and novelty might be just what the doctor ordered for you and your partner to feel more connected.

Putting It into Practice

Laura and Emma had been together for over a decade, and their relationship had settled into a comfortable but unexciting routine. Their days were filled with work, chores, and the usual grind, leaving little room for spontaneity or adventure. They both felt the spark that once ignited their passion was dimming, and their relationship was starting to feel more like a partnership of convenience rather than a loving connection.

One evening, after another mundane day, Laura turned to Emma and said, "I miss the excitement we used to have. We're like roommates now, just going through the motions."

Emma nodded. "I feel the same way. We've been so focused on work and responsibilities that we've forgotten how to have fun together."

They realized that what was missing from their relationship was play and novelty—activities that could reignite their sense of adventure and connectedness. Determined to make a change, they decided to try something new and exciting. They found a local rock-climbing facility and booked a session for the following weekend.

The day of their first rock-climbing adventure was filled with nervous anticipation. Neither of them had ever tried rock climbing before, and they were unsure what to expect. As they donned their harnesses and listened to the instructor's guidance, they felt a mixture of excitement and apprehension.

As they began to climb, they encouraged each other, laughed at their awkwardness, and celebrated each small victory. The experience was exhilarating and challenging, pushing them out of their comfort zones. By the end of the session, they were exhausted but filled with a newfound sense of accomplishment and connection.

"I can't believe we did that!" Laura exclaimed, her face glowing with joy.

Emma grinned. "Me neither. I haven't felt this alive in a long time."

Realizing the profound impact this novel experience had on their relationship, they decided to make rock climbing a regular activity. They committed to going every other week, relishing the physical challenge and the joy of supporting each other through the climbs.

They also decided to try a different restaurant on the off weeks to keep the momentum of play and novelty alive. This way, they had something new to look forward to every week, whether scaling a rock wall or exploring new culinary delights.

As weeks turned into months, Laura and Emma found that their relationship was reinvigorated. After trying rock climbing, they decided to switch things up and started playing tennis. The shared adventures and new experiences brought them closer together, reigniting the spark that routine had dimmed. They rediscovered the joy of simply being with each other, embracing both the challenges and the thrills that life had to offer. Through these activities, they strengthened their bond, proving that the key to a vibrant relationship lies in continuous growth and shared exploration.

Through play and novelty, they transformed their relationship from mundane coexistence to a vibrant, loving connection. They learned that staying connected requires intention, energy, and a willingness to step outside their comfort zones. And in doing so, they found that their love was not only rekindled but also strengthened, ready to face whatever adventures lay ahead.

Incorporating play and novelty into your relationship can rejuvenate your bond and keep your connection vibrant. Here are some ideas to help you and your partner add a sense of fun and adventure to your relationship:

1. **Explore New Hobbies Together:** Take up new activities like dancing, painting, or cooking classes. Learning something new together can create a shared sense of achievement and discovery.

2. **Engage in Physical Activities:** Try hiking, cycling, or even a new sport. Physical activities not only promote health but also foster teamwork and create memorable experiences.

3. **Plan Spontaneous Getaways:** Surprise each other with weekend trips or day-long road trips to unexplored places. These adventures can break the monotony of daily routines and provide fresh environments in which to connect.

4. **Attend Local Events:** Check out local festivals, concerts, or community events. These outings can be a great way to experience new things together and feel part of a larger community.

5. **Game Nights and Competitions:** Host game nights or engage in friendly competitions. Whether it's board games, video games, or sports, playful competition can strengthen your bond and add laughter to your relationship.

6. **Try New Restaurants:** Make a list of restaurants you've never been to and visit one each week. This not only satisfies

culinary curiosity but also gives you both something to look forward to regularly.

7. **Engage in Playful Banter:** Don't underestimate the power of humor and playful teasing. Lighthearted interactions can keep the atmosphere in your relationship fun and relaxed.

8. **Participate in Novelty Activities:** Activities like escape rooms, amusement parks, or even trying out a new form of exercise like rock climbing or yoga can be exciting and bond-strengthening.

9. **Creative Projects:** Work on creative projects together, such as building something, gardening, or writing a story. These activities can be deeply satisfying and give you both a sense of shared accomplishment.

10. **Revisit Favorite Childhood Activities:** Whether flying kites, playing catch, or visiting a zoo, engaging in activities you loved as children can bring a sense of nostalgia and joy to your relationship.

11. **Celebrate Random Occasions:** Invent your own holidays and traditions. Celebrate half-birthdays, the anniversary of your first date, or even "just because" days. These little celebrations can add fun and excitement to your relationship.

12. **Travel and Explore:** Whether exploring a distant destination or your own city, travel can bring a sense of adventure and discovery into your relationship. Try visiting new places and experiencing different cultures together.

13. **Educational Adventures:** Attend workshops or classes on topics that interest you both. This could be anything from photography to astronomy, fostering mutual growth and learning.

14. **Outdoor Activities:** Spend time in nature together. Activities like camping, fishing, or simply picnicking in the park can provide a refreshing change from your daily routine.

15. **DIY Projects:** Take on do-it-yourself projects around the house. Whether redecorating a room, building furniture, or

crafting, working together on a project can be a fun and rewarding experience.

16. **Spiritual and Mindfulness Practices:** Explore mindfulness, meditation, or yoga together. These practices can deepen your emotional connection and provide a sense of peace and balance.

17. **Surprise Date Nights:** Take turns planning surprise date nights for each other. The anticipation and mystery can bring a new level of excitement to your routine.

18. **Volunteer Together:** Spend time giving back to the community. Volunteering for a cause you both care about can be fulfilling and strengthen your bond through shared values and efforts.

19. **Seasonal Activities:** Embrace seasonal activities like apple picking in the fall, ice skating in the winter, or beach outings in the summer. These activities can create lasting memories and add variety to your time together.

20. **Learning Each Other's Interests:** Take time to learn more about each other's hobbies and interests. Whether watching a favorite movie series, reading a book one loves, or participating in a beloved hobby, showing interest in each other's passions can deepen your connection.

Chapter Six Wrap-Up

As we wrap up this chapter, let's remind ourselves that the heart of a thriving relationship lies in those everyday moments of connection. Sure, it's not always easy—life throws countless challenges our way, but by pushing through the pressures, we can proactively make a pact to maintain and protect our emotional bond. Understanding and navigating our operating system, unique love languages, and relational tendencies while creating launchings and landings that bind our hearts and lives together sets the stage for healthy relationship dynamics.

The practices we've explored here aren't just lofty ideas—they're actionable steps to fortify your relationship. By weaving these principles into the fabric of your daily lives, you'll discover that love, connection, and joy are within reach, even in the most mundane moments. May you and your partner embrace these relational lifelines with openness and courage, forging a path to a deeply connected and harmonious relationship.

Key Takeaways

1. Proactive Commitment to Connection: Maintaining and protecting emotional contact with your partner is crucial. Regularly revisiting and reaffirming your relationship vision helps prevent the erosion of intimacy and strengthen your bond.

2. The Importance of Friendship: A strong friendship forms the foundation of a lasting relationship. Prioritizing emotional intimacy and consistently supporting each other as friends can buffer against negative cycles and conflicts.

3. Understand Relational Tendencies: Recognizing and respecting each other's relational tendencies—whether anxious or avoidant—allows for more compassionate interactions. Tailoring your approach to meet your partner's emotional needs can foster a more secure and loving relationship.

4. Fill Each Other's Love Tank: Identifying and actively meeting your partner's love language needs ensures that your expressions of love are well-received. This practice keeps the relational reservoir full, reducing conflicts and increasing satisfaction.

5. Meaningful Rituals of Connection: Implementing daily rituals such as morning launchings and evening landings can significantly enhance emotional closeness. These small but consistent gestures create a sense of stability and reinforce your importance to each other.

6. Incorporate Play and Novelty: Regularly engaging in playful activities and seeking new experiences together can reignite passion and strengthen your connection. Embracing spontaneity and adventure adds vitality and prevents the relationship from becoming stagnant.

Chapter 7
Employing Effective Communication

"Anything that's human is mentionable, and anything that is mentionable can be more manageable. When we can talk about our feelings, they become less overwhelming, less upsetting, and less scary. The people we trust with that important talk can help us know that we are not alone."

— Mr. Fred Rogers

I firmly believe that learning communication skills without fostering connection is a recipe for failure. Why? Because when we don't feel connected, our threat systems are primed to trigger negative cycles. In such situations, even the most well-learned communication skills can become ineffective. The truth is communication often comes with ease when we're feeling connected. As noted relationship expert John Howard writes, "Connection is what we're really looking for, and it facilitates communication, not the other way around."[1] While this is true, and much of this book is geared toward helping us build a deeper connection with our partner, I also think **connection + savvy communication skills = a more effective communicator**. In this chapter I'll share several communication principles and practices that not only promote connection but also help keep that sneaky negative cycle from gradually creeping up on us, suffocating the oxygen of love in our relationship.

Set an Intention to Eliminate the Four Horsemen

John Gottman, one of the world's leading researchers on couples, has identified four behaviors that, when repeatedly present during conflict, indicate that couples are likely to divorce within five years of marriage. So, we probably want to pay attention to them. These are known as the *Four Horsemen of the Apocalypse*: criticism, defensiveness, contempt, and stonewalling.[2]

Criticism occurs when verbal comments attack a partner's character or personality traits rather than addressing specific behaviors. For example, instead of saying, "I feel hurt and alone when you don't do your fair share of the household responsibilities," a partner might say critically, "You're so lazy. You don't do anything around here." Other critical statements are more obvious, such as "You're such an asshole," "You are an emotional basket case," or "You are a cold and heartless person."

Criticism often includes phrases like "you always" or "you never," which can feel like personal assaults. Statements like "You always hurt me!" or "You never follow through with what I ask" imply that all the good the person has ever done has vanished, and only their failings are remembered. In reality, there were certainly moments when their partner didn't hurt them or did follow through on some requests over the years—at least, I would hope so.

This phenomenon is explained by Rick Hanson, a renowned psychologist and author of *Hardwiring Happiness*, who writes, "The brain evolved a negativity bias that makes it like Velcro for bad experiences and Teflon for good ones."[3] Stan Tatkin also highlights a key neuroscience insight, noting that the hippocampus—the part of our brain that tracks events in time, sequence, and context—goes a bit offline when we're fighting.[4] In other words, when we are hurt and in a threat state, we don't have access to all of our memories and experience tunnel vision, remembering only the bad. The loss of full access to our memories, including the positive ones, combined with the negativity bias, makes it easy to fall into the trap of criticism. However, recognizing this tendency can help us communicate more constructively.

Defensiveness is an arising impulse shielding us from the verbal spotlight cast on our actions or inactions. Defensiveness typically follows criticism. However, a partner may become so accustomed to criticism that even a simple expression of a desire or sharing a hurt—even when done healthily by their partner—can trigger a defensive reaction. This quick response often manifests as the sentiment "What are you talking about? That's not true."

Additionally, if a partner harbors core shame—a persistent, low-level feeling of being unlovable and flawed—they may react angrily to criticism or perceived criticism. Those prone to shame often respond with anger, a secondary emotion, as it masks the pain of their deep-seated shame wounds. Alternatively, they may avoid addressing the issue their partner raised by resorting to self-attack, saying, "I know. I know. I am a terrible husband. What else is new."

Here's an example of how a conversation where defensiveness shows up might unfold:

Alexa: (calmly) Hey, I've been feeling a bit overwhelmed with the household chores lately. Could we talk about maybe splitting these tasks a bit more evenly?

Jamie: (immediately defensive with a tinge of anger) What are you talking about? I do more than my share around here! You're just trying to blame me for something again.

Alexa: I'm not trying to blame you; I just feel like I've been taking on a lot and need a little more help.

Jamie: (feeling criticized and reacting from a place of shame) This is just like you, always pointing fingers. It's like nothing I do matters. I guess I'm just not good enough, am I?

In this situation, Jamie's shame spiral causes the original concern—Alexa's need for help with household chores—to vanish, shifting the focus to how terrible Jamie feels about themselves. Defensiveness not only leaves the initial issue unresolved but also deepens the emotional distance between them.

Contempt, meanwhile, is like riding an angry horse with flames bursting from its nostrils, a pointed spear in one hand and a jagged rock in the other. It involves assuming a superior stance and treating a partner with disrespect, mockery, and sarcasm. Contempt may include hostile humor, name-calling, cynicism, sneering, scoffing, and body language such as eye-rolling—all conveying disgust and a sense of superiority that can poison the relationship.

It sounds like (following an eye roll), "You're crazy, just like your mom. All you do is complain about what I'm doing and not doing. Focus on yourself. See a therapist and leave me the fuck alone!" Contempt is a deadly poison that erodes relationships, often proving to be a key factor in their unfortunate demise.

Stonewalling, also called *flooding*, is what happens when someone gets so overwhelmed that they feel like they're drowning in emotions (or *flooded*). It's that moment when their nervous system kicks into gear, saying, "Enough!" and shuts down to avoid the pain. They withdraw from the conversation, avoiding conflict and emotional engagement like it's a raging hot stove. If you or your partner have ever gone silent, stopped responding, or even walked out of the room during a heated argument or a regular chat, you've experienced stonewalling. It's a way of coping when emotions get too intense to handle.

Flooding hijacks any productive interaction, causing heart rates to skyrocket—women's from 76 beats per minute and men's from 82 beats per minute to as high as 100 to 195 bpm.[5] In this overwhelmed state, individuals might either appear frozen, like a deer caught in the headlights, or withdraw entirely, retreating in silence out of frustration. In writing about flooding, John Gottman observes, "Like animals being hunted, we go into fight, flight, or freeze mode; now we are more controlled by the racing of our heart and the dump of cortisol and adrenaline into our bloodstream than we are by rational or empathetic mental processes."[6]

Over time, this response can become automatic, often as a result of repeated experiences with a partner perceived as overreactive or relentless in their verbal lashings. Consequently, when one partner stonewalls, the other partner may feel abandoned, believing their partner doesn't care about them, which fuels further hurt and anger. As you may have guessed, this dynamic is commonly observed in the Pull Back and Protest cycle.

You can see why it's important to set an intention to proactively eliminate these Four Horsemen: criticism, defensiveness, contempt, and stonewalling. Before we learn the effective communication strategies that we'll be replacing these relationship-damaging behaviors with, there are two techniques to help us knock these sabotaging horsemen off their unruly horses for good.

Make an Explicit Agreement

One of the most beneficial commitments a couple can make is actively identifying and eliminating the Four Horsemen of the Apocalypse from their relationship. Start by understanding what these behaviors look and sound like, using the descriptions provided earlier. Once you both recognize the devastating impact these behaviors have on your relationship, come together and agree to do everything in your power to avoid them in the future. There's something powerful about a couple functioning from their shared values around communication. While agreeing to eradicate these behaviors won't make them disappear overnight, setting an intention to communicate more effectively is a step in the right direction.

Come Up with a Mantra

After you both come together and agree to eliminate the Four Horsemen from your relationship, you can engage in a mantra to help solidify your newfound agreement. It's hard to eliminate behaviors if you don't have something to replace them with. While I encourage you to come up with your own, here are some examples:

- "Instead of criticism, contempt, stonewalling, and defensiveness, I will speak with love, honor my partner, stay engaged, and own my actions."

- "Instead of criticism, contempt, stonewalling, and defensiveness, I will offer understanding, appreciation, connection, and accountability."
- "Instead of criticism, contempt, stonewalling, and defensiveness, I will communicate gently, cherish my partner, remain present, and take responsibility."
- "Instead of criticism, contempt, stonewalling, and defensiveness, I will choose to uplift, value, connect, and be responsible in my relationship."

Once you have your mantra, you can embed it more deeply into your nervous system by practicing embodied reflection a few times a week. This practice helps shift the mantra from the logical part of your mind to become ingrained in your heart and body. Here's a brief yet powerful meditative exercise to guide you (for the best experience, narrate this meditation into a recorder and use it as your guide). Replace the second part of the mantra with the version that reflects your aspiration. An audio file of the meditation below can be found at: https://markgregorykarris.-com/meditations-from-beyond-fairy-tales/.

Take a slow, deep breath in, and as you exhale, close your eyes and allow your body to relax. Feel the ground beneath you, supporting you, anchoring you in the present moment. In this space of calm and safety, silently repeat the mantra: "Instead of criticism, contempt, stonewalling, and defensiveness, I will speak with love, honor my partner, stay engaged, and own my actions." Visualize these words as a gentle wave washing over you, cleansing away any negative energy and replacing it with warmth and understanding. Picture yourself in moments of a relationship challenge, choosing love over criticism, showing honor instead of contempt, remaining engaged rather than stonewalling, and owning your actions instead of being defensive. Feel this commitment deeply in your heart, knowing that with each breath, your resolve aligns with your highest values in your relationship. Stay with this feeling of peace and intention for a few moments. When you're ready, gently open your eyes. Carry this precious agreement into your daily life, letting it inform how you meet relationship challenges.

Engage in the Fine Art of Effective Communication

Eliminating the Four Horsemen makes room for effective communication practices within your relationship. While I could fill a whole volume on this topic, I'll highlight the most important techniques here. Remember, effective communication is more of an art than a science, and like any fine art, it requires regular fine-tuning for optimal effectiveness.

Use Affirmative Language

A powerful tool for expressing emotions and needs without placing blame or causing defensiveness is the "I feel ... when you" communication technique. This approach involves starting a statement with "I feel" followed by the specific emotion you are experiencing. Then, describe the behavior or situation that triggered this feeling by using "when you."

For example, instead of saying angrily, "You never listen to me," which is an accusatory generalization, you might say, "*I feel* ignored and frustrated *when you* look at your phone while I'm talking to you." *Addressing any issue with "You" automatically puts your partner on the defensive.* Starting with our experience makes it more about us first and lessens the potential for a negative reaction. The "I feel ... when you" practice focuses on sharing personal feelings and the impact of the other person's actions, fostering a more open and empathetic dialogue. Clearly communicating how specific behaviors affect you encourages understanding and helps both parties work toward more positive interactions.

Here are some examples:

Instead of...	Say...
"You never listen to me"	"I feel ignored and frustrated when you look at your phone while I'm talking to you."
"You always leave me alone"	"I feel lonely when you go out with your friends without inviting me."
"You don't help me with anything"	"I feel overwhelmed when you don't help with the household chores."

Instead of... Say this... (*continued*)

Instead of...	Say...
"You're always smothering me"	"I feel overwhelmed when you expect constant communication throughout the day."
"You're too emotional"	"I feel uncomfortable when you express intense emotions."
"You're too needy"	"I feel anxious when you expect me to share my deepest feelings."

The "I feel ... when you" method works well, but it's good to mix things up sometimes. Howard makes a great point when he says using "I feel" statements too often can "create polarization in relationships and reinforce separate camps."[7] Instead of angry criticism or the "I feel ... when you" method, he recommends a *team-based narrative*. For example, there are times when it's appropriate to share something like "We have an issue that doesn't feel good. How can we come together and be more effective here?" Howard writes, "That collective mindset takes the burden off each individual, minimizes blame in both directions, and shares resources to address problems."[8] This approach fosters a sense of partnership and collaboration, minimizing a felt sense of criticism and helping couples tackle issues together rather than from opposing sides.

Here are some examples of using a more *we-centered* approach:

Instead of... Say...

Instead of...	Say...
"You never pay attention to me when you're on your phone"	"We seem to have a communication issue that doesn't feel good. How can we come together and be more attentive to each other when we're talking?"

Instead of... Say this... (*continued*)

Instead of...	Say...
"You don't care about the effort I put into cooking"	"We both work hard to take care of each other, but it seems like we sometimes miss appreciating each other's efforts. How can we be more mindful of showing appreciation?"
"You always embarrass me in front of others"	"We both want to feel respected and supported in public. How can we handle disagreements or feedback in a way that feels good for both of us?"
"You never help around the house"	"We both want a clean and organized home, but sometimes it feels like the chores aren't balanced. How can we create a system that works for both of us and feels fair?"
"You're too emotional"	"Emotional closeness seems to be a challenge for us. What can we do as a team to ensure we respect each other's boundaries while also nurturing our relationship?"
"You never give me space"	"We sometimes experience tension around social activities. How can we ensure we both feel included and respected in our social plans?"

Work on Your Tone, Timing, and Trimming

Megan and Tom had been married for seven years. They loved each other deeply, but their communication had deteriorated, leading to frequent arguments and misunderstandings.

One evening, Tom was working late on an important project with an urgent deadline. He was fully engrossed, typing away on his laptop in their home office. Meanwhile, Megan, feeling increasingly frustrated about their growing political and religious differences, decided it was the perfect time to address an incident that had occurred at Tom's parents' house over the weekend.

Without considering Tom's current state, Megan walked into the office and started speaking angrily. "Tom, we need to talk about what happened at your parents' place. The way they reacted to my views was really upsetting. You just sat there and said nothing while they accused me of walking down a dangerous path and expressed concern for my salvation," she said, her voice tight with concern.

Tom glanced up, his eyes tired. "Can we talk about this later, Megan? I'm in the middle of something really important."

But Megan, feeling ignored, pressed on. "No, this can't wait. You always say 'later,' and later never comes!"

Tom rolled his eyes and sighed, the sudden confrontation compounding the stress of his work. "Fine, let's talk," he said reluctantly.

Megan launched into a detailed explanation of her evolving liberal views, discussing recent political events, social issues, and her shifting perspective on religion. She recounted how she had shared these views at Tom's parents' house, shocking and upsetting his conservative parents. As she went on and on, Tom's mind drifted, overwhelmed by the sheer volume of information. He tried to keep up, but the details overloaded him.

"Can we simplify this?" Tom finally interrupted. "I can't process all this right now."

But Megan, intent on sharing everything at once, continued, "No, it's important you understand all these points. We need to address our differences and how your parents reacted."

Let's just say no effective communication was had that evening. The negative cycle had gotten the best of them. Megan felt unheard, alone, and frustrated. Feeling angry and too depleted to respond constructively, Tom ended the conversation with both feeling disconnected and upset.

Megan and Tom's communication issues were a recipe for disaster with a heaping spoonful of ineffective behaviors, especially Megan's oversight of tone, timing, and trimming. Her hurt and pain were completely understandable—Tom didn't protect her emotionally, leaving her feeling utterly alone in that moment. But the way she brought up the conversation, with a harsh, accusatory *tone*, only triggered his defensiveness and escalated their conflicts rather than fostering any kind of understanding or resolution.

Megan chose to discuss their political and religious differences and the upsetting incident when Tom was already stressed and busy with work, demonstrating poor *timing*. And instead of *trimming* her message to the essentials, she overwhelmed Tom with a lengthy and detailed explanation of her views and the incident at his parents' house rather than zeroing in on the main points.

Instead of coming in hot with a harsh, accusatory tone, she could have started the conversation calmly and empathetically, expressing her feelings without pointing fingers—something like "Tom, I need to talk about something that's been bothering me. Can we calmly discuss our views and how your parents received them?" The timing was crucial, too —instead of addressing the issue while Tom was busy and stressed with work, Megan could have chosen a better moment, maybe after dinner or on a weekend when they both had time to talk without distractions.

Lastly, instead of overwhelming Tom with a lengthy and detailed explanation, Megan could have focused on the most critical points, keeping her message concise and clear. She might have said, "I felt very alone and unsupported when your parents reacted negatively to my views. It hurt me that you didn't say anything to support me. Can we talk about how we can handle similar situations better in the future?" By considering tone, timing, and trimming, Megan would have created a more conducive environment for a constructive conversation, increasing the likelihood of understanding and resolution.

If you want to avoid the negative cycle and communicate effectively, consider tone, timing, and trimming the next time you dive into a challenging discussion. Our tone is crucial in determining how a conversation will end. According to John Gottman, if we start a conversation harshly—what he calls a "harsh startup"—it will go nowhere 96% of the time and typically lead to a negative cycle.[9] That's why I tell couples, "Soft and slow makes the relationship grow; hard and fast makes the relationship crash." If we start a conversation gently and slowly, there's a much better chance we'll engage our partner's caregiving system, making them more likely to listen and be attentive. But if we start harshly, it's almost guaranteed to trigger our partner's threat system, creating a reactive loop and leading straight into the negative cycle. I often tell couples, "Stop sabotaging the very thing you want—your partner's attention—by how you communicate with them." Tone really does matter!

With regard to timing, we can't expect our partners to be ready to engage just because we are. We must honor their subjectivity and what's happening in their world, just as we'd want them to do for us. That's why I encourage permission-seeking. If we want to talk about something important, we can ask them if it's a good time. This also sets up their nervous system for success, especially those with avoidant tendencies.

Asking, "Is this a good time to talk?" or "Can you be present with me?" will likely lead to a productive conversation. If they can't be present, they can say, "Not right now. Can you give me fifteen minutes?" or whatever time works for them.

When we finally get that time to talk, we should trim what we have to say and keep it short. Too much information can overwhelm our partners, making it hard for them to focus on the heart of the matter when too many issues are brought up simultaneously. When expressing your feelings about what you need, keep it concise and to the point.

Remember, the next time you're gearing up for a tough talk with your partner, think about your tone, timing, and trimming. It's like fine-tuning a recipe: a little tweak here and there can turn something bitter into something beautifully sweet. The healthier ingredients we put into our communication, the better our chances of truly being heard and understood.

Be BRAVE

While using "I feel … when you" and we-centric statements and considering tone, timing, and trimming are crucial for the one speaking, it's equally important for the listener to employ effective communication skills. I'd like to introduce you to these key skills through the acronym **BRAVE**:

- Beginner's Mind (approach without preconceived notions)
- Reflection (mirror the speaker's words and emotions)
- Active Listening (give full attention and presence)
- Validation (acknowledge and affirm their feelings)
- Engaging with Love (respond with empathy, validation, or a comforting gesture)

Let's take a closer look at these skills:

Adopting a *Beginner's Mind* means approaching each conversation without preconceived notions and remaining open to truly understanding the speaker's perspective. In this way, we encounter them on their terms, free from our own agenda or projections.

Reflection is about holding up a mirror to your partner's words and emotions, letting them know they've been truly heard. It's like saying, "I'm right here with you, and I get it." You're not just parroting back what they said but really absorbing it and then gently tossing it back to show you've caught the essence of their feelings. This simple yet profound act can make them feel deeply understood and valued.

Active Listening requires setting an intention to slow down and attuning to the frequency of our partner's energy, nonverbal cues, and verbal communication. It means giving your full attention and presence to show your partner that you genuinely care about what they're saying. It's not just about hearing the words but really tuning in, nodding, making eye contact, and maybe even leaning in a bit to show you're right there with them.

Validation is like giving your partner's feelings a big, warm hug. It's saying, "Your feelings matter. I can handle them, big or small. Your core concerns are important." It's about acknowledging their experiences and emotions, affirming their significance, and letting them know they're not alone in whatever they're going through.

Finally, *Engaging with Love* emphasizes responding with empathy, whether through validating their feelings, offering a comforting gesture like a hug, or simply showing warmth and compassion. Together, these skills help us as listeners to connect deeply, respond thoughtfully, and foster a positive and nurturing dialogue with our partners.

Let's pick up the story with Megan and Tom to see **BRAVE** in action.

A few days after they got caught in their negative cycle, Megan approached Tom, mindful of tone, timing, and trimming. She chose a calm evening when they both had free time and gently started the conversation. "Tom, can we talk for a bit? I wanted to try again and see if we can discuss what happened at your parents' house. I'd like to share how I felt."

Tom looked up from his book, appreciating Megan's considerate approach. "Sure, Megan," he said, setting the book aside and giving her his full attention.

Megan began with a calm and empathetic tone, "When your parents questioned my views with such a condescending tone, I felt really alone and judged. It hurt that you didn't say anything to support me. You are my rock, and I needed you to protect me in that moment. When you didn't, I felt so alone." She kept her message concise and focused on the most important points, demonstrating good trimming.

Determined to engage in **BRAVE**, Tom started with a *beginner's mind*, setting aside his previous judgments and frustrations. "Megan, I am present with you. I do care. I would really like to understand more about your experience at my parents' house," he began, maintaining a calm and open demeanor.

As Megan began to speak, Tom practiced *active listening*. He put down his phone, made eye contact, and gave her his full attention. He *reflected* back what he heard, saying, "It sounds like you felt unsupported, hurt, and alone when my parents reacted negatively. Am I getting it right?"

After Megan acknowledged that Tom understood the heart of the matter, Tom *validated* Megan's feelings, saying, "I can see why you felt alone and upset. It must have been tough to feel judged and not have my support."

To deepen the conversation, Tom *engaged with love* by asking curious questions and showing empathy. "Can you tell me more about what specifically my parents said that upset you? And what kind of support would have helped you in that moment?" he asked, genuinely interested in understanding her perspective. Then, further attempting to engage her with love, he asked, "Is there anything you need from me right now and especially in the future?"

Megan's attention to tone, timing, and trimming smoothed the way for a genuinely constructive dialogue. By using **BRAVE**, Tom created a space where Megan genuinely felt heard and valued. This approach allowed them to move beyond their previous miscommunications and work toward a deeper understanding of each other's perspectives. Their conversation became much more productive and connected, showcasing just how powerful these communication skills can be in nurturing a healthy relationship.

May you and your partner be **BRAVE** with one another, embracing the art of embodied listening and forging pathways to deeper, more profound connections.

Chapter Seven Wrap-Up

By understanding and eliminating those pesky Four Horsemen; by using affirmative language such as "I feel ... when you" and we-centric statements; by mindfully choosing our tone, timing, and succinctness; and by practicing the art of being **BRAVE** (approaching each other with a beginner's mind, reflecting, actively listening, validating, and engaging with love), we can build a relationship that creates a loop of love. The more we feel connected, the healthier we communicate. And the healthier we communicate and avoid the negative cycle, the more connected we feel.

Remember, the goal isn't perfection; it's progress. It's about journeying toward secure and meaningful connections. Yes, this path demands effort. Many of us grew up without models of healthy communication, making these practices feel unfamiliar, even daunting. Yet, it is profoundly worth the effort. Consider all the hours we waste in arguments, battling for dominance, and asserting our perceived truths as absolute. Such conflicts drain our energy and time.

Imagine if, instead, we could transform those moments with a few minutes of mindful, intentional communication. The arguments that once took hours or days to heal could be gently averted, leading us closer to the harmony we seek.

Key Takeaways

1. Connection Facilitates Communication: Effective communication stems from a strong sense of connection. When we feel connected to our partner, our communication flows more easily, helping us avoid negative cycles and fostering a deeper bond.

2. Eliminate the Four Horsemen: Criticism, contempt, defensiveness, and stonewalling are detrimental behaviors that can erode a relationship. Understanding and intentionally avoiding these behaviors can significantly improve your communication and relationship satisfaction.

3. Use "I Feel ... When You" Statements: This communication technique helps you express emotions and needs without placing blame, fostering a more open and empathetic dialogue. By sharing personal feelings and the impact of specific behaviors, you and your partner can work toward more positive interactions.

4. Adopt a Team-Based Approach: Using "we-centered" language and focusing on mutual goals can help you and your partner address issues collaboratively. This approach minimizes blame, promotes partnership, and strengthens the bond between you.

5. Consider Tone, Timing, and Trimming: Effective communication requires a gentle tone, appropriate timing, and concise messages. These elements help create a conducive environment for understanding and resolution, reducing the likelihood of conflict escalation.

6. Be BRAVE in Listening: Employ the **BRAVE** approach—Beginner's Mind, Reflection, Active Listening, Validation, and Engaging with Love—to deepen understanding and foster a nurturing dialogue. These skills will help you as a listener connect deeply and respond thoughtfully to your partner's needs and emotions.

Chapter 8
Unleashing Your Inner Cycle Slayer

"Little by little, they helped each other to stop their previously predictable interactions, to step off their well-worn path, to take some risks to engage in new interactions and thus create a new and positive relationship."

— Veronica Kallos-Lilly and Jennifer Fitzgerald, *The Two of Us*

We can make a proactive pact to maintain and protect our sense of connection, love each other with an awareness of each other's needs, set an intention to eliminate the Four Horsemen, and strive to communicate effectively. But let's be real—sometimes, the negative cycle of communication will get the best of us. When the reactivity starts to rear its ugly head, we can join forces and tackle this cycle head-on, stopping it before it gains momentum and grows larger and, like a tornado, sweeps us up into its devastating effects.

Once you can identify your negative cycle—whether it's Blame and Bash; Fracture and Fortify; Wend, Whirl, and Withdraw; or Pull Back and Protest—it loses its element of surprise. The hope is that you and your partner can be "cycle slayers" and recognize the negative cycle as the enemy with a life of its own.[1] Whether it continues to grow or dissipates depends on your ability to prevent it from gaining momentum. By standing together and addressing it early, you can stop the tornado before it builds into a destructive force. So get ready to unleash your inner cycle slayer because we're about to put it to work.

Keeping SANE: Stopping the Cycle Before it Gets Bigger

In Part Two, you took the crucial step of identifying the anatomy of your negative cycle. An important follow-up step is to give it a name. Naming your cycle externalizes it, transforming it into a separate entity you and your partner can team up against and conquer. After you've understood and named this pesky intruder and fully accepted that it's the real enemy of your relationship, you'll be better equipped to stop it in its tracks by launching the **SANE** approach:

- **See what is happening:** Be mindful that you are caught in the negative cycle.
- **Accept your part in the cycle:** Pause and acknowledge your role in the situation.
- **Name the cycle:** Identify and call out the negative pattern by name.
- **Engage toward healthy relating:** Take steps to engage in healthier, loving behaviors.

This approach helps us to notice the behaviors and recognize that the negative cycle is starting, accept our part in the cycle, call out the negative cycle with our partner, and make an effort to engage in healthier ways of relating. Let's look at an example.

Josh and Priscilla sat at their cozy dinner table, the aroma of a homemade meal filling the room. Despite the warm atmosphere, an underlying tension lingered, waiting to surface. Having anxious tendencies, Josh found it difficult to relax because he and Priscilla had to discuss their finances. These types of conversations triggered Priscilla's avoidant tendencies, which often overwhelmed her. So, she preferred to steer clear of conflict but left those conversations with a lot of shame.

As they started eating, Josh hesitated but then brought up the topic weighing on his mind. "Priscilla, I've been thinking about our finances," he began, trying to keep an even tone. "I feel like we need to figure out a way for you to contribute more."

Priscilla's shoulders tensed. She put down her fork and sighed. "Josh, you know I'm doing the best I can. I don't make as much as you. I don't have answers for you. What do you want from me?"

Josh's rising anxiety and racing thoughts produced a harsh tone as he said, "But it's not just about how much you make. It's about finding ways to balance things better. I feel like I'm carrying most of the burden."

Priscilla's instinct was to retreat and avoid the confrontation. "I don't know what more I can do," she replied, her voice edging toward defensiveness. "I'm already stretched thin by paying off student loans, leaving me barely able to contribute what I do. Why do you always have to ruin a perfectly good meal?"

Now angered, Josh said, "Why do you always want to avoid real conversations? You never want to talk about budgeting or maybe getting another job. We need to figure it out ... now!"

They were slipping into their familiar negative cycle. Josh's anxiety and frustration led him to push harder, while Priscilla's avoidant tendencies and feelings of being overwhelmed triggered her to want to withdraw. But as they were getting sucked into the negative cycle, Josh remembered the **SANE** approach from their therapy sessions.

- **See what is happening:** Josh took a deep breath and recognized the cycle they were in. He saw his own anxiety driving the conversation and Priscilla's defensiveness building. He knew nothing good was going to result if they kept going.
- **Accept your part in the cycle:** He paused, acknowledging his role. "I'm sorry, Priscilla. I know I'm putting a lot of

pressure on you right now." Priscilla looked up, surprised by his shift in tone. She felt a slight relief but remained cautious.

- **Name the cycle:** Josh continued, "I think we're falling into the Penny Dreadful" (their agreed-upon name for the negative cycle that got the best of them, leaving them both feeling frustrated, hurt, and disconnected).
- **Engage toward healthy relating:** Josh, with a softer tone, said, "I get anxious about money, and I push you, wanting some kind of solution, which makes you feel attacked and want to pull away."

Priscilla nodded slowly. "Yeah, and then I feel like I need to defend myself because I'm already trying so hard."

Josh reached out and took Priscilla's hand. "Let's find a way to work on this together. I don't want to make you feel bad. Maybe we can sit down another time and look at our budget together, see where we can adjust things without it feeling like a blame game."

Priscilla squeezed his hand, appreciating his effort to change the dynamic. "Okay. I can do that. I want to help and don't want us to fight about this."

They finished their dinner, appreciative that they didn't allow Penny Dreadful to have the last word. The next evening, they sat down and approached the budget conversation as a team rather than adversaries. By using the **SANE** method—seeing what was happening, accepting their parts in the cycle, naming the negative pattern, and engaging in healthier behaviors—Josh and Priscilla managed to stop the negative cycle in its tracks and strengthen their connection. You and your partner can use the **SANE** approach when the negative cycle starts to rear its ugly head.

Slaying the Cycle
Through a Healthy Time-Out

There are times in our relationships when it feels like we're in full-blown code red. The negative cycle spins out of control, and just one more sharp criticism or defensive comment could tip us into chaos.

You'll know it when voices start climbing, your heart starts racing, frustration and anger are off the charts, and both of you are too overwhelmed to really hear each other. The words flying back and forth are like verbal daggers, and our muscles tense up as if we're bracing for a raging storm. What's needed now is a healthy time-out.

What I'm talking about is not as simple as just leaving the room and taking a long deep breath. That might work occasionally over a minor situational trigger that doesn't foment the negative cycle. The kind of time-out I'm talking about involves a six-step approach to slay the negative cycle once it's reared its ugly head.

Here are the steps to a healthy time-out:

Six Steps to a Healthy Time-Out

Step 1. Recognize the emotional and physiological alarm bells.

Identify when your emotions are taking over and signaling the need for a pause. Pay attention to these cues:

- **Increased heart rate:** Notice if your heart is pounding or racing.
- **Physical tension:** Be aware of clenched fists, a tight jaw, or stiff shoulders.
- **Rapid breathing:** Recognize shallow or fast breathing.
- **Negative thoughts:** Pay attention to spiraling or racing negative thoughts.
- **Withdrawal urge:** Feel the impulse to walk away or shut down emotionally.
- **Overwhelming sadness:** Notice if you experience a surge of tears or an urge to cry.
- **Intense anger:** Notice when anger is becoming overwhelming and difficult to control.

Step 2. Communicate the Need with Love

Go through the **SANE** steps. Then, gently express the need for a time-out, framing it as a step toward reconnection. Keep in mind that individuals with avoidant tendencies are more inclined to want to take time-outs. In contrast, those with anxious tendencies can find time-outs anxiety-provoking and may experience feelings of abandonment. Therefore, the person initiating the time-out must consider their partner's emotional needs and attachment style. Here are some ways you might communicate the need for a time-out:

- "I sense we're both getting overwhelmed and caught in a negative cycle (or use the name you've given it). Please know that I love you. Can we take a pause to calm down and reconnect? I promise to come back and discuss these concerns with you."
- "I care about you and want to be fully present, but right now, I'm feeling overwhelmed. Let's take a break and revisit this conversation later."
- "I care about resolving this with you, but I need a moment to gather my thoughts. Let's take a time-out and try again shortly."

Step 3. Set a Safe Time Frame

Agree on a specific, short duration for the time-out to ensure it's a step toward healing. This is a crucial step, as it prevents stonewalling and withdrawal without a clear plan to reengage. By providing a specific time to resume the conversation, you can ease your partner's nervous system, assuring them their concerns will be addressed:

- "Let's take twenty minutes to cool down and then check back in."
- "I need some time to calm myself. Can we revisit this in an hour?"

If you return and still find it difficult to discuss the issue calmly, consider these options:

- **Take another break:** Step away again to allow more time to cool down. "I know I said I would be back in twenty minutes, but I still don't feel very calm. Give me another twenty, and I promise we can talk again."
- **Schedule a follow-up:** Agree on a specific time, such as the next day, to revisit the discussion. "I know I said I'd be back in twenty minutes, but I still don't feel very calm. Can we discuss this topic tomorrow at 8:00 am? Is that okay?"

Step 4. Self-Soothe and Reflect

During a time-out, it's easy for the mind to ruminate and for negative narratives to keep looping. Use this time to calm your emotional storm and distressing thoughts. Engage in nurturing activities to restore your balance. When you feel ready, practice reflective empathy and consider the deeper needs and fears underlying the conflict between you both using any of these approaches:

- **Identifying your needs:** Consider what you need to feel safe and connected again.
- **Calming activities:** Engage in practices like deep breathing, meditation, or gentle yoga.
- **Physical exercise:** Take a walk or do some light exercise, ensuring you inform your partner when you'll be back.
- **Expressive writing:** Write down your thoughts and feelings to release pent-up emotions, then discard the letter.
- **Emotional reflection:** Reflect on what emotions are being triggered and explore why.

Step 5. Return with Vulnerability

When you come back together, approach the conversation with openness and a willingness to share your deeper feelings and more tempered thoughts. Remember that prioritizing the relationship's well-being is wiser than focusing on the need to be right. Take turns to cross the bridge into each other's experiences using this approach:

- Listen empathetically to your partner's feelings and needs.
- Share what you discovered about your emotions, thoughts, and needs during the break.
- Discuss what you can agree on.
- Articulate, in a nondefensive manner, where you differ.

Step 6. Aim for a Felt Sense of Reconnection

Ensure that the reconnection focuses on understanding and supporting each other by doing the following:

- Emphasize the goal of emotional connection and safety.
- Validate each other's emotions and express empathy.
- Take responsibility for your actions and apologize, if it feels right to do so.
- Work together to address the underlying emotional needs or problems.

We can stop the negative cycle before it escalates. Yes, change is hard—really, really hard. Yet, with enough awareness and practice, we can increase what couples expert Mona Fishbane calls "free won't," a subset of free will.[2] Fishbane states, "While much of our behavior is automatic and unconscious, conscious processes allow us to override our impulses and make behavioral choices that are in keeping with our ideals. And with enough practice, our conscious goals may themselves become automatic."[3] With enough practice, we can thwart the negative cycle and engage the **SANE** method and a healthy time-out with greater ease. While one person can learn and apply these principles and practices to make a difference in their relationship, the chances of success skyrocket when both partners jump on board.

Slaying the Cycle Through Healing Conversations

When the events in a relationship burrow into us like a stubborn splinter festering under the skin, and the slightest touch sets off pain and sends us spinning into our negative cycles, we're usually facing attachment injuries. These are the unwelcome baggage we can't seem to offload, the grievances that pop up in unrelated arguments, turning every minor conflict into a battleground of past hurts. Couples experts Jennine Estes Powell and Jacqueline Wielick describe it perfectly: "Think of lime juice: If it is squirted on a scar, it is painless. However, if you still have an open wound, the lime juice stings badly. Like the lime juice, an unresolved attachment injury from the past causes serious pain in the present, no matter how long ago the injury occurred."[4] If you find yourself revisiting the same old wounds and feeling that same raw pain, like lime juice on an open cut, you're likely grappling with attachment injuries.

Attachment injuries are a form of relational trauma. They are like a blindsided sucker punch to your mind and body, leaving you reeling and wondering, "What the heck just happened?!" It's the kind of jarring experience that overloads your nervous system, making it impossible to fully process in one day. This kind of injury messes with your beliefs about yourself, your partner, and the world around you, leaving you struggling to make sense of it all.

I meet with many folks who believe their partners should just get over it. "It happened so long ago; why are you still holding on to this? I already apologized." This kind of comment is completely invalidating and doesn't take into account that their partner *doesn't want* to react this way either. Do you think a partner chooses to react so strongly to what happened that it affects their mood, increases their stress, and makes them feel miserable? No way. The attachment injury lives in the body and has a life of its own, often beyond conscious control, as the following example illustrates.

Ananya and Arjun had been eagerly awaiting the arrival of their first child. The joy of welcoming their baby girl was immense, but the weeks following the birth were challenging. Ananya, who had anxious tendencies, struggled with postpartum depression, feeling overwhelmed and alone. Despite needing support, she felt that Arjun, who had avoidant tendencies, was emotionally distant.

Arjun, on the other hand, was also dealing with a lot. His mother, who had dementia, required constant care, and he felt torn between his responsibilities at home and his duty to his mother. In traditional Indian culture, caring for elderly parents is often seen as a primary duty, which added to Arjun's sense of obligation. He spent long hours with his mom, frequently leaving Ananya alone to cope with the newborn. Arjun believed he was doing his best by fulfilling his familial duties, but Ananya saw it differently. She felt abandoned and thought Arjun cared more about his mom than her and their baby.

Ananya's isolation grew as Arjun failed to check in on her as much as she needed. She longed for him to ask how she was feeling, to offer comfort and support, but he seemed preoccupied with his mother's care. The emotional distance between them widened, and Ananya felt profoundly betrayed. In Indian culture, the extended family plays a significant role, and Ananya felt additional pressure to navigate her relationship with Arjun's mother, which further strained her.

As a result of this relational trauma, Ananya began to have strong reactions. Minor disagreements triggered intense emotions, leading to arguments that spiraled out of control. Her anxious tendencies heightened her sensitivity to any signs of neglect. She'd often confront Arjun about perceived slights, even in unrelated situations, which pushed Arjun further away, propelled by his avoidant tendencies to withdraw from conflict.

Ananya needed Arjun to be her partner and support system. Instead, she felt like a single parent. She wanted him to be present during important rituals and family gatherings, which were crucial in their culture, but his avoidant tendencies led him to withdraw even more. Their cultural expectations and their personal attachment styles clashed, making it even harder for them to connect during this challenging time. The unresolved attachment injuries festered, affecting their interactions and deepening the emotional chasm between them. How would they bridge the deep divide between them?

To effectively address and heal attachment injuries, we need to confront them directly. Ignoring these deep-seated wounds won't make them disappear; instead, it allows them to fester and negatively impact our relationships. Thankfully, we can use research-based steps to heal these injuries and restore the fractured bonds.[5] Based on that research, I've created steps for conversations that help you both heal from relational injuries. Note that each step indicates which partner does the communicating in that step.

Eight Essential Steps to Healing Conversations

Step 1. Create a Safe Space (both partners)

A. Set the scene: Find a comfortable, private place where both of you feel safe to talk openly. This could be a quiet room at home, a peaceful spot in a park, or any location where you both feel relaxed and undisturbed. Turn off gadgets to minimize distractions.

B. Establish ground rules: Agree to listen to each other without interrupting or judging. This is about understanding, not blaming. Set specific guidelines such as taking turns to speak, using "I" statements to express feelings, and avoiding accusatory language.

C. Agree upon a structure: Recognize that both of you may have attachment injuries. Agree on who will share first and who will be the primary listener. Focus on addressing one injury at a time to avoid feeling overwhelmed.

D. Set an intention: Before you start, take a moment to breathe and set an intention to communicate effectively and engage in empathetic listening. This helps create a mindful and compassionate atmosphere for your discussion.

Step 2. Recognize and Describe the Injury (*hurt partner*)

What happened? Identify the specific incident or series of events that left you feeling hurt. It might involve betrayal, abandonment, or a moment where one you felt wounded. When sharing with your partner, be precise about the details of the events as you understand them.

Step 3. Share Your Feelings (*hurt partner*)

While you may have already shared a general overview of the event, now open up about the specific feelings you experienced. Were you angry, sad, fearful, hurt, betrayed, frustrated, or lonely? Explain how the event impacted you emotionally and affected your trust and security in the relationship. Be honest and vulnerable, sharing your deepest feelings and fears.

Examples:

"I was outraged and felt seriously betrayed when I found out you lied to me. It shattered my sense of security in our relationship, and I'm scared it will happen again."

- "Your absence during a time I needed you most left me feeling incredibly lonely and sad. It felt like you didn't care about what I was going through, and that's made it hard for me to rely on you."
- "When your family disrespected me at the dinner table, and you didn't say anything to defend me, I felt humiliated and unsupported. It felt like you didn't value me or our relationship enough to stand up for me. That moment has left me feeling hurt and vulnerable, and it's been hard for me to feel secure around your family since then."
- "When I discovered the affair, I felt utterly devastated and betrayed. It was like my whole world fell apart."

[**Note to the listening partner:** *Really* listen. Your job is to understand your partner's pain and show that you care about their feelings. Avoid interrupting or defending yourself. If you find yourself thinking, "Well, that's not how it happened," pause and return to your intention of listening to your partner. Feel into their pain. Imagine what it must have been like for them.]

Step 4. Express Your Deeper Needs (*hurt partner*)

Talk about your deeper needs and fears behind the hurt. It's not just about the event itself and the feelings it elicited, but what it meant for your sense of trust, security, and connection. Discuss the underlying issues and emotional needs that were triggered.

Examples:

- "When you didn't show up, I felt like I couldn't rely on you. I felt scared and alone. I need to know that I can rely on you to be there when you say you will."
- "When you didn't defend me in front of your family, I felt unimportant and unsupported. I need to know that you have my back and that I matter to you."
- "When you forgot our anniversary, I felt neglected and unappreciated. I need to know that our relationship is important to you and that you cherish our special moments."
- "When you had the affair, it shattered my trust. I felt worthless. I need to understand why it happened and to feel reassured that it won't happen again so I can feel secure in our relationship."

Step 5. Show Empathy, Check In, and Take Responsibility (*what the partner who did the hurting must do*)

A. Empathize: As the partner whose actions hurt the other, try to genuinely understand and feel the other's pain. Show that you truly grasp the depth of their hurt and that it matters to you.

Examples:

- "I can see how much it hurt you when I didn't show up. It pains me to know you felt so scared and alone. I'm really sorry for contributing to your pain."

- "When you say that you felt unsupported when I didn't defend you, I realize how that left you feeling unimportant. I understand now how crucial it is for you to feel I have your back."
- "I can only imagine how devastated and betrayed you felt when you found out about the affair. I see how profoundly it has affected you, causing pain and shaking the foundation of our relationship. I am deeply sorry that you're enduring this kind of hurt, and I regret the suffering it has brought into your life."
- "I understand that you felt dismissed and unloved when I didn't acknowledge your feelings during our argument. I take full responsibility for my invalidating actions. I realize now how crucial it is for you to feel heard and valued."

B. Check in: Now that you have empathized with the hurt partner, check in to ensure that you truly understand the heart of your partner's pain. This step is crucial for validating the hurt partner's feelings and ensuring effective communication.

Examples:

- "I want to make sure I'm really understanding you. Do you feel I'm getting to the heart of your pain?"
- "Can you tell me if there's anything I've missed or if there's more you need me to understand about how you felt?"
- "I hope I'm hearing you correctly. Is there anything else you want to share to better help me understand your feelings?"
- "Please let me know if there's more about how you're feeling that I need to understand. I want to make sure I'm fully here for you."

If the injured partner states that you understand their pain, proceed to step C below. If not, ask for clarification. After they share more, reflect back what they say and repeat Step A (Empathize).

C. Own up: Acknowledge your actions and their impact. Apologize sincerely, showing that you understand how your actions contributed to your partner's hurt. Avoid justifying your actions and focus on validating your partner's feelings.

Examples:

- "I am so sorry for not being there when you needed me. I understand now how my absence left you feeling abandoned and hurt."
- "I apologize for not defending you in front of my family. I see how that led to you feeling unsupported and unimportant, and it was wrong of me not to stand up for you."
- "I am deeply sorry for having the affair. I understand that my betrayal shattered your trust and left you feeling worthless. It pains me to see you hurt, and I take full responsibility for the choices I made that have brought us to this point."
- "I apologize for ignoring your feelings during our argument. I understand that it left you feeling dismissed and unloved, and I regret that you felt that way."

Step 6. Reassure and Reach Out (for the partner whose actions led to the hurt)

A. Reassure: The hurt partner needs reassurance that their feelings matter and that you are committed to making things right. Provide verbal affirmations and consistent, caring actions to rebuild trust.

Examples:

- "Your feelings are really important to me, and I'm committed to making things right between us."
- "I understand how much this hurt you, and I want you to know that I'm here for you and will do everything I can to rebuild your trust."

- "I value our relationship deeply and will work hard to ensure you feel safe and supported."
- "Your pain matters to me, and I am dedicated to changing my behavior and showing you that you can rely on me."

B. Reach out: Ask what your partner needs to be comforted in the moment.

Examples:

- "What can I do right now to help you feel more comfortable and supported?"
- "Is there something specific you need from me to feel reassured and cared for?"
- "How can I show you in this moment that I am here for you and genuinely care about your feelings?"
- "Please tell me what you need from me right now to feel more at ease and comforted."

Step 7. Respond with Appreciation and Honesty (*what the hurt partner must do*)

A. Privilege the positive: Let your partner know that you are thankful for their compassionate presence and for listening to your concerns. Highlighting the positive aspects of the interaction helps reinforce the behavior and encourages continued empathy and understanding. Acknowledge the effort your partner is making to mend the relationship, which can help build a foundation of trust and healing.

Examples:

- "Thank you for really listening to me and being here for me. It means a lot to feel heard and understood."
- "I appreciate you taking the time to understand my feelings

and showing that you care. It helps me feel more connected to you."

- "Your willingness to hear me out and empathize with my pain is very important to me. Thank you for making the effort to support me."
- "I'm grateful for your patience and effort in being present with me during this conversation. It shows me that you're committed to our relationship."

B. Be honest in love: If you still feel raw and cannot fully trust, extend appreciation while expressing your mixed feelings. Acknowledge the part of you that can take in what they said and the hurt part that finds it difficult. If you feel hopeful, share that as well.

Examples:

- "I appreciate you really trying to hear me. There's a part of me that's still struggling to trust completely. But there's also a part of me that feels reassured."
- "Thank you for your understanding and empathy. I want to believe in your commitment to change, but part of me is still hurt and finding it hard to trust. At the same time, I can feel some hope."
- "I'm grateful for your apology and efforts to make things right. While I still need time to heal and fully trust again, I do feel a sense of hope."
- "Your words mean a lot to me, but a part of me is still guarded and finding it hard to believe completely. However, I also feel some comfort and appreciate your patience as I work through these feelings."

Step 8. Reinforce Your Progress (*both partners*)

- **Celebrate wins:** Acknowledge the progress you've made. Remember, healing takes time, so celebrate small victories along the way. Recognize and appreciate each other's efforts and improvements.

• **Keep connecting:** Continue having these open, honest conversations regularly to reinforce the healing that has taken place.

Ananya and Arjun's Healing Conversation

Let's pick back up with Ananya and Arjun and explore how they engaged in a healing conversation in this way.

One evening, Ananya and Arjun found a quiet, comfortable place to talk. They chose their living room, turning off their phones and other gadgets to minimize distractions. Ananya lit some candles and placed a couple of cushions on the floor to make the environment more inviting.

Ananya began, "I know this is new for us. Thank you for taking the time to have this conversation. I know talking about conflict can be challenging for us. Let's agree to really listen to each other without interrupting or judging. We should take turns to speak and use 'I' statements to express our feelings."

Arjun nodded. "I agree. This is hard for me, but you are worth it. Let's set an intention to work through this issue. I am ready to be present."

Ananya started by pinpointing specific incidents that triggered profound hurt. She described feeling abandoned when Arjun spent long hours caring for his mother and not checking in on her during her postpartum depression.

Arjun listened intently, realizing the gravity of her feelings. He noticed some anxiety in his chest, yet took deep breaths and continued to listen.

Ananya's voice wavered as she recalled those lonely days and nights. "I was really angry and felt betrayed when you spent so much time with your mother but didn't check in on me. It shattered my sense of security in our relationship, and I'm scared that if I am in times of need, you will not be there for me again. When I needed you most, your absence brought on a lot of sadness and loneliness. It felt like you didn't care about what I was going through, and that's made it hard for me to rely on you."

Arjun focused on understanding Ananya's pain, imagining what it must have been like for her. He avoided interrupting or defending himself, showing genuine empathy.

They then dug deeper to talk about the underlying issues and emotional needs. Ananya expressed her fear of being unsupported and her need for reliable companionship. "When you didn't show up, I felt like I couldn't rely on you. I felt scared and alone. When you didn't defend me in front of your family, I felt unimportant and unsupported. I need to know that you have my back and that I matter to you."

Arjun nodded, understanding how these events had deeply shaken Ananya's sense of security and connection. He absorbed her words, letting them settle. "I see now how much it hurt you when I didn't show up the way you needed. You must have felt so scared and alone. When you tell me you felt unsupported when I didn't defend you, I've come to a deeper realization of how that left you feeling unimportant." With tears in his eyes, he said, "I understand now how crucial it is for you to feel that I have your back. I will do better."

He then checked in to ensure he truly understood the heart of Ananya's pain. "I want to make sure I'm really understanding you. Do you feel that I'm getting to the heart of your pain? Do you feel like I am present with you?"

Ananya nodded, feeling that Arjun was genuinely trying to understand her. "Yes, you are."

Arjun took responsibility for his actions. "I'm truly sorry for not being there when you needed me. I now understand how my absence brought up feelings of abandonment and sadness. I can see why you feel betrayed and unloved because of what I did."

Arjun provided verbal affirmations and consistent, caring actions to rebuild trust. He looked intently into Ananya's eyes and said, "Your feelings are really important to me, and I am committed to making things right between us. I understand how much this hurt you, and I want you to know I'm here for you and will do everything I can to rebuild your trust."

He then asked Ananya what she needed to be comforted in the moment. "What can I do right now to help you feel more comfortable and supported?"

Ananya replied, "Just being here and listening to me is already helping."

Ananya acknowledged Arjun's efforts and presence. "Thank you for really listening to me and being here for me. It means a lot to feel heard and understood."

She expressed her mixed feelings honestly. "I appreciate everything you've said, and a part of me still struggles to trust completely. But there's also a big part of me that feels reassured."

With tears in their eyes, they embraced each other. "We've come a long way," Arjun said, "and I'm committed to continuing these conversations and doing so as long as it takes."

By embracing these steps, like Ananya and Arjun, you and your partner can embark on the delicate journey of mending your past wounds. Together, you can begin to craft a relationship that feels like a sanctuary filled with the warmth of love and the security you both long for. Make a heartfelt promise to keep the lines of communication open, understanding that healing is not a final destination but a continuous voyage. Each step can bring you closer, not just to each other, but to a deeper understanding of yourselves, serving as a beautiful testament to the power of vulnerability and the resilience of the human heart.

You Are a Cycle Slayer

After reading all the examples of how to master this cycle-slaying stuff, you might be thinking, 'This is fairy-tale nonsense. Do people really talk to each other like this?' I get it. It can sound like a foreign language, and who has time to learn a new one? I admit, these communication and cycle-slaying skills can be challenging to put into practice. But you can do it. You might need to tweak the language to make it sound more like you, and that's okay. As long as you capture the essence and stay true to the heart of the steps—the cost of admission—the reward of admission—a secure relationship—will be well worth it.

Perpetual conflict drains the soul, while unresolved dragons of fire-breathing trauma can scorch the heart. Wide chasms between us and our partners echo with stark loneliness. Yet we are love-sick cycle-slayers, warriors of the heart who battle for peace and harmony, never surrendering, fighting for love as long as even the faintest embers still burn.

To those readers who feel a heaviness in their chest, knowing your partner isn't fully on board with finding clarity, doing the work, and building a lasting relationship—I see you. Truly, I do. It's exhausting to feel like you're shouldering all the effort, while your partner seems to be in la-la land, stuck in anger, being defensive, or simply indifferent. Yet, pushing past our pain, striving to be the healthiest version of ourselves, and loving to the best of our ability—while still being assertive and setting boundaries when needed—is noble. We can only control ourselves. And sometimes, even if our partners aren't on the healthy love train, our actions can still shift the relational dynamic. That's where hope lies. Each moment offers the potential for something new to happen.

Chapter Eight Wrap-Up

Recognizing and naming our corrosive negative cycles, then using strategies like the **SANE** approach and healthy time-outs, can stop them in their tracks before they escalate. Additionally, engaging in the Eight Essential Steps to Healing Conversations can be crucial when there are ruptures or attachment injuries that need repair. It's about owning your part in the dance, working together to engage in healthier behaviors, and turning conflicts into chances for growth and connection.

Incorporating these practices into your daily life takes commitment and effort from both partners. It's about doing the work. It's about those small, consistent efforts to understand, support, and love each other in ways that hit home. By doing so, you can create a positive cycle of connectivity that not only counters the negative cycle but also strengthens the foundation of your relationship, helping it thrive even when the going gets tough.

Key Takeaways

1. Name the Cycle: Externalizing the negative cycle by naming it helps you and your partner team up against it, making it feel like a separate entity to conquer together.

2. Use the SANE Approach: Using the SANE method (See what is happening, Accept your part in the cycle, Name the cycle, Engage toward healthy relating) empowers you and your partner to identify and interrupt negative cycles, fostering healthier interactions.

3. Take Healthy Time-Outs: Recognizing emotional and physiological signs of distress allows you and your partner to take constructive time-outs, using breaks to calm down and prepare for a more productive conversation later.

4. Self-Soothe and Reflect: During time-outs, engaging in self-soothing activities and reflecting on your emotions and needs helps prepare you to return to the conversation with greater clarity and empathy.

5. Heal Attachment Injuries: Addressing deep-seated attachment injuries through open, empathetic conversations is an important step in healing relational trauma, rebuilding trust, and strengthening emotional bonds in your relationship.

6. Embrace Cycle-Slaying Skills: While mastering effective communication and cycle-slaying techniques may feel challenging and unnatural initially, adapting these skills to fit your unique style is essential for creating and maintaining a secure and harmonious relationship. Overcoming perpetual conflict and trauma is worth the effort, as it leads to deeper connection and emotional resilience.

Chapter 9
Cultivating a Healthier You (For A Healthier We)

"We often feel powerless in our relationships because we spend most of our time and energy focusing on the things we can't control: other people."

— Dr. Nicole LePera, *How to Be the Love You Seek*

M ost of this book has been a journey through understanding your and your partner's operating systems, charting the negative cycle that gets you stuck, and discovering the principles and practices for connection, communication, and the skillful art of cycle-slaying—all aimed at nurturing a secure bond with your ride or die. Now, let's turn the spotlight inward. Let's devote a chapter to the dynamic, ever-evolving relationship with yourself, embracing the timeless wisdom that *a healthier me begets a healthier we*. For in the grand tapestry of love, the dance of two embodied souls is most graceful when each is on the journey to be healthy and whole. The more we cultivate our own well-being, the more our shared love blossoms into its truest, most vibrant form.

In this chapter, we'll dive into three essential areas of growth that can make our relationships flourish: boosting self-compassion, embracing our inner child, and keeping our values front and center. As we grow in these areas, the positive changes will naturally spill over, gently nurturing and strengthening our relationships to help them thrive.

Self-Compassion

In an ideal world, we and our partners are consistently there for each other, helping to soothe and calm one another in moments of distress. The thrust of most of this book is working toward that end. But let's be real—sometimes, we can't be there for each other the way we want. Sometimes, we fight and can't repair the rift right away. Sometimes, our partners are away, busy with work, or just too exhausted and don't have the bandwidth. And sometimes we feel too ashamed and haven't worked up the courage to talk about challenging internal struggles. That's where we need to bring another fabulous lover into the picture—ourselves.

Self-love, especially in the form of self-compassion, is the secret ingredient for a healthier, happier you, and by extension, a healthier, happier relationship. Think of self-compassion as a superpower that banishes toxic shame and unhealthy guilt, lightening your body and spirit and enabling you to feel freer in the world. This superpower can also transform your attitude toward those around you. When we learn to love and be kind to ourselves despite our flaws and foibles, we naturally become warmer and less judgmental toward others.

Let's take a moment to dive into some truly fascinating self-compassion research. One study had folks rank their partners' self-compassion and list the traits that influenced their rankings.[1] Those with higher self-compassion were seen as warmer, more considerate, and affectionate. Conversely, those with lower self-compassion were viewed as self-absorbed, detached, and controlling. Another study showed that by reducing negative self-judgment and boosting our ability to calm ourselves when distressed, self-compassion helps us keep healthier boundaries and communicate better.[2] This, in turn, cranks up relationship satisfaction because partners feel more understood and valued. Kristin Neff, one of the world's leading self-compassion researchers and authors, has shown that self-compassion increases motivation, forgiveness, happiness, hopefulness, positivity, wisdom, curiosity, engagement in new experiences, agreeableness, extroversion, and conscientiousness while also decreasing shame and depression.[3] So, it turns out that being gentle and loving toward ourselves is revolutionary not just for us but for everyone with whom we interact.

What Is Self-Compassion?

Kristin Neff talks about self-compassion in such a down-to-earth way: *respond to yourself in tough times like you would to a dear friend.* She breaks down self-compassion into three main ingredients: self-kindness, common humanity, and mindfulness.[4] The extent to which we integrate all three elements in our day-to-day moments, especially during the difficult ones, determines our level of self-compassion.

First, show "self-kindness." This means treating yourself as you would a loved one who is suffering and in pain—with kindness, warmth, and genuine care. Rather than engaging in self-hatred, harshness, judgment, and criticism, treat yourself gently and compassionately despite your personal shortcomings and life's challenges.

Let's say your partner comes home absolutely fried and wants to zone out alone for a bit. And there you are, feeling like yesterday's leftovers, thinking, "They are such a jerk. They don't care about spending time with me," quickly spiraling into, "If I were more fun and worthwhile, and if they really cared, they'd want to be with me." Instead, take a deep breath and practice a little self-kindness. You might say, "It's okay to feel a little hurt right now. All I wanted was some connection. Their need for alone time isn't a reflection on me. I know they love me. I'll give them the space they need, and maybe I'll soak in the tub, treat myself to a little comfort. They are not the only ones who can love me. I can love on myself too. We'll reconnect when they're ready." By doing this, you've given yourself what you need, instead of staying anxious and frazzled, waiting for your partner to fill your cup. This self-compassionate approach helps you recognize your feelings without beating yourself up and allows you to show up for yourself in a way that's kind and life-giving.

Second, become aware of your common humanity. This is the realization that everyone—yes, everyone—is imperfect, wounded, and prone to making mistakes. The opposite is feeling like you're the only person on the planet who screws up so royally.

Imagine you've just had a colossal fight with your partner. You yelled, you cursed, and now you're feeling like the worst person in the world. You might catch yourself thinking, "What's wrong with me? I'm a terrible partner. I wish I could control my feelings like everyone else." That's isolation talking, my friend. That shame-spiraling attitude just piles on the self-judgment, pushing you further away from everyone else floundering right along with you. Instead, remind yourself that you're simply human, like the rest of us.

Third, practice mindfulness. This is typically thought of as *the practice of intentionally focusing one's attention on the present moment and accepting it without judgment.*[5] In other words, mindfulness means being acutely aware of the present moment and accepting it with gentle curiosity and wonder. Before we can extend kindness to ourselves, we should understand what we're experiencing. Mindfulness lets us stay open to everything we're feeling right now: our physical sensations, thoughts, feelings, urges, and impulses. It's like turning on a light in a dark room so we can see what's there without freaking out about it.

Mindfulness is the ability to distinguish thoughts and feelings from the self. When you practice mindfulness, you observe the thoughts and feelings passing through your mind and understand that they are not you; it's you having thoughts. A lack of mindfulness can lead to overidentifying with our negative thoughts and feelings. Mindfulness allows us to step back and view our emotions and experiences from a distance, recognizing that these thoughts may not be accurate and opening up to a more flexible perspective.

You might be thinking, "That's a great concept. But what does mindfulness look like in real life?" Here's a practical example. Let's revisit that self-critical and isolating comment: "What's wrong with me? I'm a terrible partner." Instead of believing that these thoughts define who you are, try recognizing that your brain is just doing what it does best—spitting out thoughts with no sound basis.

The self-compassionate approach is to be mindfully aware of those thoughts when they occur. The phrase "I'm a terrible person. I wish I were more in control like everyone else" can be met with mindful awareness: "Right now, *I'm having the thought* that I'm a terrible partner and wish I was more in control like everyone else." The takeaway is that mindfulness creates enough space around your thoughts to make "choice" possible. You can believe your thoughts and let them take root … or not. It's your choice made possible by mindfulness.

Bringing together all the elements of self-compassion—self-kindness, common humanity, and mindfulness—imagine sitting on the couch after a big, blowout fight. You replay all the nasty things you said, feeling that sharp sting of healthy guilt because you know you didn't treat your partner right. Instead of going into a shame spiral for a few hours, you take a deep breath and remind yourself, "Hey, everyone loses it sometimes. It doesn't mean I'm the worst person ever or that my relationship is headed for disaster. It just means I'm human. And in this beautiful, messy humanness, there's room to learn, apologize, and grow into the kind of partner I want to be." With this newfound sense of lightness and compassionate clarity, you can live out your values of love and respect by thwarting a shame spiral, offering a genuine apology, positively impacting your relationship.

The Yin and Yang of Self-Compassion

In her book *Fierce Self-Compassion*, Kristin Neff distinguishes between the Yin and Yang of self-compassion.[6] This distinction is incredibly helpful. Many people perceive self-compassion as fluffy, weak, and overly feminine—something for coddling-seeking individuals or relentlessly self-indulgent narcissists. That couldn't be farther from the truth. While self-compassion can indeed be nurturing, it can also be strong, fierce, and deeply practical. Protecting ourselves from harm and standing up against oppressive dynamics in our relationships and society are also powerful forms of self-compassion.

Neff borrows from ancient Chinese philosophy to distinguish between the Yin and Yang of self-compassion. The Yin side embodies soft, nurturing energy. Imagine a mother gently cradling a crying child—that's Yin self-compassion. It's tender, soothing, and accepting. For example, if you've just had a terrible argument with your partner and you're feeling raw, practicing Yin self-compassion means acknowledging your pain and comforting yourself as you would a dear friend. This might involve taking a few deep breaths, gently placing your hand on your heart, and reassuring yourself that it's okay to feel hurt and that you will get through this.

On the flip side, we have the Yang quality of self-compassion, which is all about assertive action. Think of the fierce determination of a firefighter charging into a burning building or a mama bear protecting her cubs. Yang self-compassion asks, "In the thick of this suffering, what do I need right now?" and "What can I actively do to help myself?" Maybe you're feeling overwhelmed by your partner's constant demands. Practicing Yang self-compassion might mean setting firm boundaries to protect your emotional well-being. You could say to your partner, "I know you want to spend time with me, but I need some personal space and time to recharge," and then make sure you follow through and carve out time in a kind and respectful way to both of you.

Maybe you've discovered that your partner has been lying to you. Practicing Yang self-compassion might mean directly confronting the deceit and standing up for your emotional well-being. You could say to your partner, "I know you haven't been truthful with me, and that hurts. I need honesty and trust in our relationship," and then take concrete steps to address the issue, such as setting boundaries or seeking couples therapy. In this fierce, self-compassionate way, you ensure your needs for trust and integrity are met while taking proactive steps to heal and strengthen your relationship.

In the end, whether it's the gentle Yin or the assertive Yang, self-compassion is about taking care of yourself in a way that's both kind and strong. It's about knowing what you need and having the courage to give it to yourself, which, more often than not, benefits the relationship too. Let's dive into how self-compassion can enhance our relationships through various scenarios and applications.

Self-Compassion in Action

Below, we'll explore some common challenges in relationships and the benefits of applying self-compassion in these situations.

Example 1: *Healing Past Traumas*

Scenario: Jane and Mark have been locked in a dance of frequent arguments. Jane, with anxious tendencies, often feels anxious and unloved, while Mark, with avoidant tendencies, tends to withdraw and feel criticized. Jane is still haunted by relational trauma from her past. At the tender age of five, she experienced a heart-wrenching moment when her father left her mom and her for another woman. These wounds were reopened when a previous partner cheated on her and ran off with another woman, leaving her grappling with issues of trust and self-worth.

Application of Self-Compassion: When Jane feels her anxiety spike because she hasn't heard from Mark in a while—he's swamped at work —she takes a moment to practice mindful breathing, calming her frazzled nerves. She reminds herself that her anxieties are mostly echoes from past traumas, not a reflection of her current relationship. She then turns to her journal, spilling her feelings onto the page and responding to herself with the same kindness she would offer a friend going through something similar.

She even tries self-compassionate imagery, picturing her inner child and offering that little girl the love and reassurance she craves. This approach represents the Yin aspect of self-compassion, providing a nurturing and soothing response to her pain.

Mark, who finds it challenging to open up and be vulnerable, practices mindful self-compassion, observing his feelings without judgment. Mark also engaged in a compassionate letter-writing exercise, drafting a letter to himself from his core wise and loving self, expressing understanding and support for his struggles. This introspective practice is another example of the Yin aspect. To incorporate the Yang aspect, he and Jane start having regular check-ins and little talks where they lay their feelings and concerns on the table. This is self-compassion with a bit of grit, as he knows how hard it is to face those difficult feelings, yet he actively takes steps to break the exhausting negative cycle and strengthen their connection.

Example 2: *Managing Parenting Stress*

Scenario: María and José are new parents, overwhelmed by the demands of caring for their infant. María feels guilty for not being a "perfect" mother, while José feels inadequate for not being able to ease María's stress.

Application of Self-Compassion: María, like a wise, gentle soul who knows that life is a tangled mess of imperfections, practices self-compassion by permitting herself to be flawed. She whispers to herself affirmations like "I am doing my best, and that is good enough," and takes precious moments to care for herself. She reaches out to other parents, forming a circle of solidarity that reminds her she isn't alone in this chaotic dance of parenting. María also embraces a self-compassion meditation called the body scan. She slows down, shuts her eyes, and tenderly acknowledges each part of her body, offering it kindness and gratitude for the heavy lifting it does every single day. These tender, nurturing practices are the very essence of the Yin aspect of self-compassion, wrapping her in a soothing embrace of stress relief. However, María also practices Yang self-compassion, which involves setting boundaries and protecting herself. When she feels overwhelmed by the demands of others, she firmly but kindly says, "No, I can't take on that task right now," recognizing her need to prioritize her well-being.

Then there's José. He looks at his feelings of inadequacy and nods, recognizing them as part of the messy human experience. José acknowledges that his feelings of inadequacy are normal and engages in self-care activities like exercise or hobbies to maintain his well-being. José practices loving-kindness meditation, sending ripples of warmth and goodwill to himself and others, which makes him feel connected and less isolated. José also uses mindful walking, taking a few minutes each day to walk slowly and mindfully, appreciating the present moment. He channels the Yang aspect of self-compassion by taking action—organizing a support group for new fathers. José knows he can't navigate this fatherhood journey alone, so the community serves as a lifeline to swap stories and strategies, actively working to ease the collective stress.

Example 3: *Coping with Infidelity*

Scenario: Lisa and John are trying to rebuild their relationship after John had an affair. Feeling hurt and betrayed, Lisa questions her self-worth. John is wracked with guilt and self-loathing.

Application of Self-Compassion: In her beautifully messy human way, Lisa practices self-compassion by acknowledging her pain and letting herself grieve instead of criticizing herself for being unable to "get over it." She uses mindfulness to stay present with her emotions, allowing them to exist without letting them drown her. She attends therapy and support groups to reinforce that this betrayal does not define her worth and to empower her to work through this relational trauma. This proactive approach embodies the Yang aspect of self-compassion as Lisa takes solid and decisive steps to heal and reclaim her life.

Lisa, who values her faith, also embraces self-compassionate journaling, pouring all her raw, unfiltered feelings onto the page and imagining what kind, encouraging words God would whisper to her. These tender practices embody the Yin aspect, gently cradling her wounded soul with the care it desperately needs.

John, amid his traumatizing betrayal, practices self-compassion to avoid collapsing into debilitating shame. He recognizes his guilt and accepts it as part of his messy journey toward healing. He dives deep into self-reflection and seeks forgiveness through actions showing his commitment to change. By treating himself kindly, he finds the strength to support Lisa better and rebuild their trust. John also embraces compassionate touch, placing a hand on his heart and whispering to himself words of kindness and reassurance to help navigate the storm of his turbulent emotions. Embracing the Yang aspect, John takes proactive steps to make amends. He sets up regular couples counseling sessions, seeks individual therapy, and engages in transparent, honest communication with Lisa, all in the hope of rebuilding the fragile bridge of trust between them.

Example 4: *Navigating Political and Gender Differences*

Scenario: Hyejin and Jisoo have been together for several years but have recently found themselves clashing over their differing political views and beliefs about sexuality and gender. Hyejin is passionate about advocating for LGBTQI+ rights and progressive policies, while Jisoo holds more conservative views. This difference has led to frequent and heated arguments, creating a rift in their relationship.

Application of Self-Compassion: Hyejin practices self-compassion by acknowledging her frustration and the emotional toll these disagreements take on her. She uses mindfulness to stay present and not get carried away by anger. Engaging in self-soothing activities like yoga or painting helps her maintain emotional balance. With a touch of Yang compassion, she reminds herself that having differing opinions is okay and that Jisoo's acceptance does not define her worth. These practices embody the Yin aspect of self-compassion, providing gentle care and understanding.

Although Jisoo remains more defensive and reactive, Hyejin's consistent practice of self-compassion serves as a model. She listens to Jisoo without judgment and validates his feelings even when she disagrees. This approach creates a safer space for Jisoo, potentially encouraging him to lower his defenses and engage in more constructive dialogue over time. Hyejin also engages in internal self-compassion breaks, taking a few moments during heated discussions to step back, breathe, and remind herself of her commitment to kindness and understanding.

To incorporate the Yang aspect of self-compassion, Hyejin takes action by asserting her boundaries clearly and firmly. During a particularly heated discussion, she tells Jisoo, "I understand that we have different views, but it's not okay to speak to me disrespectfully. We need to communicate with respect." By speaking assertively, Hyejin protects herself from disrespect and models how to maintain dignity and respect in their conversations. Additionally, she suggests structured dialogue sessions where each person has a set time to speak without interruption, creating a more balanced and respectful discussion. This proactive stance embodies the Yang aspect, demonstrating that self-compassion also involves taking courageous and decisive actions to protect oneself and the relationship.

These examples show how a broad assortment of self-compassion skills—think mindful breathing, compassionate letter writing, loving-kindness meditation, mindful self-compassion, self-compassion body scan, compassionate touch, compassionate listening, and self-compassion breaks—can flip our relationships on their heads in the best way possible. We're talking about fostering empathy, understanding, and the kind of emotional resilience that makes you feel like you can weather any storm. By weaving in Kristin Neff's Yin and Yang aspects of self-compassion, we strike a beautiful balance between nurturing and proactive elements. That way, self-compassion is no longer just a feel-good principle but a powerful tool for healing and growing our connection with ourselves and our partners.

Instead of being overly harsh on yourself during those "self-at-worst" moments, letting those self-critical voices tear you down and spiraling into shame, try engaging in self-compassion. Instead of drowning in substances to numb emotional pain, you can determine whether you need the gentle, nurturing Yin compassion or the firm, protective Yang compassion, then treat yourself like you would a dear friend in the same boat. Instead of feeling adrift and disconnected from your partner, desperately needing love and reassurance but not knowing where to find it, give self-compassion a shot. It's a well-researched principle and practice that can truly transform your life. Embrace self-compassion and become a healthier you, paving the way for a healthier relationship.

With your newfound grasp of self-compassion, you can now reach out to that often-forgotten part of yourself—your tender, wounded inner child—and offer it the love and care it has always needed.

Your Inner Child

Before we focus on our inner child, I want to take a few moments to talk about how we view our partners, particularly during challenging times. This part gets a little abstract, but stay with me, and I trust you'll find it brings some valuable insights.

Our Beloved, Annoying Mirror

Let's kick things off with a thought-provoking question: If you could paint a picture using a metaphor of what you want your partner to be in your life, what would it look like? Maybe you'd see them as a lighthouse, shining brightly to guide you through life's stormy seas. Or perhaps they're your co-architect designing a shared existence of responsibilities and routines or fellow adventurers embracing the joys and thrills of life's journey. Deep down, you may crave them to be a sanctuary, a peaceful haven amidst life's chaos.

Let's play with some other ideas, too.

What if your partner were a therapist, helping you untangle the knots of your emotions and offering a safe, calming space where you feel genuinely understood? Or a coach walking beside you as you both strive to become your best selves? Maybe you envision them as a guru, dispensing just the right doses of wisdom and care to keep your relationship healthy and thriving. Or perhaps they're your co-pilot, sharing the ups and downs of raising kids together.

Maybe your response is, "I want all of them!"

Now, let's toss in a wild card: the metaphor of the *beloved, annoying mirror*. Imagine this: your partner is the magic mirror from Snow White, but instead of merely revealing who's the fairest, they reflect your true self—flaws, grandeur, warts, wounds, and all. This mirror doesn't sugarcoat or flatter; it reveals the unvarnished truth. Not only does the reflection show your undistorted, raw emotional and behavioral reactions, but it's also a guide to healing and growth—that is, if we choose to follow its lead.

In our most challenging moments, our beloved partners hold up a mirror to us, often without even knowing it. They might provoke, anger, frustrate us, or bring out our deepest fears and insecurities. But in doing so, they allow us to confront and address the parts of ourselves we'd rather ignore. They reflect the shadows of our psyche that need healing, exposing old wounds that existed long before we met them. However, we have a choice. We can continue pointing judgmental fingers at our partners or see them as beloved annoying mirrors, revealing that we're actually pointing at ourselves. Then, we can listen to the wisdom of where the mirror directs us—the triggers within.

Triggers, Our Sacred Guides

It's completely natural to have a strong aversion to our partners when they trigger us. Who in their right mind wants to lean into pain? No one. We aren't masochists. Our nervous systems are hardwired to alert us to danger and throw us into self-protection mode. Dodging pain and pointing fingers—that's just our nervous systems and our minds doing their thing.

After we get hurt, especially if we have insecure relational tendencies, we often start ruminating about how our partner seems unloving and uncaring. We convince ourselves that our relationship would be incredible if only they would change. We imagine that if they morphed into the ideal version we fantasize about, we'd get the love we deserve, the intimacy we need (or the loving "space" for those with avoidant tendencies), and the ever-doting supportive partner we crave. But reality never quite matches the fantasy, and we're left with a deep sense of internal angst and pain. To cope, we might withdraw into apathy, put up walls, settle for the status quo, or harbor bubbling resentment. These reactions are understandable, yet they only deepen our hurt and disconnect us further from our partners.

But what if we stopped pointing the finger at our partner? What if, instead, we allowed them to be our beloved, annoying mirror, reflecting back our triggers, which are in fact sacred guides into the depths of our psyches? What if we viewed these triggers as a ferryman, like Charon from mythology, guiding us across the tumultuous waters of our inner world to the places that need healing? What if the very places our triggers lead us to are the sites of our salvation—the areas in our psyche that reveal the core wounds, guiding us to become more mature and healthier versions of ourselves? And what if the ferryman doesn't lead us to a place but to a person—to a small, wounded child, the younger, hurting version of ourselves? That's precisely what I am proposing.

The Wounded Inner Child and Their Invisible Lenses

There's no denying that our partners can sometimes do things that hurt us. It's crucial to acknowledge this reality. Some triggers have nothing to do with our past and are solely due to our partner's behaviors. However, while holding our partner accountable for their actions is important, we must also recognize the significant influence of our unresolved childhood wounds. These wounds, often inflicted by our parents or primary caregivers, shape our emotional responses and magnify the pain evoked by our partner's actions. When our partners trigger us, our past wounds can escalate our emotional response from what would possibly be a mild 3 or 4 on a hypothetical Emotional Reactivity Scale to an intense 8 or 10. In order to cultivate a healthier self and relationship (a healthier *me* and *we*), it's critical to address and heal our wounded inner child. First, since the inner child is a *part* of us, we need to have a brief introduction to "parts" work through the lens of internal family systems (IFS).

The inner child, or *exile*, represents the vulnerable, younger part of you that carry the burdens of past traumas, unmet needs, and painful emotions. This part was once full of life, curiosity, friendliness, and a desire for play and adventure. However, due to their experiences during particular moments in life, they may now bear the scars of painful, traumatic events.

Imagine this tender child part now sitting in a locked bedroom, feeling the heavy weight of loneliness, isolation, anxiety, shame, and pain from those original wounds. They're frozen in time, stuck at the age when the hurt first struck. It's daunting to face their suffering, so we tuck them away, out of sight and out of mind, hoping they won't interfere with our daily lives. We fear that acknowledging them will derail and overwhelm us, affecting our work, relationships, parenting, or just our ability to manage the mundane tasks of life, so we keep the door shut tight. Meanwhile, this younger part is desperate to be nurtured and cared for.

We often carry multiple exiles within us, though many people mainly identify with and relate to a single "inner child." These exiles commonly hold painful negative *schemas*, or internal beliefs (e.g., "I'm not lovable," "I'm broken," "I'm worthless," "I must be perfect," "Others can't be trusted"). These deeply ingrained patterns of thought and emotion latched onto us during childhood and have stubbornly influenced our adult lives. It's like wearing invisible contact lenses tinted by old, sometimes painful stories that dictate how we see and react to the world.

These lenses are so seamlessly integrated into our vision that we often forget they are there, yet they color every interaction and relationship we have. Among the most common schemas I encounter with folks include Abandonment/Instability, Mistrust/Abuse, Emotional Deprivation, Defectiveness/Shame, Social Isolation/Alienation, and Dependency/Incompetence.[7]

The *Abandonment/Instability* schema is that gnawing fear that everyone you love will eventually leave you. It's the voice in your head that makes you anxious and clingy in relationships, always waiting for the other shoe to drop. For example, if your partner cancels plans at the last minute, you might spiral into anxiety, convinced they're losing interest and will soon leave you.

Mistrust/Abuse is the wary expectation that others will harm or manipulate you, making you tiptoe through interactions, always on the lookout for danger. If your partner forgets to mention a conversation with an ex, you might immediately suspect deceit and feel a surge of distrust, even if their intention was innocent.

The *Emotional Deprivation* schema whispers that your emotional needs will never be met, leaving you feeling lonely and struggling to form close connections. You might feel this acutely if your partner seems distracted when you share something important, leading you to believe no one will ever truly be there for you.

Defectiveness/Shame is that cruel inner critic that convinces you you're fundamentally flawed and unworthy, making you hypersensitive to criticism and prone to low self-esteem. If your partner points out a mistake you made, you might internalize it deeply, feeling like a complete failure and fearing they'll see you as incompetent.

The *Social Isolation/Alienation* schema plants the idea that you're different and disconnected from others, fostering a sense of loneliness and leading you to withdraw socially. When your partner seamlessly socializes at a party, you might feel like an outsider, convinced you don't belong and that people don't really like you.

Dependence/Incompetence is the nagging belief that you can't handle responsibilities or make decisions independently, keeping you reliant on others and hesitant to take initiative. If your partner suggests you handle an important task, you might feel overwhelmed and anxious, doubting your ability to manage it without their help.

Do you recognize a core schema your inner child may be carrying that affects your relationship?

These schemas, triggered by interactions with your partner, can profoundly influence your behavior and feelings within the relationship. Recognizing them allows you to challenge and reshape these ingrained patterns, fostering healthier, more fulfilling connections and a more compassionate view of yourself.

Protector Parts

The inner child parts, those tender little exiles, are often pushed into the farthest corners of our psyches by our well-meaning *protector parts*. These parts act like overly cautious parents who want to keep everything calm and suppress any potential disruption that might occur with emotionally dysregulated, loud and unruly children. The protector parts fear that the raw pain and vulnerability of our inner child might over-whelm us. To prevent this, they take control, ensuring we maintain the status quo and avoid confronting the room where our inner child resides. Protector parts come in two forms: managers and firefighters.

Managers are like vigilant hall monitors, always on high alert to maintain order and prevent chaos. They're proactive and strategic, thrive on checklists, and embody our inner control freaks, who rely on logic and rational thinking. In couple dynamics, these can manifest as critical voices or controlling behaviors, where one partner constantly criticizes or micromanages the other to maintain a sense of control and avoid failure or rejection, thereby avoiding the vulnerability of their inner child. Another partner's manager might swoop in to avoid tough conversations and the vulnerability of their inner child feeling shame by putting up walls of defensiveness and rationalizing, maintaining a safe emotional distance.

Firefighters react with urgency and desperation to smother emotional distress. They use any means necessary to numb or distract from the pain, such as addictive behaviors (e.g., drinking, overeating, mindless scrolling) or compulsive activities (e.g., shopping, overworking, binge-watching). In couple dynamics, this can create distance or avoidance of underlying issues, keeping the inner child's pain at bay. Explosive outbursts are another tactic, where anger and rage are used to deflect from deeper, vulnerable feelings, protecting the inner child from exposure. Firefighters seek immediate relief, often in messy and over-the-top ways, to prevent emotional overwhelm and shield the inner child from resurfacing distress.

Awareness of our inner child parts and protectors, which become triggered in the eye of the damaging conflict cycle storm, is vital for understanding ourselves and the health of our relationships. To gain a bit more clarity on how these parts manifest, let's take a stroll through a couple's story and see how these parts show up in their interactions.

Jason and Charlotte

Jason and Charlotte met during their senior year of college. Jason, a reserved and introspective computer science major, carried the weight of avoidant tendencies from growing up in a household where emotions were buried beneath a façade of tough love. His parents believed in stern rationality over softness, and Jason learned early on to tuck his feelings away, relying on himself for comfort and stability. This emotional deprivation schema contributed to him feeling that his needs would never be met, leading his inner manager parts to take charge with constant vigilance. That way, Jason maintained order and control in his life, steering clear of conflict and seeking solitude when tensions rose.

Charlotte, on the other hand, was diving into the world of psychology. She hailed from a lively, expressive family that valued open communication but was no stranger to chaos. Her parents' relationship was a tempest of arguments and reconciliations. Her mother's emotional distance and inconsistency, paired with her father's unpredictable outbursts, left Charlotte with a deep-seated fear of abandonment and an unquenchable thirst for reassurance. She developed anxious relational tendencies, always on the lookout for signs of disconnection, a direct result of her abandonment/instability schema. From a young age, Charlotte became a mediator in her parents' conflicts, constantly striving to earn their attention and validation. Her need for connection and fear of being left behind followed Charlotte into adulthood, making her hypervigilant about any signs of distance in her relationships.

When Jason and Charlotte first met, their attraction was electric. Jason was drawn to Charlotte's warmth and vivacity, while Charlotte found Jason's calmness and depth intriguing. They seemed to balance each other out perfectly. But as their relationship deepened and life presented its inevitable challenges, their childhood wounds began to creep into the foreground.

When his father passed away unexpectedly, Jason was unable to openly process his grief, so he retreated into himself. Charlotte, desperate to support him, found herself locked out. Her efforts to connect were met with Jason's silence and withdrawal, triggering her inner child's fear of abandonment. Her firefighter parts kicked in, leading her to angrily criticize Jason for his emotional unavailability, hoping to provoke a reaction and break through his walls.

Jason, overwhelmed by his grief and Charlotte's demands, felt attacked and controlled. His manager parts went into overdrive, rationalizing his need for space and reinforcing his emotional barriers. He saw Charlotte's criticism not as a plea for connection but as an additional burden, adding to his stress.

This cycle of Pull Back and Protest became their recurring dance routine. Charlotte's attempts to reach out, driven by her firefighter part, were met with Jason's withdrawal, driven by his manager. Their reactions stemmed from their wounded inner children: Charlotte's fear of abandonment and Jason's fear of being smothered or controlled.

Their relationship hit a breaking point when Charlotte lost her job. Feeling vulnerable and needing support, she turned to Jason, only to find him emotionally distant. Her inner child's pain was too much to bear, leading to an explosive argument. Jason, feeling overwhelmed, shut down completely, retreating further into his shell.

Through couples therapy, Jason and Charlotte began to unearth these deeper layers of their relationship dynamics. They learned about their inner child wounds and that the protective parts had been steering their behaviors. Jason started to see his avoidance as a defense mechanism, shielding his inner child from the pain of past traumas. Charlotte recognized that her criticisms were desperate attempts to avoid the pain of feeling unloved and abandoned.

With this new understanding, they began to approach their conflicts differently. Jason started nurturing his inner child, listening to its needs, valuing its voice, and providing the reassurance and comfort that the young part of him never received from his parents. He learned to stay present and communicate his need for space without shutting Charlotte out completely. Charlotte began to reparent her inner child, acknowledging its fears, validating its feelings, and offering the consistent love and attention her inner child had longed for. She learned to express her needs without resorting to criticism, finding healthier ways to soothe her inner child and address her anxiety.

By embracing and loving their inner children, Jason and Charlotte experienced a profound shift in their relationship. They began to see each other as beloved, albeit annoying, mirrors reflecting back their deepest triggers and guiding them to the parts of themselves that needed healing. They became less reactive to each other's behaviors and more compassionate toward their own and each other's vulnerabilities. This acceptance and care for their inner children reduced the emotional charge around their partner's actions, allowing them to approach conflicts with greater patience and empathy. By following the wisdom of their triggers and addressing the wounds revealed by their partner's reflections, they created a foundation of self-love and mutual respect, paving the way for a healthier and more fulfilling partnership.

Connecting with Your Inner Child

In our relationships, conflicts can often stir up deep-seated emotions and beliefs rooted in our childhood experiences. Sometimes, the reactive energy we direct at our partners can be about 25% due to them and 75% due to the past wounds our inner child carries. Embracing our inner child with the love, care, and protection they may never have received from our primary caregivers could reduce the painful energy we bring to our relationships. In this section, you'll learn some powerful ways to embrace your inner child, beginning with a guided meditation.

Guided Meditation: Discovering Your Inner Child

This meditation is designed to help you connect with that inner child by revisiting a moment of conflict with your partner. An audio file of this meditation can be found at: https://markgregorykarris.com/meditations-from-beyond-fairy-tales/

Find a quiet and comfortable place where you won't be disturbed. Remember that this practice may bring up strong emotions. Be gentle with yourself as you explore these memories and feelings. Sit or lie down in a relaxed position and gently close your eyes. Take a few deep breaths, allowing yourself to settle into this moment. Let go of any tension or distractions and bring your focus inward.

Recall a Moment of Conflict

- Begin by bringing to mind a recent moment of conflict with your partner. Visualize the situation as vividly as you can. Notice where you are, what is happening, and how you interact with your partner.

Notice the Worst Part

- As you revisit this conflict, focus on the worst part of the experience. What aspect of the conflict felt most distressing or painful? Allow yourself to fully experience that moment again.

Observe Your Feelings

- Notice the feelings that arise as you focus on this moment. What emotions come up for you? Is it anger, sadness, fear, frustration, or something else? Simply observe these emotions without judgment.

Sense Your Body

- Shift your attention to your body. Notice any sensations that accompany these feelings. Where do you feel tension or discomfort? Is it in your chest, stomach, throat, or elsewhere? Pay close attention to these physical sensations.

Identify Self-Beliefs

- Now, identify what you believe about yourself in this moment of conflict. Complete the sentence: "I am _____." Do you feel unloved, unworthy, unsafe, powerless, or something else? Allow this belief to come to the surface.

Journey Back in Time

- Take all of the sensations, feelings, and beliefs about yourself, and gently allow your mind to take you back to when you were a child. Try to remember a moment from your childhood when you felt a similar way. What memory comes to mind?

Explore the Memory

- Once a memory emerges, stay with it for a while. Notice the details of the memory. Where are you? Who is with you? What is happening? Allow yourself to fully experience this memory as if you are there again. If remaining in the memory becomes too overwhelming, take a pause and engage in a calming activity.

Connect with Your Inner Child

- As you connect with this memory, recognize that this is your inner child, a younger version of yourself who holds these feelings and beliefs. Notice what your inner child needs in this moment. Is it comfort, reassurance, love, or something else?

Offer Compassion and Understanding

Take a moment to offer compassion and understanding to your inner child. Imagine giving them what they need. Visualize yourself holding them, comforting them, and providing the love and support they may not have received at the time.

Integration

- When you are ready, gently bring your awareness back to the present moment. Take a few deep breaths, and slowly open your eyes. Reflect on the insights you have gained from this meditation. Observe any similarities between your feelings with your partner and those you have with the person or persons in your memory. How can understanding your inner child's experience help you navigate conflicts with your partner more compassionately?

As you finish this meditation, take a moment to honor the work you've done. Recognize the courage it takes to face these tender parts of yourself. Remember, each step toward understanding and nurturing your inner child brings more compassion into your relationships. By caring for your inner child, you're fostering a healthier, more loving connection with yourself. Take a deep breath, and as you exhale, release any remaining tension, feeling a sense of peace and connection within.

If taking part in this meditation didn't dredge up any early childhood memories, I get it. I really do. Sometimes, tapping into our imaginative selves feels like trying to catch smoke with our bare hands. And for some of us, our deepest wounds and the pesky beliefs they plant aren't anchored in our earliest years. They might be tangled up in later experiences, shaped by those influential moments or relationships as we stumbled through life.

So, if a childhood memory didn't bubble to the surface, don't worry. Maybe take a detour through the backroads of your adolescent or adult life. Think about those moments that packed an emotional punch and felt like a traumatic incident, whether they involved friends, romantic partners, mentors, or other family members. These memories can be like little treasure maps, offering clues about your core schemas and how you navigate relationships today.

Next, let's look at some other ways to connect with our inner child.

Healing Forward

Embracing, loving, and healing our inner child—often referred to as reparenting—can be a transformative journey that profoundly enhances our ability to connect with our partners. Here are some practical ways to nurture this inner healing process within the context of your relationship:

1. **Journaling:** When conflict arises, take the time to write letters to your inner child, expressing understanding, love, and reassurance. Share some of these reflections with your partner to help them understand your emotional landscape and childhood influences. Encourage your partner to do the same

and discuss your insights together, fostering empathy and deeper connection.

2. **Self-Compassion:** Practice self-compassion by speaking to your inner child kindly, especially when you feel vulnerable or triggered during conflicts. Offer the same compassion to your partner when they are struggling, keeping their inner child in mind to create a more supportive and understanding environment.

3. **Visualization:** During or after conflicts, visualize yourself comforting and nurturing your inner child. If it feels emotionally safe, share these experiences with your partner and invite them to create their own.

4. **Regular Check-Ins:** Make it a habit to check in with your inner child regularly throughout the week. Spend a few moments each day tuning into your inner child's voice, listening to its needs, and offering it encouragement and love. If your relationship feels emotionally safe, share with your partner what you learned or offered during these check-ins, and encourage them to check in with their inner child as well. This ongoing practice can help you stay connected to your inner child's needs and foster a deeper understanding and support within your relationship.

5. **Therapeutic Support:** Consider seeking support from a therapist who specializes in inner child work or trauma, especially if you experience recurring or particularly intense conflicts. Couples therapy can provide a safe space for both you and your partner to explore and heal deep-seated wounds together. Working with a therapist can also equip you with tools to better support each other's healing journeys and manage conflicts more effectively.

Nurturing Our Inner Children Together

We cannot expect our partners to shoulder the responsibility of being the primary caregivers for our inner child—it's unfair. That's a heavy load to drop on them, especially since they're often clueless about our inner child's traumas and needs (and many times their own). We end up putting them in an impossible position, hoping they'll reparent our inner child and fill in the gaps left by our parents. The truth is, it's up to us to be primarily responsible for bringing love, tenderness, and healing to our own inner child.

Still, an incredibly beautiful dimension is added to partnerships when we bravely introduce our wounded inner child to them. This level of intimacy brings a new layer of understanding and depth to the relationship. Often, we begin to see past their controlling, critical, or avoidant behavior and recognize that, while their actions may hurt, there's some room for compassion, knowing there is a little boy or girl within them acting out of desperation. We get a peek behind the curtain of their reactions and see a little boy or girl inside them, too, longing to be heard, loved, protected, and valued. We also see their protective parts—the managers and firefighters—working overtime to shield that vulnerable young one inside.

Once we step into that sacred space of intimately be introduced to our partner's inner child, we can agree not to save them but to support them. We commit to honoring them, not judging them, and offering love and kindness whenever we can, while asking them to do the same with ours. Real depth and intimacy occur here—in the mutual recognition and care of our inner children.

When we consistently apply inner child practices within our relationship, especially during conflicts, we can create a loving and supportive environment for both inner children. This mutual understanding and compassion fosters healing and growth, making navigating and resolving conflicts easier, thereby minimizing the negative cycle. In this way, we ultimately strengthen our bonds and enhance our overall well-being as a couple.

Having explored the transformative power of self-compassion and the nurturing of our inner child, we're ready to dive deeper into the foundation of a resilient relationship. Now, let's turn our attention to discovering and embracing our core values.

Core Values

Core values serve as anchors, providing strength and stability during the inevitable storms of conflict. By identifying and living out these values, we not only weather relational challenges more effectively but also bring greater meaning and purpose to our lives, knowing we are living authentically.

What Are Your Core Values?

Many people confuse values with goals, so let me start by making the distinction. Goals are the tangible, check-it-off-your-list kind of things: starting a new business, publishing that book, hitting six figures. Values, though, are about the journey, not the destination. They're the essence of how we move through life, qualities like inclusivity, connectivity, authenticity, and creativity. They're not endpoints; they're the compass guiding us in our everyday decisions and actions, helping us navigate this beautifully messy thing called life. Values lead us toward lives rich with meaning and purpose, reminding us of what truly matters along the way.[8]

Imagine, in some distant future, you get the rare opportunity to attend your own funeral. You've lived a long, rich life filled with love, laughter, adventure, and perhaps some well-placed sarcasm. As you sit quietly in the back, listening to the heartfelt eulogies from those who knew you best, what do you hope they say about you? Especially about how you related to others and, most importantly, your partner?

Picture, too, your tombstone. What words do you want to be etched there for eternity? What strengths, qualities, and characteristics do you hope are carved into the stone, reflecting the essence of who you were?

Our core values are the invisible threads that weave through our lives, shaping how we interact with ourselves and the world. They are our true north. The words spoken about us at our funeral and those inscribed on our tombstone offer profound insights into our deepest values.

Valued Loving

In relationships, truly loving your partner goes beyond mere emotions; it involves embodying your deepest values and living them out daily. By knowing and committing to these values, you create a foundation of trust, respect, and meaningful connection, not only with yourself but also with your partner. "Valued loving" invites us to remain true to our values, regardless of how we feel or what our partner does or doesn't do.

"Mark, you are nuts!"

Yes, I know that's a hard ask. When our partner is yelling at us, that part of our mind that wants to attack back is strong. When our partner makes a passive-aggressive comment, it's natural to want to snap back with a quick-witted retort. After we get sucked into the negative cycle, it's natural for us to think, "Screw them, I'm going to ignore them and see how they like it." I get it. The more primitive parts of our brains are designed for war, not for fostering loving and warm relationships.

However, imagine being true to your core self and living out your values anyway, no matter what your partner is doing or not doing. That's real empowerment. That means you're not reactive or dependent on someone else's behavior to determine your actions. It's about maintaining your integrity and sense of self, which fosters inner strength and confidence. Living your values can also be incredibly empowering because it means you are not at the mercy of someone else's moods or actions. You are acting from a place of purpose and intention, which can lead to greater personal satisfaction and fulfillment. And guess what? It will benefit your relationship, too. If you strive to live by your values, and your partner also aims to embody their loving ideals, that's a recipe for more secure and loving relating.

In case you're unaware of your values, here's a list to help you. As you consider each, identify your top five in terms of their importance to you within your relationship. Then, rank them in order.

- **Respect:** Treating your partner with dignity and

consideration, valuing their opinions and feelings, even
during disagreements.

- **Trust:** Building and maintaining a foundation of reliability
  and honesty, ensuring your partner feels safe and secure in the
  relationship.
- **Empathy:** Understanding and sharing your partner's
  emotions, showing genuine care and concern for their
  experiences and perspectives.
- **Patience:** Allowing your partner the time and space to grow,
  make mistakes, and learn without rushing or pressuring
  them.
- **Kindness:** Consistently demonstrating thoughtfulness and
  compassion, making a daily habit of small acts of love and
  consideration.
- **Authenticity:** Being your true self with your partner,
  fostering a relationship based on honesty and genuine
  connection.
- **Support:** Actively encouraging and uplifting your partner in
  their personal and professional endeavors, standing by them
  through challenges and successes.
- **Forgiveness:** Letting go of grudges and resentments and
  being willing to move forward after misunderstandings or
  conflicts.
- **Commitment:** Showing dedication and loyalty to your
  partner, prioritizing the relationship, and working together to
  overcome obstacles.
- **Communication:** Engaging in open, honest, and respectful
  dialogue with your partner, ensuring both voices are heard
  and understood.
- **Gratitude:** Regularly expressing appreciation for your
  partner and the relationship, recognizing and celebrating the
  positives.
- **Flexibility:** Being willing to adapt and compromise,
  understanding that relationships require give and take to
  thrive.

- **Integrity:** Upholding strong moral principles in your actions and decisions, ensuring your behavior aligns with your values.
- **Joy:** Creating and sharing moments of happiness and fun, bringing lightness and positivity into the relationship.
- **Generosity:** Giving your time, energy, and resources freely, showing your partner that their well-being is important to you.
- **Humility:** Acknowledging your own flaws and mistakes, being open to feedback, and striving to improve the relationship.
- **Responsibility:** Taking ownership of your actions and their impact on your partner, being accountable for maintaining a healthy relationship.
- **Adventurousness:** Embracing new experiences and challenges together to foster a sense of excitement and growth in the relationship.
- **Justice:** Treating your partner fairly and standing up for what is right, ensuring equity and fairness in your relationship dynamics.
- **Intimacy:** Cultivating a deep emotional and physical connection, ensuring that both of you feel loved, cherished, and understood.
- **Spirituality:** Sharing and supporting each other's spiritual beliefs and practices, fostering a sense of shared purpose and deeper connection.
- **Intellectual Stimulation:** Engaging in meaningful and thought-provoking conversations, challenging each other's minds, and fostering a dynamic intellectual connection.

Incorporating the concept of valued loving into your relationship can be profoundly transformative. Start by identifying your core values. You could also share them with your partner, inviting genuine and open conversations about what really matters to each of you. Maybe even jot them down and stick them on the fridge, or set a reminder on your phone to keep them front and center. Then, make a conscious effort to embody these values in your daily interactions.

Remember, you are not just your knee-jerk reactions. Deep down, you have a core self that wants to be healthy, loving, and kind. When things get rough, take a breath, and remind yourself who you really are at your center, what your values are, and let that guide how you respond.

Choice Points and Values

At any given moment, we are doing something. Whether we are engaged in contemplative meditation, eating, taking a shower, working, sitting still, sleeping, or reading, we're always engaged in some form of activity. When our actions move us *toward* a life that feels authentic and meaningful, we might call those "toward moves."[9] When our actions pull us *away* from an authentic and meaningful life, those are "away moves."[10]

Visualize an image of a fork in the road. If you go left, that's an *away move*, moving you away from your values and the life you want to build with your partner. If you go right, that's a *toward move*, moving you toward your values and the life you want to live with them.

When veering right and engaging in toward moves, you choose activities based on your values that feel good to your core self. Toward moves might include having an open and honest conversation with your partner, spending quality time together, sharing in household responsibilities, showing appreciation and kindness, practicing active listening, and making time for shared hobbies or interests.

Away moves, by contrast, do not enhance your partnership in the long run. They might include avoiding difficult conversations with your partner, resorting to criticism or stonewalling, engaging in passive-aggressive behavior, ignoring household responsibilities, neglecting to spend time together, or dismissing your partner's feelings.

Each day, we are faced with dozens of "choice points"—moments to choose which way to go on that proverbial fork in the road. When life goes according to plan, it is easier to make toward moves that align with our values. However, when we encounter life stressors, some of us are more prone to veer left, moving away from our values down a well-worn pathway to unhelpful responses.

Here, though, we have a choice. We can choose away moves, such as avoiding meaningful communication, taking our frustrations out on our partner, or withdrawing emotionally. Alternatively, we could choose a toward move on a trajectory in the direction of our values.

For instance, if you value kindness, practice small acts of consideration and thoughtfulness, like leaving a sweet note or doing a chore your partner dislikes. If intellectual stimulation is your thing, carve out time for deep conversations or dive into new topics together. If empathy is a core value, try active listening when your partner shares their feelings, showing understanding and compassion by really getting where they're coming from. Even during a fight, when your partner acts like a not-so-healthy version of themselves, you can still practice empathy.

Show your commitment to secure relating by consistently being there for your partner, especially when times get tough. Make sure to prioritize quality time even when life gets busy. If self-respect is one of your values, set healthy boundaries and communicate your needs clearly, showing that you value and take care of yourself, too.

Remember, don't beat yourself up if you're not always living according to your values. It's not about perfection; it's about heading in the right direction. Values are what we're aiming for, guiding us like a trusty compass. By consistently choosing toward moves, we align our actions with our values and true selves, creating a more authentic and meaningful relationship.

Chapter Nine Wrap-Up

As we draw the curtains on this exploration of self-compassion and connection, let's hold onto this gentle truth: loving yourself isn't a detour from loving your partner; it's the very path that deepens and enriches that love. Imagine self-compassion as the sturdy roots of a tree, grounding you so you can stand firm in the fiercest of storms. When we nurture these roots, we find the strength to love more fully, to forgive more readily, and to embrace each messy, beautiful moment with our partner.

Embracing your inner child isn't just about digging up old wounds; it's about offering the tender care and understanding that "little you" has always needed. By recognizing and soothing these young parts of ourselves, we bring a compassionate, healing presence into our relationships. This act of reparenting softens our own hearts and paves the way for deeper empathy, lightening the load on our partners so they're not solely responsible for reparenting us. We also start to see our partners not just as adults in conflict but as fellow travelers with their own inner children, longing to be loved, accepted, valued, and empowered. Such a sacred way of seeing transforms our approach to each other's vulnerabilities, allowing us to connect on a profoundly human level.

And then there's valued loving, this beautiful practice of aligning our actions with our deepest values. It's about making choices that reflect the essence of who we are, regardless of the stormy seas around us. Committing to living out our values creates a relationship rooted in integrity, respect, and genuine connection. Imagine the power of consistently choosing our values—even when it's hard. By doing so, we not only build a stronger, more resilient partnership but also craft a life together that is rich with meaning and purpose.

Ultimately, a healthier me creates a healthier we. The more we show compassion to ourselves, embrace our inner child with tenderness, and love according to our values, the healthier and more whole we become. And when we do this inner work, our relationship can't help but thrive.

Key Takeaways

1. Self-Compassion Is a Superpower: Embracing self-compassion is like discovering a secret ingredient that transforms your inner world and, by extension, your relationship. Treat yourself with the same kindness and understanding you'd offer a dear friend. This superpower helps banish toxic shame and unhealthy guilt, making you lighter and more connected to those around you.

2. Balance Yin and Yang Self-Compassion: Kristin Neff's concept of Yin and Yang self-compassion shows us that being kind to ourselves isn't just soft and nurturing—it can also be fierce and protective.

Whether it's soothing yourself after a tough day or setting firm boundaries to protect your emotional well-being, self-compassion is about knowing what you need and having the courage to provide it.

3. Embrace Your Inner Child: Tending to your inner child isn't just about healing old wounds. It's about offering that younger version of yourself the love and reassurance they've always needed. This compassionate act reduces the burden on your partner to unknowingly reparent you and helps you see them as a fellow traveler with their own inner child, longing for love and acceptance.

4. Living Your Values Transforms Relationships: Valued loving means aligning your actions with your deepest values, even when it's hard. It's about making choices that reflect who you truly are, fostering a relationship rooted in integrity and genuine connection. This practice not only strengthens your partnership but also enriches your life with meaning and purpose.

5. Choice Points and Values: Every moment offers a choice: to move toward or away from your values. By consistently choosing actions that align with your values—whether it's a kind word, an act of patience, or a moment of empathy—you create a more authentic and fulfilling relationship. These small, daily choices build the foundation for a resilient, loving partnership.

6. A Healthier Me Creates a Healthier We: Ultimately, the work you do on yourself—showing compassion, nurturing your inner child, and living your values—creates a healthier, more whole you. By doing this inner work, you not only transform your own life but also pave the way for a deeper, more meaningful connection with your partner.

Chapter 10
Revitalizing Your Sexual Connection

"Your sexuality is not a problem you have to solve or a disorder that needs to be treated. Your sexuality is a garden you can cultivate."

— Emily Nagoski, *Come Together*

Sex. What is it, really? It's way more than just intercourse. It's this wild, beautiful adventure into an orgasmic wonderland where our passionate, sacred bodies excitedly dance with one another. It's about tangled psyches and intertwined nervous systems coming together in those blissful moments when it feels like heaven touches earth. It's those pulsating moments of connection where time seems to stand still, and love emanates from our lustful eyes as we gaze into each other with radical acceptance.

Alright, so here's the thing. Yes, some lucky souls out there are living in this perpetual blissful state of tantric ecstasy, clocking in hours of multiple orgasms and gleefully rating their sex lives at a solid 11 out of 10. But for the rest of us, those moments of sheer, unadulterated bliss are more like delightful little surprises—rare, wonderful, and certainly not the everyday norm. Work, kids, household responsibilities, overall exhaustion and stress, and entrenched negative cycles can be obstacles to such consistent Edenic sexcapades.

And then, for some, sex can feel like navigating a minefield, where every anxious and shame-filled step—or in this case, thrust—is an effort to avoid stumbling over some invisible tripwire. Some folks fret about maintaining an erection; others tense up, hoping they have enough lubrication, bracing themselves against the possibility of pain. And then there are those just trying to keep their partners happy, faking their way through the sexual experience, screaming, "You're so amazing, honey," while internally praying, "Please, God, let this be over quick."

Add to these sexual obstacles the nagging fear of comparison, haunted by the thought that you might not measure up to your partner's past lovers. Or the frustration of mismatched desires, where one partner craves intimacy while the other feels pressured, creating a cycle of guilt and resentment. And let's not forget the mismatched preferences, where one partner enjoys the comfort of vanilla intimacy in the missionary position, while the other seeks a more adventurous experience with an array of toys, whips, and elaborate moves as if they were playing tantric Twister.

Sex can be a tangled mess of worry, self-doubt, pressure, disappointment, and perfectionistic standards that choke the life out of true, uninhibited sexual expression and pleasure. All of these layers turn what should be a pleasurable connection into a stressful ordeal.

In this chapter, we will uncover the barriers that often stand in the way of genuinely connective and pleasurable sex. We'll dive into how the demands of everyday life, the deep wounds from attachment injuries, those nagging internal narratives and beliefs, and the insidious negative cycle can all sabotage sexual connection. But don't worry, we'll face those obstacles head-on and then dive into some principles and practices that can breathe new life into our intimacy. Together, we'll journey through the messy and beautiful experiences of sex, seeking ways to turn moments of disconnection into opportunities for deeper understanding and love.

Blocks to Sexual Intimacy

In order to revive the sexual intimacy in our relationships, we need to first take a look at what's blocking us. Let's start with the obvious one: stress.

Stress, the Libido Killer

Stress is like your old laptop with ten tabs open, four programs running, and an update in progress. It gets all slow and cranky, heating up to the point where you worry it might just spontaneously combust. It sputters along, barely able to keep up, making you want to throw your hands up and scream, all while your to-do list keeps growing.

Life's pressures pile on stress, from demanding jobs and family obligations to paying bills, social media overload, health worries, financial uncertainties, household chores, parenting challenges, relationship issues, and global conflicts. Those pressures can become all-consuming, squeezing the life out of your once-vibrant sexual life. We get so tangled up in the daily whirlwind that sex morphs into just another item on the to-do list—if it even makes the list. Then there's the dilemma: one partner craves intimacy precisely because life is so stressful, while the other feels overwhelmed and exhausted, considering it another duty to tick off. This mismatch creates a frustrating dance where desire and exhaustion collide, making the quest for connection even more elusive.

When you have children, maintaining intimacy can be extra challenging. While they are a life-affirming gift, they can also inadvertently disrupt the intimacy between parents. Children often become the focal point of our lives when they arrive with their boundless energy and constant needs, pushing our personal needs to the background. Late-night feedings, school projects, and numerous extracurricular activities can leave us exhausted, with little time or energy for romantic evenings. The spontaneous and carefree moments of intimacy we used to enjoy feel like a distant memory, overshadowed by the relentless demands of parenting.

Husbands often find themselves in a tricky spot, feeling guilty for longing for the touch and attention their wives now lavish on the children and are afraid to voice it. Meanwhile, women, especially those with young kids, can feel utterly "touched out" by the mental, emotional, and physical demands of motherhood. With little ones constantly clinging to them, the thought of a partner's touch can be overwhelming. The wives are left feeling guilty or resentful, convinced that their husbands are clueless about the toll mothering takes on them. It's a complex dance where both partners yearn for connection but are often too exhausted or emotionally drained to reach out and grab it.

LGBTQI+ couples, in particular, can face unique stressors that further complicate their intimate lives.[1] Research highlights that discrimination, social stigma, and internalized homophobia can significantly elevate stress levels among LGBTQI+ individuals. These stressors can lead to a higher prevalence of mental health challenges, such as anxiety and depression, which are known libido killers. Additionally, LGBTQI+ couples might navigate complex family dynamics and societal pressures that heterosexual couples may not experience to the same degree. These external and internal pressures can intensify the already challenging task of maintaining a healthy sexual relationship, making the quest for intimacy feel like an uphill battle.

The weight of our responsibilities and relational dilemmas can drain our energy, making it hard to switch gears and feel sexy or desired. Our bodies, designed to handle short bursts of stress, are not meant to be in a constant state of high alert. These stressful dynamics can flood our systems with cortisol—a hormone that, while essential in the right amounts, can wreak havoc on our libido when levels remain elevated. Research reveals a clear pattern: as stress levels rise, libido plummets, dragging the frequency and quality of sexual activity down with it.[2] This decline doesn't just affect our personal well-being; it also undermines relationship satisfaction. It's a vicious cycle: the more stressed we are, the less we connect, and the less we connect, the more stressed we feel.

Cortisol isn't the only troublemaker in town. High stress levels can also rob our bodies of serotonin and dopamine, those delightful neurochemicals that keep our mood buoyant and our sexual desire alive. When cortisol is up, serotonin and dopamine can take a nosedive, leaving us with feelings of depression and anxiety—not exactly the stuff that gets you in the mood. On top of that, stress activates the fight-or-flight response, sending blood rushing away from nonessential functions like digestion and, you guessed it, sexual arousal. It's like our bodies are saying, "Sorry, no time for romance; we're busy surviving here!"

Keep this in mind: if your sexual desire has been waning, maybe there's nothing wrong with you. Perhaps you are deeply and wonderfully sexual, and there might not be anything wrong with your relationship, either. Stress is the real enemy here, not each other. We only have so much bandwidth. Sex takes time and energy. When we're juggling work, kids, bills, and the rest of life's relentless demands, our sexual desire often diminishes. Add some depression and consistent overwhelm to the mix, and our brains and bodies become so busy keeping us afloat in the stormy seas of daily life that our sexual selves are shoved to the backseat.

So, if stress is our biggest intimacy buster, the obvious solution is to decrease stress. I hear you saying, "Yeah right, Mark. No problem!" I know that lessening your stress feels impossible, but let me propose some ways that are doable.

Find Small and Big Ways to Destress

In our wildly busy lives, we seldom have the luxury of weekly yoga and massage sessions, hour-long meditations, consistent date nights, and stress-free vacations every other month. In this context, little is the new big. Find those small micro-moments to destress, which will make a big impact over time. You can take a quick self-compassion break, putting your hand on your heart, noticing the busyness of your life, like everyone else, and saying to yourself, "May I know that I will get through this. May I know I will be okay." You can also close your eyes, slow down, and notice your breath for twenty seconds, breathing in calm and breathing out negative energy.

Then, there are these beautiful, connective acts that weave threads of closeness between you and your partner, acting as natural stress relievers. They don't need to be grand gestures. You can try to find a rhythm for your landings and launchings—providing a simple, brief moment to reconnect as you leave or return home. Imagine a thirty-second hug, powering up your relationship, boosting oxytocin, and lowering stress hormones, all while refueling your love tanks. Or perhaps it's sending a loving text, a virtual hug that whispers, "I'm thinking of you." You can try spreading some humor with a ridiculous meme. Maybe it's taking a short stroll together, even if it's just around the block—walking side by side, enjoying the conversation and the view. Even small gestures, like leaving little notes for each other or sharing what you're grateful for during the day or before bed, can help dissolve some of the stress in your stress tank.

And when you carve out those larger slices of time, be adventurous. Dive into play and novelty, as we discussed in Chapter Six. Finding ways, both big and small, to destress—especially with your partner—can actually boost your chances of connecting in the bedroom.

Schedule Sex

There may be times when your life is so stressful and busy that scheduling sexual intimacy might be a wise move.

"What! *Scheduling* intimacy?!"

I get it. For some, scheduling romance can feel like trying to wedge yet another appointment into your already jam-packed calendar. The very idea of scheduling sex can create too much pressure, making it feel forced, like a chore rather than a cherished moment.

However, let's flip the script for a moment. What if we saw scheduled sex as a precious gift, a love letter to your partnership, precisely *because* you're both so busy and stressed? What if it becomes a powerful, subversive act? A middle finger to the stress all around you? Imagine it as an intentional act of love where you carve out sacred time to shut off the world, dim the lights, put on some mood music, and truly enjoy each other.

For those with "spontaneous" desire, the readiness to engage is often there before you even hit the bedroom, like a spark waiting to ignite. But for those with "responsive" desire, the flame of passion often lights up while being touched. Then, it is as if the body whispers in delight, "Yes, this is what I've been needing."[3] Creating intentional moments of intimacy can be a powerful way to cultivate these sparks into fireworks of delight. Of course, for scheduled sex to work well, some may need to feel the lubricant of emotional connection well before the planned time. As the saying goes, "Some people need to have sex to feel loved, and some need to feel loved to have sex."

Scheduled intimacy doesn't have to be a rigid, joyless task. Think of it as an invitation to rediscover each other, to let the day's stresses melt away, and to see where the moment takes you. In this busy world, creating these intentional moments can deepen your bond and remind you both why you chose each other in the first place.

Attachment Injuries and Emotional Disconnect

Attachment injuries can throw a wrench into sexual intimacy in relationships. When partners experience these deep emotional wounds—often rooted in betrayal, abandonment, or neglect—it can completely undermine their sense of security and trust in the relationship. This breach of trust creates an emotional disconnect, a chasm where open communication and vulnerability once thrived.

Without the crucial elements of trust and openness, sexual intimacy becomes a real challenge. The emotional safety required for genuine connection and intimacy is compromised, leaving partners feeling distant and cautious. The cold and silent bedroom can turn into a stark reminder of the emotional gap. Even if they do engage in sex despite this rift, it often becomes an act driven by pure physical pleasure rather than a mutual entanglement of physical enjoyment and emotional connection.

Even when hurt or angry, some people use sex to bridge the gap. Others are wired differently. If they feel emotionally unsafe, they can't let go and be free in the bedroom. For many, sexual intimacy is deeply tied to emotional safety and connection. The bottom line is: "How can I give you my body if I don't feel emotionally safe and connected to you?" They just can't. Until there are healing conversations, reparative actions, and an increase in emotional safety, vibrant sexual expression will be stifled. Let's look at the stories of four couples to see how attachment injuries and emotional disconnection have affected their sexual intimacy differently.

Story #1: The Weight of Words: Lily and James had been married for eight years. In the early years, their relationship was filled with laughter, adventure, and a deep sense of connection. They thrived on shared experiences, late-night conversations, and an easy, natural intimacy. Their bond seemed unbreakable, and they felt like they could face any challenge together. However, the birth of their second child brought a palpable shift.

Lily struggled with the weight she gained during pregnancy. She juggled the demands of motherhood, work, and maintaining their household and often felt overwhelmed. Instead of feeling supported, she faced critical comments from James. He had always been direct, but now his words had a sharper edge. He started losing patience with her weight concerns and felt she should just work out and take care of herself more.

One evening, while they were getting ready for a rare night out, Lily expressed disappointment that her dress didn't fit right. Feeling frustrated, James said, "If I could be blunt, you should start working out more. And to be honest, I'm just not as attracted to you with all this weight."

His words cut deep, leaving Lily feeling ashamed and insecure. These comments created an emotional barrier between them, making Lily self-conscious and distant. Physical intimacy became rare and forced as Lily feared his judgment.

Nights once filled with affection and connection were now moments of silence and distance. Lily longed for the days when she felt cherished and adored, but now she felt like a stranger in her own marriage. Anxiety and self-doubt replaced the emotional safety she once felt, making it impossible for her to relax and connect with James in the bedroom.

Story #2: Choices Have Consequences: Emma and Jack had been married for ten years, a milestone marked by quiet celebrations and shared memories. They once thrived on their deep emotional connection until Jack had an affair. Though his affair was brief, and he ended it quickly, the betrayal cut Emma deeply.

Despite their attempts to rebuild, an invisible wall had been erected between them. Jack sought her out in the bedroom, his touches tender and apologetic, but Emma felt a cold numbness each time. Her wounded heart didn't allow her to be vulnerable with Jack again. She couldn't shake off thoughts about those few sexual encounters he had with that other woman. The injury and disconnect were profound. She longed to feel the connection they once had, but with each passing night, she withdrew further.

Story #3: Men Get Hurt Too: Samantha and Eric were the couple everyone admired, with a seemingly unbreakable bond and an enviable love story. In the early days of their marriage, their sex life was a whirlwind of passion and joy, the kind that makes you believe in happily ever after. They weathered life's storms together, always finding their way back to each other, no matter what. But recently, a shadow had crept into their bedroom. Eric had been struggling with maintaining an erection, a problem that left him feeling embarrassed and vulnerable. Their once easy intimacy turned into a minefield of anxiety.

Initially, Samantha was supportive, assuring Eric that it wasn't a big deal and that they could work through it together. But as the issue persisted, frustration began to creep into her responses. One night, after a few glasses of wine, as they were in the middle of trying to have sex, Samantha sighed and said, "What is wrong with you? This is really getting annoying. Can't you just fix this?" Her words were sharp and laced with impatience and disappointment.

Eric's heart sank. He had already been feeling insecure, and Samantha's critical comments only deepened his anxiety. He tried to laugh it off, but her words were a deep attachment injury. He began to dread their intimate moments, fearing another failure and more criticism. Once a place of connection and love, the bedroom became a minefield of stress and self-doubt.

Story #4: Listening Matters: Keisha and Darnell had been married for six years. On the surface, they seemed like the perfect couple, always smiling at family gatherings and holding hands in public. But beneath the façade, Keisha felt growing frustration and emotional disconnection.

Keisha had always been the one to manage the household responsibilities, juggling work, taking care of the kids, and keeping everything in order. She tried talking to Darnell about sharing the load, but he never took her concerns seriously. "You're overreacting," he'd say dismissively. "I do plenty around here. Who the heck do you think pays the bills around here?" His words stung, invalidating her feelings, which left her feeling unheard and unappreciated.

This emotional disconnect seeped into their sex life. Darnell's focus was always on his own pleasure, rarely considering Keisha's desires. She longed for him to slow down, to engage in foreplay and make her feel desired, but he seemed more interested in rushing to the finish line. Each encounter left her feeling used and unseen, a stark contrast to the connection she craved.

One evening, after another rushed and unsatisfying attempt at intimacy, Keisha could no longer hold back her frustration. "Darnell, I need you to understand how I feel. You don't listen to me about the house, and in bed, it's like my needs don't even matter to you. I can't keep doing this."

Once again, Darnell minimized what she was saying, creating even more emotional distance between them. Feeling invalidated and neglected, Keisha started to avoid having sex altogether. The bedroom, once a place of connection, became a symbol of her unmet desires and emotional loneliness. Darnell's attempts at intimacy were met with avoidance, and the gap between them grew wider.

In the landscape of relationships, attachment injuries and emotional disconnects are the potholes that can turn a smooth journey into a jarring ride. These wounds—born of betrayal, neglect, or harsh words—don't just bruise our hearts; they fracture the delicate trust that forms the bedrock of intimacy. When trust is compromised, it's as if a once vibrant garden of emotional connection withers, leaving behind barren soil where communication and vulnerability struggle to take root.

Sexual intimacy, often seen as the ultimate expression of closeness, suffers in this barren landscape. It's not just about the physical act; it's about the safety and trust that allow us and our partners to let down our guard and be truly present with each other. Without this emotional safety, physical closeness can feel like a forced performance, a hollow echo of what once was.

If attachment injuries prevent you and your partner from feeling safe enough to open up in the bedroom, dining room, car, or wherever you like to have sex, it's time to take action. What has your partner done that you can't let go of, that feels painful to even think about, that is a barrier to intimacy? Or perhaps it's not what your partner has done, but past attachment injuries you're dealing with that you need to face head-on. Either way, ignoring those emotional injuries and hoping they'll magically disappear is like trying to drive a car with a flat tire and expecting a smooth ride. Sometimes, you have to choose to deal, feel, and then reveal so you can heal.

I get it—healing isn't a tidy, straight line; it's more of a wild zigzag, like riding a rollercoaster at night when you can barely see. But let's be real: what's the point of being in a relationship if you can't be your true, messy, authentic self with your partner? Take a moment to think about what steps you've tried, and what additional steps you'd be willing to try. Have you given the eight-step healing conversation process from Chapter Eight a real go? If not, I encourage you to reread that section and initiate a conversation with your partner related to intimacy issues. Attending to all the steps is important to have the greatest chance of success.

And if you're thinking, "No way, it's not safe enough to even start that," then maybe it's time to consider couples therapy or reach out to a wise, trusted friend for support and perspective. Holding onto hurt, anger, and resentment is like carrying a threadbare backpack full of heavy bricks up a steep hill every day. Trust me, I know how hard it can be to heal from emotional wounds. I've been there. And I know the idea of seeking therapy or confiding in a friend can be scary. But imagine how much lighter and freer you'd feel if you could put down that two-ton backpack. Picture the joy and connection that could blossom if you redirected all that energy toward creating meaningful moments with your partner.

Negative Narratives

Often, we lug around old stories and beliefs into our relationships, stories that have nothing to do with our partners and everything to do with the baggage we've been carrying since we were young. These oppressive ideas come from all sorts of places—our families, cultures, religions—and shape how we see ourselves and each other, often stifling us and squashing the spark of sexual intimacy. They create walls where there should be windows, keeping us from loving ourselves, talking openly, savoring pleasure, respecting each other, and truly connecting. Here are some of the outdated, constricting, and frequently destructive narratives that individuals and couples have shared with me:

1. **"Women should be submissive and pleasing."** The expectation that women must always prioritize their partner's pleasure over their own diminishes fulfillment and autonomy. It suppresses their true selves, reducing vibrant individuals to mere shadows. This obsolete narrative confines women to outdated roles, stifling personal growth, happiness, and genuine sexual intimacy.

2. **"Real men don't express vulnerability."** This harmful narrative discourages men from showing emotional vulnerability, creating a barrier to deep emotional and sexual intimacy. This constricting narrative forces them into solitary confinement with their own emotions, perpetuating a damaging ideal of masculinity. As a result, men become isolated from genuine, holistic connections, reducing their ability to be fully present and embodied lovers.

3. **"Women's bodies belong to their husbands."** This belief, often found in religious communities, disregards a woman's autonomy and consent, treating her body as her husband's property. It strips away her sense of self, turning partnership into ownership. This narrative undermines mutual respect and equality, degrading the foundation of healthy sexual intimacy.

4. **"Men desire sex more than women do."** This tired old cliché not only dismisses women's sexual preferences but also heaps on a load of unnecessary shame for women who happen to have a strong sex drive. And let's not forget the poor guys who don't feel like they're constantly ready for action—they

end up feeling like something's wrong with them, too. The idea that men desire more sex than women reduces the rich spectrum of sexual expression to a simplistic and harmful stereotype, undermining mutual satisfaction and understanding.

5. **"Sex should always be perfect."** The unrealistic expectation that every sexual encounter must be flawless creates pressure and disappointment. Porn is a significant contributor to this narrative as it overlooks the beauty of imperfection, turning intimacy into a performance. This narrative places undue stress on partners, detracting from genuine, enjoyable sexual experiences.

6. **"Having sexual fantasies is wrong."** Shame or guilt associated with sexual fantasies can inhibit open communication and sexual expression. It locks away a part of our imagination that can bring excitement and connection. This narrative stifles creativity and honest dialogue in intimate relationships, limiting sexual fulfillment.

7. **"My sexual past defines my sexual future."** Allowing previous negative experiences or mistakes to dictate future sexual relationships traps individuals in a story already written without a chance to write new chapters. It denies the possibility of growth, healing, and starting afresh. This narrative chains individuals to their past, preventing them from embracing a hopeful and fulfilling sexual future.

8. **"There's a 'normal' amount of sex couples should have."** Comparing one's sex life to perceived norms creates unnecessary pressure and dissatisfaction. Such comparisons often make individuals feel either less than or better than others, reducing intimacy to a numbers game instead of reveling in the unique rhythm of each relationship. This narrative fosters unrealistic comparisons that undermine sexual satisfaction and intimacy.

9. **"Talking about sex is embarrassing or taboo."** Avoiding open communication about sexual desires, and boundaries

stifles intimacy. It creates a barrier to understanding and deeply connecting with each other. This narrative perpetuates shame, silence, and misunderstanding—a formula for undermining intimate bonds and sexual fulfillment.

10. **"Purity or punishment awaits."** Emphasizing abstinence to the point of instilling fear and shame around sexuality, as seen in the religious context of "purity culture," leads to difficulties in sexual relationships even after marriage. It plants seeds of anxiety that grow into barriers to intimacy. This narrative leverages the power of fear, resulting in long-term sexual and emotional issues.

11. **"Divorce and remarriage are immoral, even in cases of abuse."** Trapping individuals in harmful, abusive, or dysfunctional relationships due to religious prohibitions against divorce and remarriage is deeply damaging. It prioritizes dogma over individual well-being, perpetuating harm. This narrative sacrifices personal safety and happiness, severely impacting sexual and emotional intimacy.

12. **"Homosexuality is an abomination."** Denying and stigmatizing LGBTQI+ identities and relationships leading to significant emotional and psychological harm. It marginalizes people for who they love, creating unnecessary suffering. This narrative spreads intolerance and pain, blocking the path to acceptance, equality, and healthy sexual intimacy.

13. **"Sexual pleasure is sinful."** Associating pleasure with sin creates fear and discomfort around sexual experiences. It shrouds a natural part of life in shame, hindering healthy sexual expression. This narrative condemns joy and connection, promoting guilt instead of acceptance and fulfilling intimacy.

14. **"Men can't control their sexual urges."** This belief is often touted to justify male promiscuity and inappropriate behavior, usually blaming women for "provoking" men. It excuses harmful behavior instead of promoting respect and self-control. This narrative absolves accountability, reinforcing

damaging stereotypes and behaviors that undermine respectful and consensual intimacy.

I imagine you cringed when you read many of these beliefs. And I also suspect that a couple of them might have rung a bell to you, at least to some degree. Our relationships are shaped by stories and beliefs we've carried long before we met our current partners. These old narratives are often stifling and shame-inducing, trapping us in patterns that prevent us from living pleasureful lives in our bodies and being our authentic selves. Family, culture, and religion are just a few sources of these oppressive ideas. To build healthier, more fulfilling relationships, we must recognize and challenge these damaging beliefs while crafting our own unique narratives.

Identify and Challenge Your Damaging Beliefs

Below are some questions to help kickstart this healing journey. Take some time to reflect on them. If it feels comfortable to you, consider opening up a dialogue with your partner surrounding these harmful narratives, using these questions as a springboard:

1. Can you identify any specific beliefs or stereotypes from the list that have impacted your own experiences or behaviors in relationships?
2. How do you feel when encountering these harmful narratives in your life or society? How do you typically respond to them?
3. How can self-compassion help you heal from the effects of these oppressive narratives?
4. What practical steps can you and your partner take to cultivate mutual respect, equality, and genuine intimacy in your relationship?
5. What empowering and positive narratives would you like to adopt to inspire your sexual journey, and how can these new

beliefs enhance your intimacy and connection with your partner?

Marie Kondo Your Sex Life

Marie Kondo, the tidying guru we know and love from Netflix's *Tidying Up with Marie Kondo*, teaches us to declutter our homes by only keeping what sparks joy. Now, imagine taking this transformative magic wand and waving it over your sex life, beliefs, and shared habits with your partner. Yes, it's time to declutter.

First, take a deep, honest inventory of your intimate moments and your habits and behaviors. Ask yourself: What truly brings you joy and pleasure? What feels more like a chore or routine and no longer thrills you? Let go of behaviors that are blocking intimacy and pleasure.

Next, look at the habits and behaviors your partner brings to the mix. It's crucial to have open and heartfelt conversations about your desires, boundaries, and fantasies. It is okay to be assertive and to say, "I like this," or "I don't like that."

Consider the concept of "accelerators" and "brakes."[4] Accelerators are those delightful little things that ignite your passion and make sex feel like a gift. Imagine this: deep conversations that make your hearts beat in sync, setting a romantic mood with soft lighting and scented candles, or simply being mindful and present with each other. Picture gentle caresses and warm hugs, those non-sexual touches that create a bubble of closeness and safety around you. Deep, meaningful talks can weave an emotional connection that's just magical. Maybe it's the scene set with soft lights, the aroma of your favorite candle, and soothing music playing softly in the background. The playful teasing and affectionate flirtation throughout the day, little acts of love that build up excitement.

Trust and admiration are like secret ingredients; feeling genuinely trusted and admired by your partner can send waves of desire and pleasure through you. Dancing together, sharing inside jokes, practicing mindfulness—these fun, shared moments can make your senses tingle. Opening up about your fantasies can draw you even closer, and activities like dancing or working out together can get those endorphins and attraction levels soaring. And don't forget the importance of a private, uninterrupted space where it's just the two of you, focusing solely on each other —pure bliss.

Now, let's talk about brakes, those pesky things that throw cold water on your desire and pleasure.[5] Picture the stress of a busy workday, or that gnawing self-consciousness about your body—it's like throwing a wet blanket over your enthusiasm. Unresolved arguments can hang in the air, creating invisible walls between you. Feeling pressured to perform or obliged to engage turns what should be delightful into a chore. Distractions from electronic devices or a noisy environment can shatter the mood in an instant. Those negative beliefs about sex, ingrained by cultural norms, can become powerful brakes. Physical pain, illness, or health concerns add layers of difficulty. The relentless demands of children and the weight of financial worries can drain the energy out of the room. And when you feel emotionally disconnected from your partner, it's like trying to light a fire with wet matches. Identify these in your relationship. In Marie Kondo fashion, eliminate your behaviors that act as brakes, blocking intimacy and pleasure. Embrace and nurture those that act as accelerators, sparking joy and excitement.

The Negative Cycle

We've come to the last major common barrier to sexual intimacy: that noxious negative cycle. Having read about all the ways your and your partner's negative cycle impacts your relationship, it's no surprise that sexual intimacy is another way—and often a major one. Let's see how this holds true for one couple.

Jenna and Marcus

Jenna and Marcus had a whirlwind romance that led to a quick engagement and marriage. Both came from close-knit families where open communication and emotional expressiveness were encouraged. Their strong emotional bond initially translated into a fulfilling sex life, which they both saw as a natural extension of their intimacy and connection.

As the demands of their professional lives increased, Jenna and Marcus found themselves spending less quality time together. Jenna, an ambitious architect, often worked late nights on demanding projects, while Marcus, a dedicated social worker, was emotionally drained by his daily encounters with clients in distress. The stress and exhaustion from their jobs began to seep into their relationship, leading to a subtle yet insidious erosion of their connection.

Their arguments started subtly—first about household chores, then about financial planning, and gradually about the lack of time spent together. While these issues are common among many couples, Jenna and Marcus began to experience a negative cycle around sex that neither had anticipated. Jenna felt increasingly resentful of Marcus' emotional unavailability when she needed support, leading her to withdraw emotionally and physically. She often felt overwhelmed and underval-ued, struggling with the pressure of her work and feeling that her emotional needs were being overlooked. Marcus, on the other hand, felt neglected and unimportant, which led him to seek physical intimacy even more as a way to reconnect.

In their attempts to communicate their needs, they often ended up feeling misunderstood, hurt, and annoyed at one another. Jenna, feeling overwhelmed and undervalued, would become distant, finding it hard to relax and be intimate. She would make comments like "How in the world do you expect me to want to have sex when you completely disregard the things I ask you to do?" Marcus would try to do more chores and listen to her more, but his efforts were always short-lived.

Feeling rejected and lonely, Marcus would try to initiate sex more frequently, hoping it would bridge the growing gap between them. When Jenna turned him down for sex, noting how exhausted she felt, Marcus would throw jabs at her, like "All you care about is everything else but me," and then take a dig at her sex drive: "What is wrong with you? Did you become asexual or something?" This only added to Jenna's feelings of hurt, sense of pressure, and perception of sex as another task on her to-do list, further diminishing her desire.

Their negative cycle around sex intensified. Jenna would acquiesce to Marcus' advances out of a sense of duty rather than desire, which left her feeling even more disconnected and resentful. Marcus, although recognizing Jenna's lack of enthusiasm, felt too hurt and desperate for connection to address the underlying emotional issues directly.

As this Pull Back and Protest pattern continued, their sex life became a battleground for their unresolved emotional conflicts. Jenna's withdrawal led Marcus to pursue more aggressively, which in turn propelled Jenna pull away even further. They were both caught in a cycle where their conflicting desires and feelings surrounding sex only highlighted their emotional disconnection.

Jenna and Marcus' negative cycle wasn't just about the frequency of sex; it was about the underlying emotional needs that were not being met. Jenna desired emotional security and support, while Marcus desired affirmation and closeness. Without addressing these core attachment needs, their sexual relationship suffered, creating a painful loop of pursuit and withdrawal.

Slay Your Negative Cycle

Back in Part Two, we mapped out your negative cycle or dance of disconnection: What are your dance steps? Who is pursuing more connection; who is avoiding? It's like a tenacious tango where your rhythms and feet are getting stepped on. Neither of you feels truly heard or loved. Recognizing the cycle is crucial. You can't fix what you don't understand. It's not about blaming one partner or the other but about seeing how your patterns feed into each other and then coming together to defeat it. That's where those cycle-slaying tools come in: using the **SANE** approach (See what's happening, Accept your part in the cycle, Name the cycle, Engage toward healthy relating) to stop the negative cycle in its tracks; taking a healthy time-out when the cycle rears its ugly head; and initiating healing conversations to restore a healthier connection. This last strategy—communication—is key when it comes to your sexual relationship.

I'm not talking about just any communication. I'm talking about the deep, vulnerable kind where you lay your heart on the table, even if it feels messy and raw. You say, "I feel alone and disconnected when ..." or "I desire to feel close to you in this way ..." It's scary, and it might make you feel like you're standing naked in the middle of a crowded room, but it's the only way to break free from the negative cycle. Create a safe space where both of you can express your deepest fears and desires without judgment. And then there's empathy—for yourself and each other. It's realizing that your partner isn't intentionally trying to hurt you.

Emily Nagoski, a well-known author, speaker, and educator in the field of sexual health and well-being, identifies four primary needs underlying our sexual desires: connection, shared pleasure, being wanted, and freedom. Understanding these core needs can foster a deeper connection, promote a more compassionate and supportive relationship, and prevent the negative cycle from consuming your relationship.

Connection is about forming a deep emotional bond where we feel truly seen, heard, and valued by our partners. This enhances our sense of closeness and mutual understanding. *Shared pleasure* emphasizes the joy derived from mutual satisfaction. It's about taking delight not just in our own pleasure but in the pleasure we give and receive, creating a joyful, shared, intimate experience. *Being wanted* addresses the need to feel desired and cherished by our partner. It provides validation and boosts self-esteem, making us feel attractive and appreciated. Finally, *freedom* represents the desire to let go of everyday stresses and fully immerse ourselves in the moment. It's about experiencing a sense of liberation and presence that enables total relaxation and uninhibited expression.

These needs—connection, shared pleasure, being wanted, and freedom—are not just about the physical act of sex. They touch on the very essence of what we seek in our deepest, most intimate relationships, bringing us closer and enriching our bond. What is it you are looking for? What is it that your partner is looking for? Approach each other with the understanding that you're both in this together as teammates rather than adversaries. Remember why you fell in love in the first place and hold on to those moments of connection like a lifeline.

This is worth repeating: don't be afraid to seek help. Sometimes, the best thing you can do is to invite a third party into your dance—a therapist who can help you see the steps you can't see on your own and guide you to create a new, healthier pattern. It takes time, patience, and a lot of practice, but it's worth it.

Jenna and Marcus navigated this maze of miscommunication and mismatched expectations by bravely learning to voice their desires regarding sex and intimacy more openly and honestly. They delved into the intricacies of their unique user manuals, discovering what revved their sexual engines and what threw on the brakes, unraveling the deep-seated motivations that drove their desires for intimacy. But it wasn't just about what happened between the sheets. They learned to support each other in ways that resonated far beyond the bedroom.

They faced their inner child parts—the ones that kicked up a fuss in tough moments—and began to understand the attachment fears and long-ings that danced in their cycle. Together, they sifted through the family and cultural baggage that had long stifled their self-love and genuine self-expression. They poured effort into fortifying their emotional connection, knowing that their sexual relationship would flourish as a natural byproduct of this deeper bond.

So, take a deep breath, hold your partner's hand, and start this journey together. Slay that negative cycle not with swords of blame but with the gentle power of understanding, curiosity, patience, and love. You've got this.

The Canvas of Sexuality:
Crafting Our Own Masterpiece

Imagine your sexuality as a pristine, blank canvas. From the moment you were born, this canvas began to take shape, absorbing the influences of those around you. Family, friends, media, culture, and society—all of these forces have contributed to the strokes and colors that have formed your sexual self. Sometimes, these external influences are positive, enriching your canvas with vibrant hues and beautiful patterns. Other times, the marks left by others can feel intrusive, confusing, or even damaging, creating dark spots or chaotic splashes that obscure your true desires and identity.

As you grow older, you can break free from the matrix of influence. You can break free from the bondage of lies that were pumped into you and inscribed upon you. Although daunting, you realize that you now wield the creative brush. As you become more aware of your authentic sexuality, you now have the power to apply linseed oil and remove the old paint, or you can just paint over those old layers to blend and transform them into something uniquely yours. This process is about reclaiming your canvas and intentionally creating your own masterpiece.

So, the first step is to recognize the existing layers on your canvas. Acknowledge the influence of early experiences, cultural messages, and past relationships. Reflect on how these layers have shaped your perceptions, beliefs, and feelings about your sexuality. Understanding these influences allows you to see where you want to make changes.

As you begin to paint your own masterpiece, it's crucial to identify and embrace your true colors. What are your genuine motivations, desires, fantasies, boundaries, and expressions of sexuality? This self-discovery may involve exploring new experiences, educating yourself, and communicating openly with your partner. Embracing your true colors means honoring your authentic self and allowing it to shine through in safe and wise ways.

For many, the canvas of sexuality may have dark and uncomely spots and splashes brought about by negative experiences, trauma, or shame-infused messages. Healing these areas is an essential part of creating your masterpiece. This healing can come from self-compassion, therapy, yoga, meditation, or supportive relationships. As you heal, you may find that these dark spots can be transformed into areas of strength and resilience, adding depth and richness to your canvas.

In a relationship, your partner also contributes to the canvas. This collaboration requires communication, trust, and mutual respect. Together, you can blend your colors and create something beautiful that reflects both of your sexual identities and desires. This joint effort enhances the masterpiece, making it a dynamic and evolving work of art.

The reality is your canvas is never truly finished. Sexuality is a fluid and evolving aspect of who you are. As you grow and change, so too will your masterpiece. New desires can become outdated ones in the future.

Embrace this continual creation process, allowing yourself the freedom to repaint, redesign, and reinvent as you journey through life.

By reclaiming your canvas, you transform your sexuality into a vibrant, expressive, and personal masterpiece. You honor the layers that have shaped you, heal the wounds that have hindered you, and celebrate the unique beauty of your own sexual identity. In doing so, you not only create a more fulfilling and authentic sexual self but also enrich your relationship and your overall sense of well-being.

Chapter Ten—and Final—Wrap-Up

Well, you've made it to the end of the book, and you're hopefully on your way to enhanced connection and intimacy with your partner, both emotionally and physically. It's been quite a journey to get here. We started out in Part One with some serious myth-busting to replace our fairy-tale fantasies with the hard truths about relationships. We then took a crash course in attachment theory, discovering how our earliest relationships engender attachment tendencies that impact our relationships throughout life—unless we become aware of them and learn to alter our deep-seated response patterns. Lastly, we explored the power of reflective empathic compassion and how you and your partner can incorporate it into your relationship.

In Part Two, we took a deep dive into the negative cycles that nearly all of us get caught up in and that often wreak havoc on our once blissful and easygoing unions. You reflected upon your own negative cycle with your partner: Is it Blame and Bash? Fracture and Fortify? Wend, Whirl, and Withdraw? Or Pull Back and Protest? Once you recognized the particular dance you and your partner perform on this dance floor of life, we pulled apart all of its components: the triggers, emotions, behaviors, negative narratives, and contextual factors that keep that dance going. While this in-depth exploration may have touched some sensitive nerves, it prepared you to break the deeply entrenched negative cycle that harms and threatens your relationship.

Then, in Part Three, we rolled up our sleeves and got to work learning principles and practices that serve as a roadmap for maintaining and enhancing your relationship. From proactively making a pact to protect your emotional contact to understanding and accommodating each other's love languages and relational tendencies, these strategies are designed to foster deeper connection and resilience against negative cycles. It's also vital to be mindful of the Four Horsemen—criticism, contempt, stonewalling, and defensiveness—and work actively to eliminate these behaviors from your interactions.

Genuine connection is the heartbeat of a thriving relationship. Pair it with savvy communication skills, and it's like finding that perfect pair of shoes that go with everything. Suddenly, navigating life's challenges feels a whole lot easier. Practicing the "I feel ... when you" technique; considering tone, timing, and trimming in your conversations; and adopting a we-centered approach can seriously improve the quality of your interactions. Don't forget that starting a conversation with a softer tone and choosing the right moment can make all the difference in how your message is received.

Armed with stronger communication skills, you then unleashed your inner cycle slayer to stop the negative cycle right from the get-go and prevent it from escalating out of control. Taking a healthy time-out and following the eight essential steps to healing conversations are the cornerstones of cycle slaying, and you, my friend, are now a cycle slayer.

To have and maintain a healthy relationship, we need to care for ourselves. We need to have and demonstrate self-compassion, connect with and nurture our inner child, know what our core values are, and act according to those values. Remember, *a healthier me makes a healthier we*.

And that brought us to this final topic of revitalizing your sexual connection. So, before you turn to the epilogue, here are some takeaways from this last chapter.

Key Takeaways

1. Understand Barriers to Sexual Intimacy: Recognizing the everyday stressors, attachment injuries, and internal narratives that can hinder sexual connection is the first step toward overcoming these barriers and fostering a more intimate relationship.

2. The Role of Stress and Mismatched Desires: Acknowledge how stress, parenting, and the mismatch in sexual desires can impact intimacy. Finding ways to manage stress individually and as a couple can enhance your sexual connection.

3. Schedule Intimacy as an Act of Love: While spontaneous intimacy is ideal, scheduling sexual time can be a powerful way to prioritize your relationship amidst busy lives. This approach ensures that intimacy remains a cherished part of your partnership.

4. Heal Attachment Injuries: Emotional wounds can significantly affect sexual intimacy. Healing these attachment injuries through open communication, empathy, and possibly therapy can restore trust and closeness in your relationship.

5. Expose and Challenge Harmful Narratives: Identify and challenge the shame-infused beliefs and cultural narratives that negatively impact your sexual expression. Embrace empowering and positive narratives that support a healthy and fulfilling sexual relationship.

6. Create Your Sexual Masterpiece: View your sexuality as a dynamic and evolving canvas. By acknowledging past influences, embracing your true desires, and healing old wounds, you and your partner can collaboratively create a vibrant, authentic, and fulfilling sexual relationship.

Epilogue

I n this topsy-turvy world, where headlines often read like a dystopian novel, I've found that protecting my relationship becomes an anchor in the storm. Why? Because there's nothing quite like the sanctuary of a secure relationship. It's where your heart feels at home, your nervous system finally gets a breather, and you exist in a space filled with love, respect, and mutual understanding. Knowing, without a shadow of a doubt, that your partner has your back is priceless. Cultivating this kind of connection is how we build a lasting relationship and worth every effort.

But let's be real here. Even in the healthiest of relationships, those dreaded negative cycles of communication will sneak in, and we will hurt one another. It's just part of the package deal of being human. Our partners will feel pain because of us—not out of malice, but simply because we are imperfect beings trying to stay in sync in a world that often feels like it's trying to knock us off balance. With our nervous systems acting like overzealous security guards, always on high alert, reactivity is inevitable, and when we're wobbly on our feet, stepping on our partners' toes is just bound to happen.

When we sense a threat—a dismissive eye roll, a stony silence, a cutting remark—the vulnerable child inside us feels the sting, and our inner protectors spring into action. This is how the negative cycle starts, spinning faster and faster out of control the more our dance steps fuel its fire.

Yet, here I am, a hopeless romantic and an eternal optimist. I don't believe that our partners can swoop in like superheroes to heal all our childhood wounds or fill every emotional gap our parents left. But they can be our greatest allies. Together, we can support each other, align with our values, and fight against those negative cycles and life's relentless stresses. This is the essence of my work with couples, and this is why I wrote this book—to help you form a resilient, loving partnership. We can absolutely make choices that contribute to the health of our relationship.

Yes, it takes time. Shifting the dynamics in our relationships doesn't happen overnight. But with hard work, intentional play, and creating moments of deep connection, we can break those stubborn generational patterns, elevate love to new heights, and face life's challenges with a united front. So, let's roll up our sleeves; embrace the messy, beautiful journey; love well; and kick life's ass together.

Notes

1. The End of Fairy Tales and Embracing the Real Us

1. Fraenkel, Peter. *Last Chance Couple Therapy: Bringing Relationships Back from the Brink.* W.W. Norton & Company, 2023, 193.
2. Young-Eisendrath, Polly. *Love between Equals: Relationship as a Spiritual Path.* Boston, MA. Shambhala Publications, 2019, 117.
3. Real, Terrence, and Springsteen, Bruce. *Us: How Moving Relationships Beyond You and Me Creates More Love, Passion, and Understanding.* Emmaus, PA. Rodale Books, 2022, 174.
4. See Louis J. Cozolino, *The Neuroscience of Human Relationships: Attachment and the Developing Social Brain*, New York: Norton, 2006.
5. Ibid.

2. Discovering Each Other's Operating Manual

1. See Cassidy, Jude, and Phillip R. Shaver, editors. *Handbook of Attachment: Theory, research, and clinical implications.* Guilford Press, 2008.
2. This acronym is taken from a training I did with couples expert Rebecca Jorgensen.
3. Mikulincer, Mario, and Phillip Shaver. *Attachment in Adulthood: Structure, Dynamics, and Change.* New York: Guilford Press, 2007.
4. Tatkin, Stan M. *Wired for Love: How Understanding Your Partner's Brain and Attachment Style Can Help You Defuse Conflict and Build a.* 2nd ed. Oakland, CA: New Harbinger Publications, 2024, 79.

3. Awakening the Gift of Reflective Empathic Compassion

1. Becker, Michelle. *Compassion for Couples: Building the Skills of Loving Connection.* London, England: Guilford Press, 2023, 22.
2. Gilbert, Paul, and Chodin. *Mindful Compassion: How the Science of Compassion Can Help You Understand Your Emotions, Live in the Present, and Connect Deeply with Others.* Oakland, CA: New Harbinger Publications, 2014.
3. See Gilbert, Paul. *Compassion Focused Therapy: Distinctive Features.* London, UK: Routledge, 2010.
4. Johnson, Sue. *Hold Me Tight: Seven Conversations for a Lifetime of Love.* Little, Brown & Co., 2008, glossary.
5. I have had the privilege of participating in David Mars' training for several years, where I learned about the seven channels of experience through his exceptional instruction. You can check out his website here: https://www.cfttsite.com/. For more

information on his channels, see Mars, David. 'Dr. Mars Explains the Seven Channels of Experience for Couples.' *Center for Transformative Therapy*. Accessed August 26, 2024. https://www.cfttsite.com/papers-articles-and-podcasts/dr-mars-explains-the-seven-channels-of-experience-for-couples.

4. What Is Your Negative Cycle?

1. Sun Tzu. *The Art of War*. Translated by Lionel Giles. Dover Publications, 2002. Chapter 3.
2. Johnson, Susan M. *Attachment Theory in Practice: Emotionally Focused Therapy (EFT) with Individuals, Couples, and Families*. 1st ed. New York/London: The Guilford Press, 2019.

5. What Is the Anatomy of Your Negative Cycle?

1. Porges, Stephen W. *Polyvagal Safety: Attachment, Communication, Self-Regulation*. New York: W.W. Norton & Company, 2021.
2. I adapted material from worksheets by Scott Woolley, Douglas Tilley, Matt Angelstorf, Karen Shore, Kallos-Lilly & Fitzgerald, and from Sue Johnson's 'Hold Me Tight' curriculum
3. Ibid.

6. Strengthening Your Connection

1. Gottman, John M., Silver, Nan, and Gottmann, John. *The Seven Principles for Making Marriage Work*. Oxford, England: Weidenfeld & Nicolson, 1999, 19.
2. Ibid.
3. Tatkin, Stan. *In Each Other's Care: A Guide to the Most Common Relationship Conflicts and How to Work through Them*. Louisville, CO: Sounds True, 2023, 7.
4. Chapman, Gary. *The Five Love Languages: How to Express Heartfelt Commitment to Your Mate*. Chicago: Northfield Publishing, 1995.
5. Tatkin, Stan M. *Wired for Love: How Understanding Your Partner's Brain and Attachment Style Can Help You Defuse Conflict and Build a Secure Relationship*. 2nd ed. Oakland, CA: New Harbinger Publications, 2024, 109.
6. Ibid.
7. Proyer, René T., Karin Brauer, Andrea Wolf, and Garry Chick. "Adult Playfulness and Relationship Satisfaction: An APIM Analysis of Romantic Couples." *Journal of Research in Personality* 79 (2019): 10-23.

7. Employing Effective Communication

1. Howard, John. 2023. *More than Words: The Science of Deepening Love and Connection in Any Relationship*. New York, NY: Simon & Schuster, xvii.
2. Gottman, Julie Schwartz and John Gottman. *Fight Right: How Successful Couples Turn Conflict into Connection*. Harmony, 2024.

3. Rick Hanson, *Hardwiring Happiness: The New Brain Science of Contentment, Calm, And Confidence* (New York: Harmony Books, 2016), xxvi.

4. Tatkin, Stan M. *Wired for Love: How Understanding Your Partner's Brain and Attachment Style Can Help You Defuse Conflict and Build a.* 2nd ed. Oakland, CA: New Harbinger Publications, 2024, 61.

5. Ibid, p. 151

6. Ibid.

7. Howard, John. *More than Words.* 63

8. Ibid.

9. Gottman, Julie Schwartz and John Gottman. *Fight Right: How Successful Couples Turn Conflict into Connection.* Harmony, 2024, 121.

8. Unleashing Your Inner Cycle Slayer

1. I first heard the term "Cycle Slayer" in an EFT training by Lisa Palmer Olsen.

2. Fishbane, Mona DeKoven. *Loving with the Brain in Mind: Neurobiology and Couple Therapy.* New York: W.W. Norton & Company, 2013, 148.

3. Ibid.

4. Powell, Jennine Estes LMFT, and Jacqueline Wielick LMFT. *Help for High-Conflict Couples: Using Emotionally Focused Therapy and the Science of Attachment to Build Lasting Connection.* New Harbinger Publications, 2024, 128.

5. Brubacher, L. (2018). *Attachment Injury Resolution Model in Emotionally Focused Therapy.* In: Lebow, J., Chambers, A., Breunlin, D. (eds) Encyclopedia of Couple and Family Therapy. Springer, Cham. https://doi.org/10.1007/978-3-319-15877-8_903-1

9. Cultivating a Healthier You (For A Healthier We)

1. Neff, Kristin D., and S. Natasha Beretvas. "The Role of Self-Compassion in Romantic Relationships." Self and Identity 12, 1 (2013): 78–98. doi:10.1080/15298868.2011.639548.

2. Yarnell, Lisa M., and Kristin D. Neff. *Self-Compassion, Interpersonal Conflict Resolutions, and Well-being.* Self and Identity 12, no. 2 (2013): 146-159.

3. Neff, Kristin D. "Self-Compassion: Theory, Method, Research, and Intervention." *Annual Review of Psychology* 74 (2023): 365-396.

4. Ibid.

5. Kabat-Zinn, Jon. *Wherever You Go, There You Are: Mindfulness Meditation in Everyday Life.* New York: Hachette Books, 1994.

6. Neff, Kristin. *Fierce Self-Compassion: How Women Can Harness Kindness to Speak Up, Claim Their Power, and Thrive.* New York: Penguin Life, 2022.

7. Young, Jeffrey E., Janet S. Klosko, and Marjorie E. Weishaar. *Schema Therapy: A Practitioner's Guide.* New York: Guilford Press, 2003.

8. Acceptance and Commitment Therapy, particularly the writings of Russ Harris, greatly influences my work with values.

9. Russ Harris explores Toward and Away Moves and what he calls The Choice Point in detail in: Harris, Russ. *The Happiness Trap: How to Stop Struggling and Start Living.* 2nd ed. Boulder, CO: Shambhala, 2022.

10. Ibid.

10. Revitalizing Your Sexual Connection

1. Meyer, Ilan H., and Mary E. Northridge, eds. *The Health of Sexual Minorities: Public Health Perspectives on Lesbian, Gay, Bisexual, and Transgender Populations*. New York: Springer, 2007.

2. Bodenmann, Guy, David C. Atkins, Markus Schär, and Thomas G. Poffet. "The Association Between Daily Stress and Sexual Activity." *Journal of Family Psychology* 24, no. 3 (2010): 245-252. https://doi.org/10.1037/a0019365.

3. Nagoski, Emily. *Come Together: The Science (and Art!) of Creating Lasting Sexual Connections*. New York: Ballantine Books, 2024, 23.

4. Ibid, 16-17.

5. Ibid, 16-17.

Acknowledgments

I extend my deepest gratitude to the courageous couples I have had the privilege to work with over the years. Your challenges, resilience, love for one another, and trust in me have shaped me into the therapist I am today.

To the pioneers in the field—Sue Johnson, John and Julie Gottman, Terry Real, David Mars, Esther Perel, Stan Tatkin, Kathryn de Bruin, and many others—thank you for your groundbreaking work that has profoundly influenced my life and practice.

Special thanks to Laura Castro, Jessica Lagos, Debra Fogle, and Julie Sykora for your invaluable editing and feedback on several chapters. Your insights were instrumental in refining my ideas. Thank you to Grammarly, ChatGPT, and Hemingway Editor for their valuable assistance. To my main editor extraordinaire, Rona Bernstein, your exceptional wisdom and guidance elevated my entire manuscript to new heights, and for that, I am forever grateful.

Lastly, to my wife, Bianca, and my son, Alex, my greatest teachers, thank you for your endless love and support.

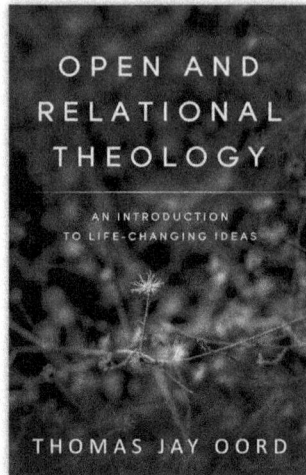

About the Author

Dr. Mark Gregory Karris is a compassionate and dedicated licensed marriage and family therapist committed to guiding individuals and couples on transformative journeys of self-discovery and healing. Based in the vibrant city of San Diego, California, Mark brings extensive expertise in couples therapy, men's issues, and religious trauma.

Mark's therapeutic approach is holistic, integrative, and deeply experiential. He engages the mind, body, spirit, and emotions, drawing from a diverse array of therapeutic modalities, including psychodynamic therapy, Intensive Short-Term Dynamic Psychotherapy, Internal Family Systems, cognitive-behavioral therapy, somatic practices, and spiritual approaches. He has also undergone extensive training in Emotionally Focused Therapy and is enthusiastically learning from David Mars and his Transformational Couples Therapy ®. For Mark, guiding couples is not just a profession—it's a heartfelt journey where he pours his soul into nurturing love and connection.

To learn more about Mark's work, visit MarkGregoryKarris.com

www.ingramcontent.com/pod-product-compliance
Lightning Source LLC
Chambersburg PA
CBHW032052020426
42335CB00011B/303